what did you eat yesterday? 2
fumi yoshinaga

VERTICAL.

#9.   3

#10.   23

#11.   41

#12.   61

#13.   79

#14.   97

#15.   115

#16.   133

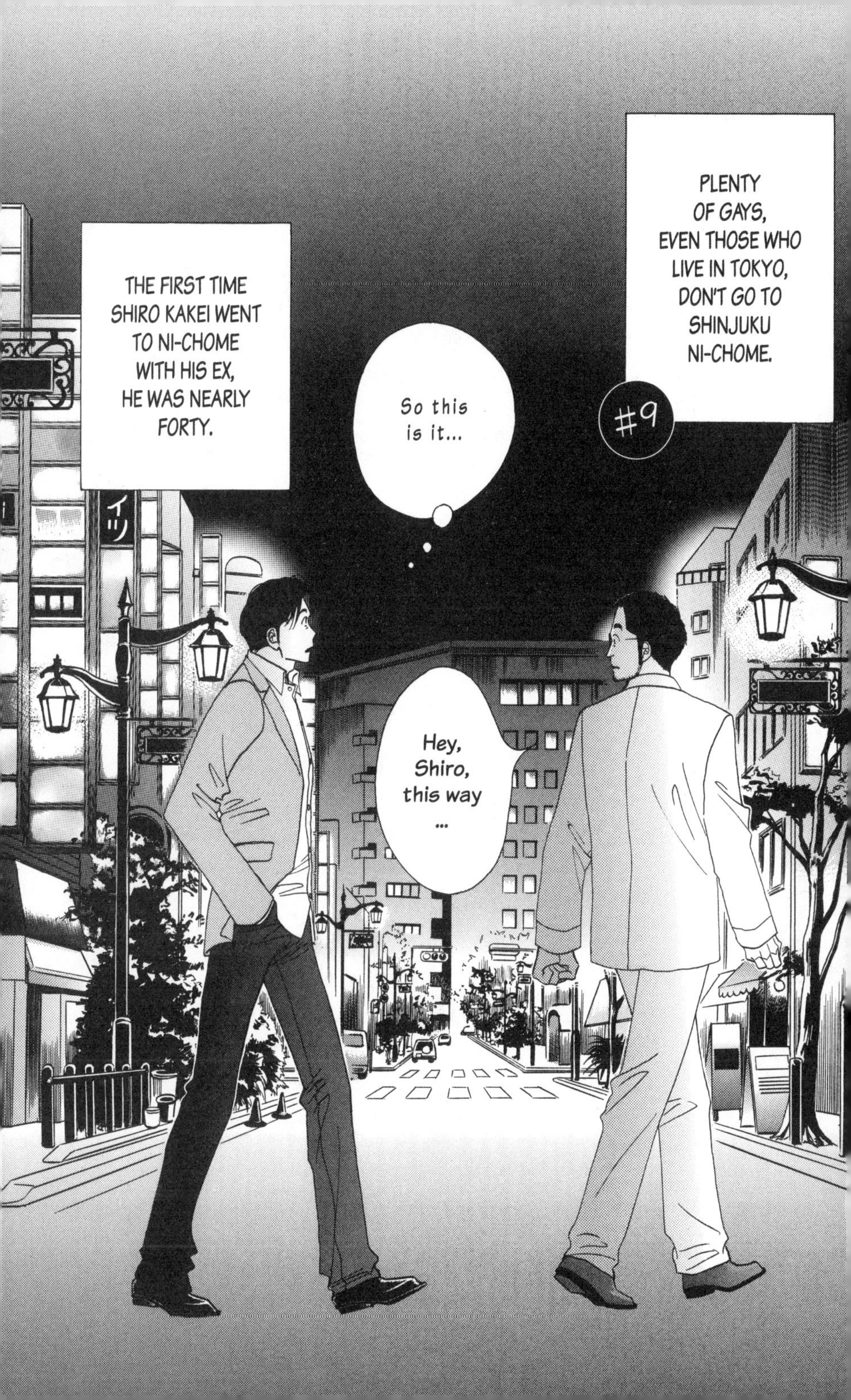
PLENTY OF GAYS, EVEN THOSE WHO LIVE IN TOKYO, DON'T GO TO SHINJUKU NI-CHOME.
#9
THE FIRST TIME SHIRO KAKEI WENT TO NI-CHOME WITH HIS EX, HE WAS NEARLY FORTY.
So this is it...
Hey, Shiro, this way ...

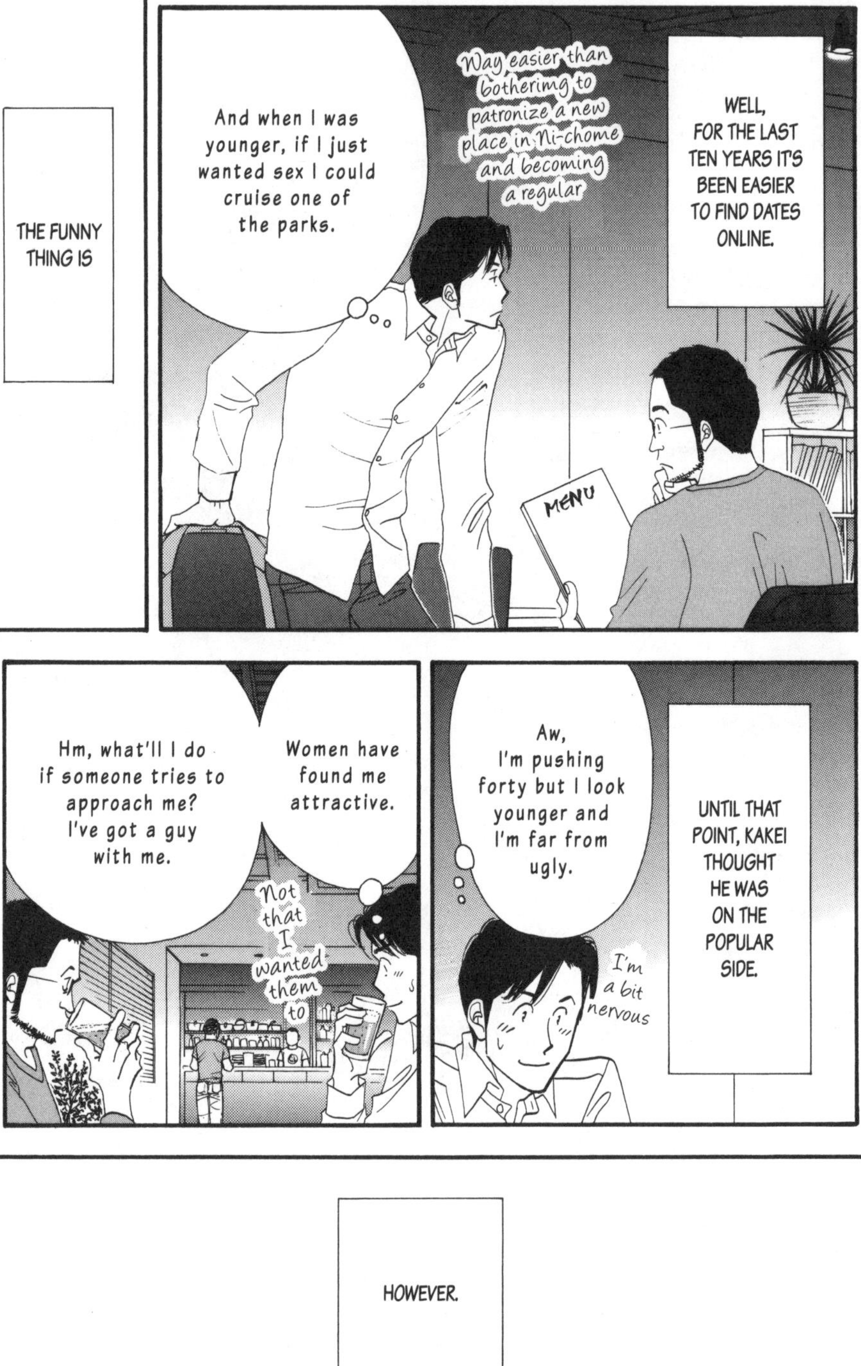
WELL, FOR THE LAST TEN YEARS IT'S BEEN EASIER TO FIND DATES ONLINE.
Way easier than botherimg to patronize a new place in Ni-chome and becoming a regular
And when I was younger, if I just wanted sex I could cruise one of the parks.
MENU
THE FUNNY THING IS
UNTIL THAT POINT, KAKEI THOUGHT HE WAS ON THE POPULAR SIDE.
Aw, I'm pushing forty but I look younger and I'm far from ugly.
I'm a bit nervous
Women have found me attractive.
Hm, what'll I do if someone tries to approach me? I've got a guy with me.
Not that I wanted them to
HOWEVER.

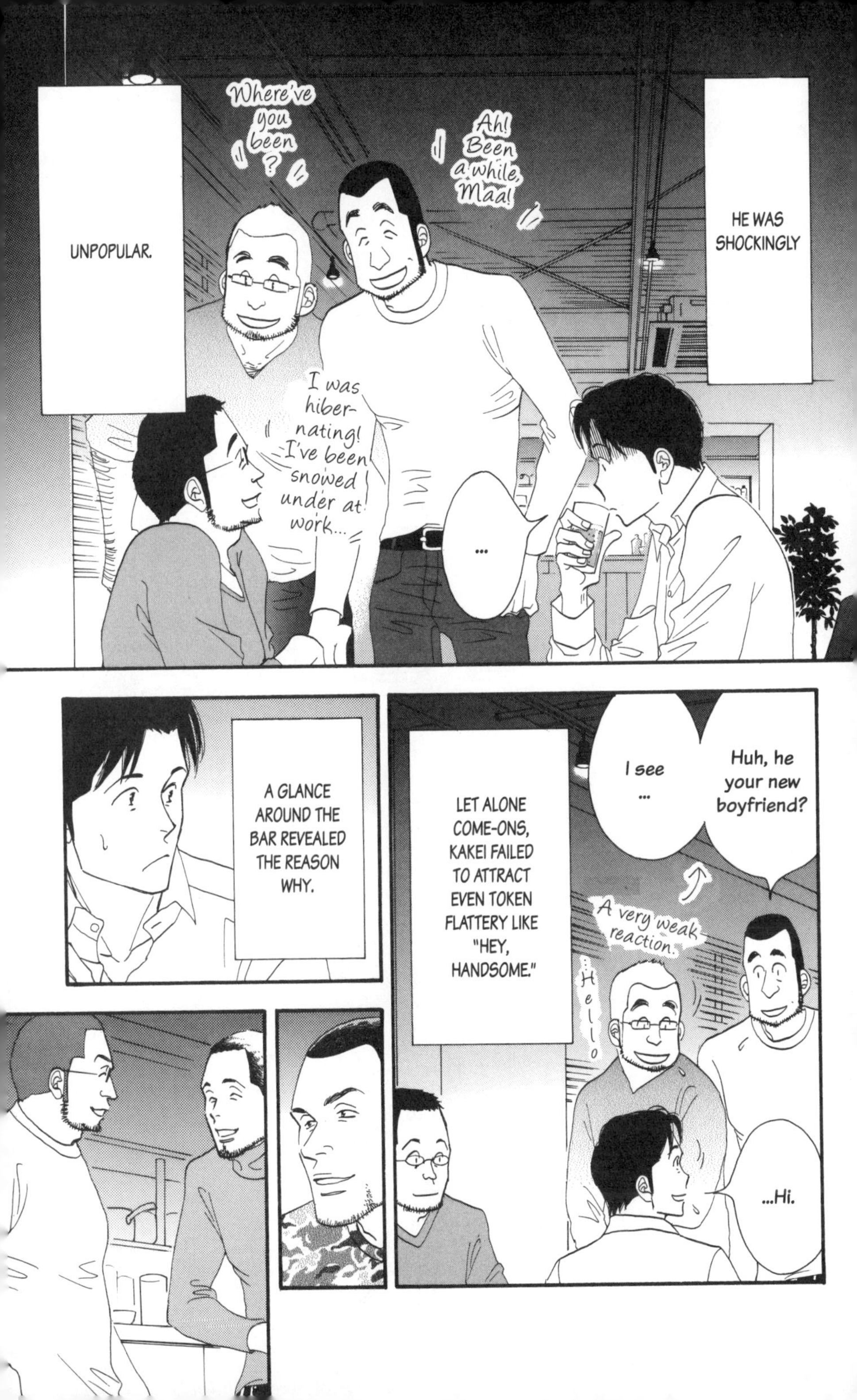
HE WAS SHOCKINGLY
UNPOPULAR.
Ah! Been a while, Maa!
Where've you been?
...
I was hibernating! I've been snowed under at work...
Huh, he your new boyfriend?
I see ...
LET ALONE COME-ONS, KAKEI FAILED TO ATTRACT EVEN TOKEN FLATTERY LIKE "HEY, HANDSOME."
A very weak reaction.
...Hello
...Hi.
A GLANCE AROUND THE BAR REVEALED THE REASON WHY.

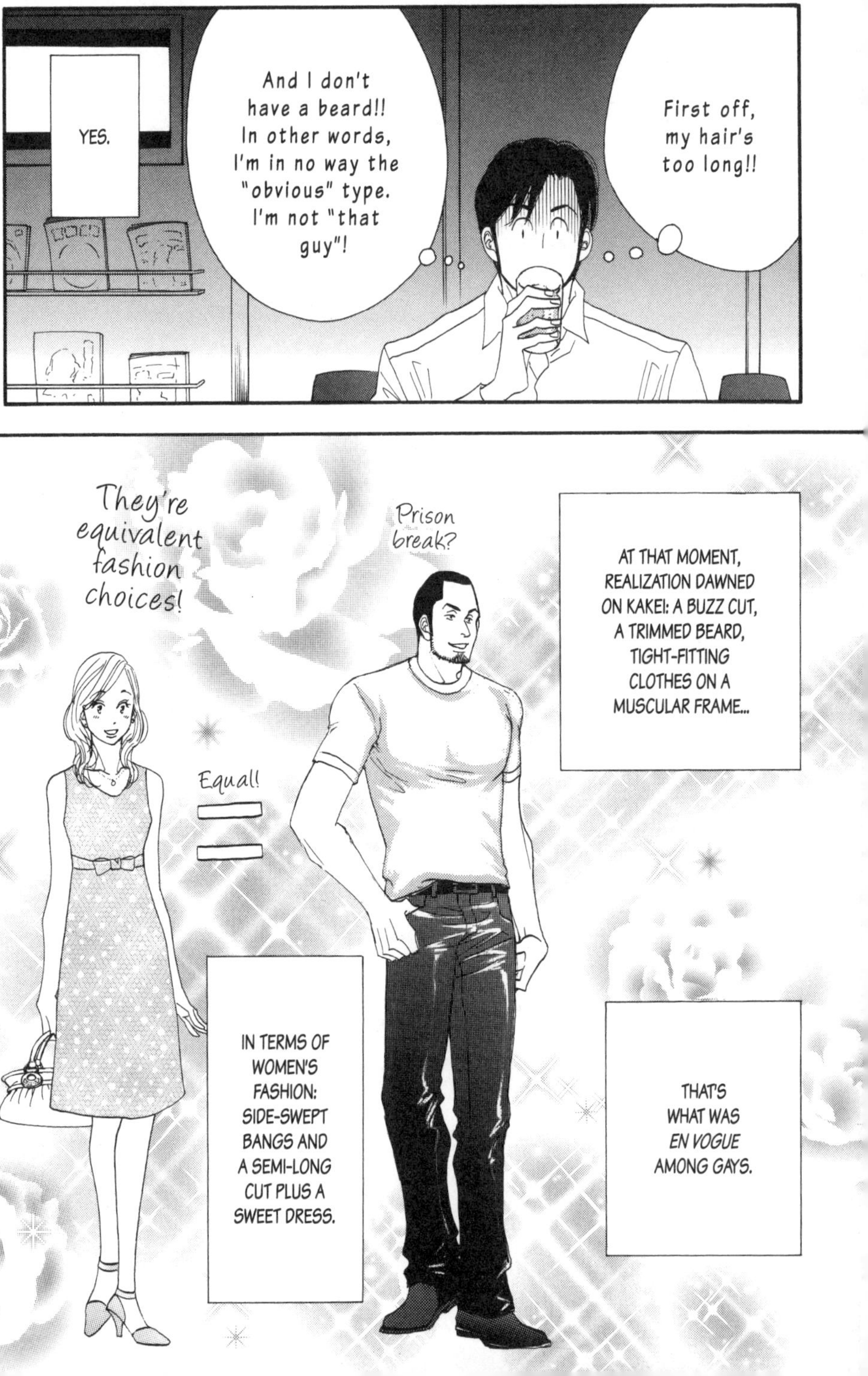
First off, my hair's too long!!
And I don't have a beard!! In other words, I'm in no way the "obvious" type. I'm not "that guy"!
YES.
AT THAT MOMENT, REALIZATION DAWNED ON KAKEI: A BUZZ CUT, A TRIMMED BEARD, TIGHT-FITTING CLOTHES ON A MUSCULAR FRAME...
Prison break?
THAT'S WHAT WAS *EN VOGUE* AMONG GAYS.
They're equivalent fashion choices!
Equal!
IN TERMS OF WOMEN'S FASHION: SIDE-SWEPT BANGS AND A SEMI-LONG CUT PLUS A SWEET DRESS.

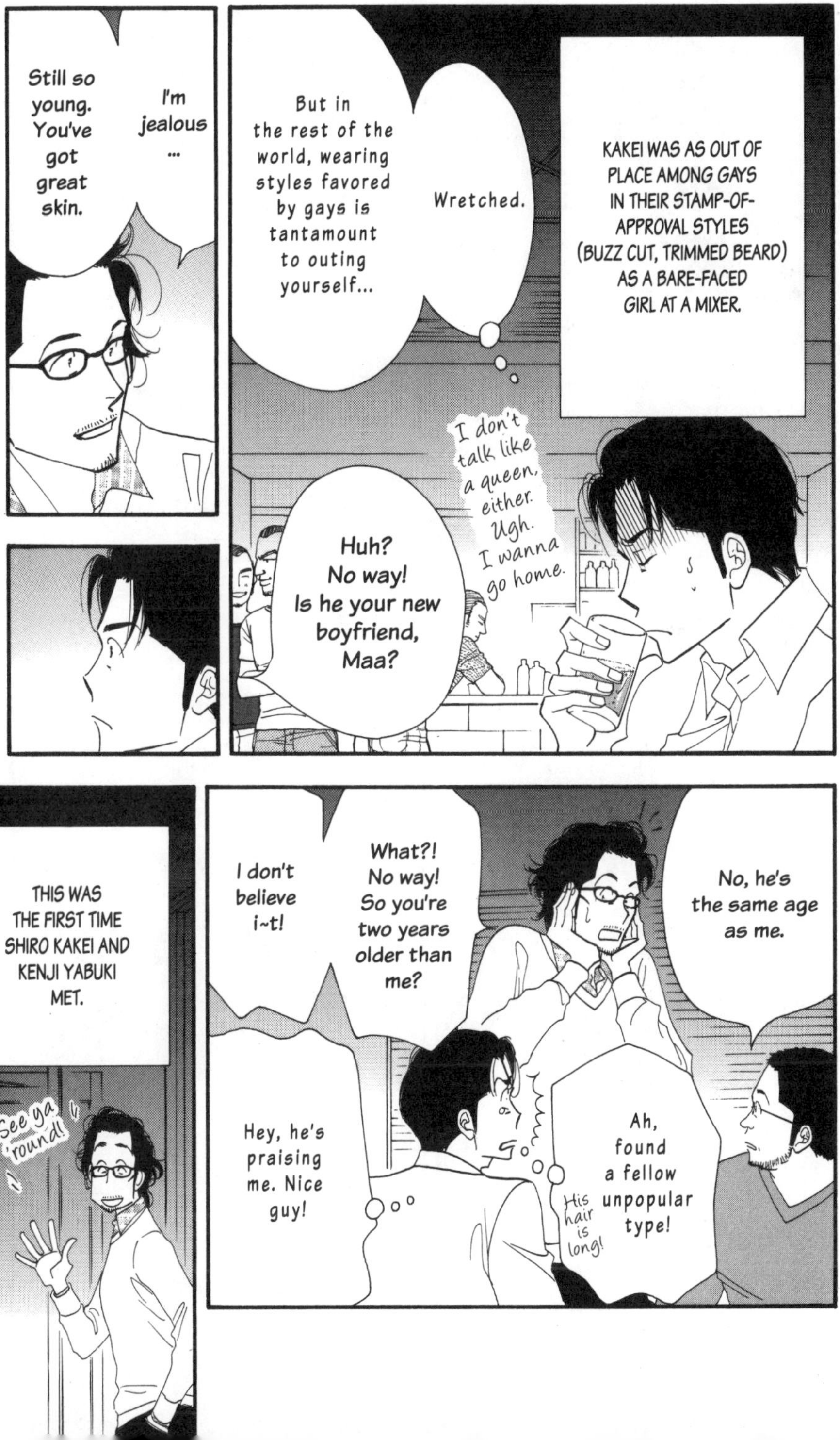
KAKEI WAS AS OUT OF PLACE AMONG GAYS IN THEIR STAMP-OF-APPROVAL STYLES (BUZZ CUT, TRIMMED BEARD) AS A BARE-FACED GIRL AT A MIXER.
Wretched.
But in the rest of the world, wearing styles favored by gays is tantamount to outing yourself...
I don't talk like a queen, either. Ugh. I wanna go home.
Huh? No way! Is he your new boyfriend, Maa?
I'm jealous ...
Still so young. You've got great skin.
No, he's the same age as me.
What?! No way! So you're two years older than me?
I don't believe i~t!
Ah, found a fellow unpopular type!
His hair is long!
Hey, he's praising me. Nice guy!
THIS WAS THE FIRST TIME SHIRO KAKEI AND KENJI YABUKI MET.
See ya 'round!

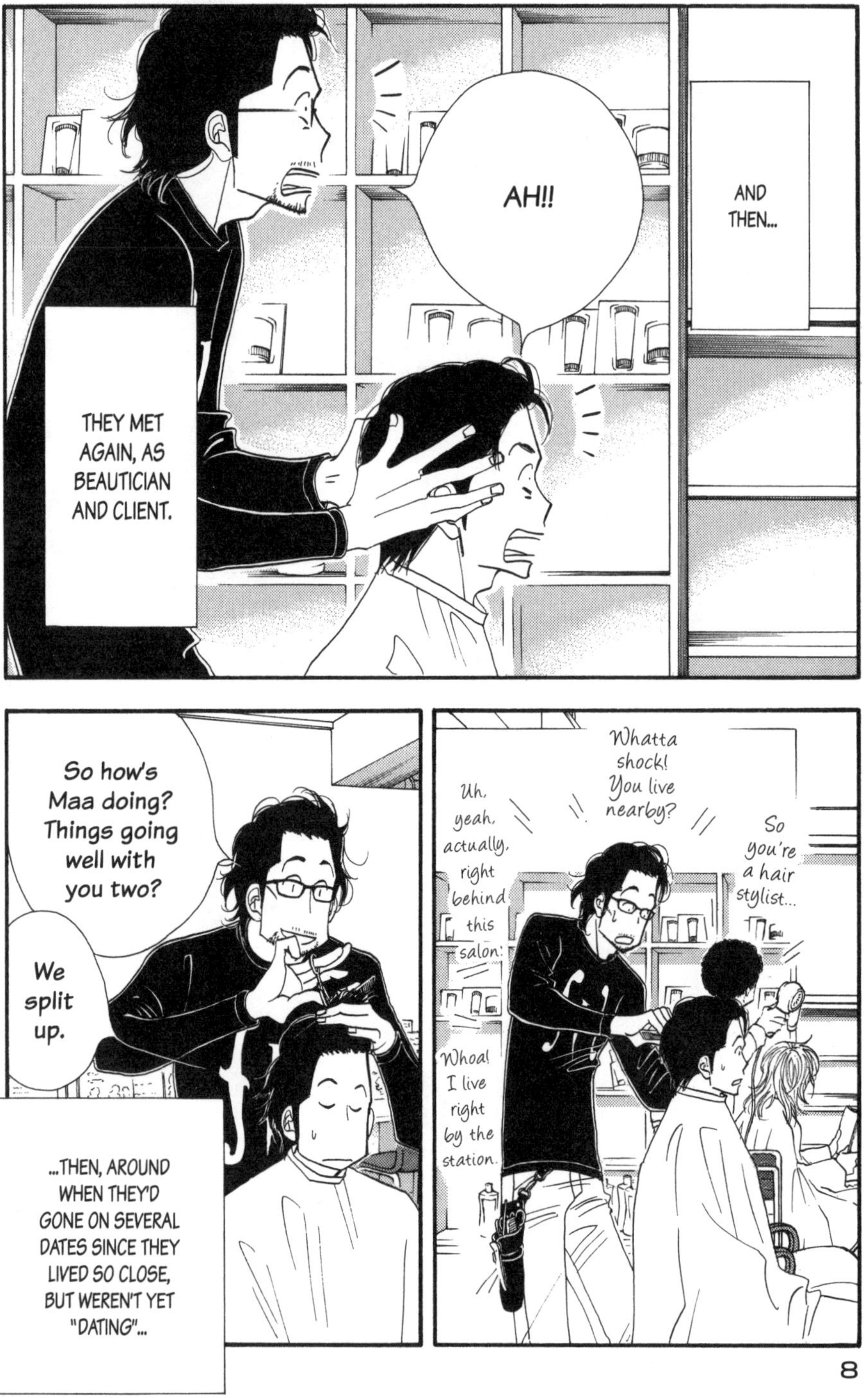
AND THEN...
AH!!
THEY MET AGAIN, AS BEAUTICIAN AND CLIENT.
So you're a hair stylist...
Whatta shock! You live nearby?
Uh, yeah, actually, right behind this salon.
Whoa! I live right by the station.
So how's Maa doing? Things going well with you two?
We split up.
...THEN, AROUND WHEN THEY'D GONE ON SEVERAL DATES SINCE THEY LIVED SO CLOSE, BUT WEREN'T YET "DATING"...

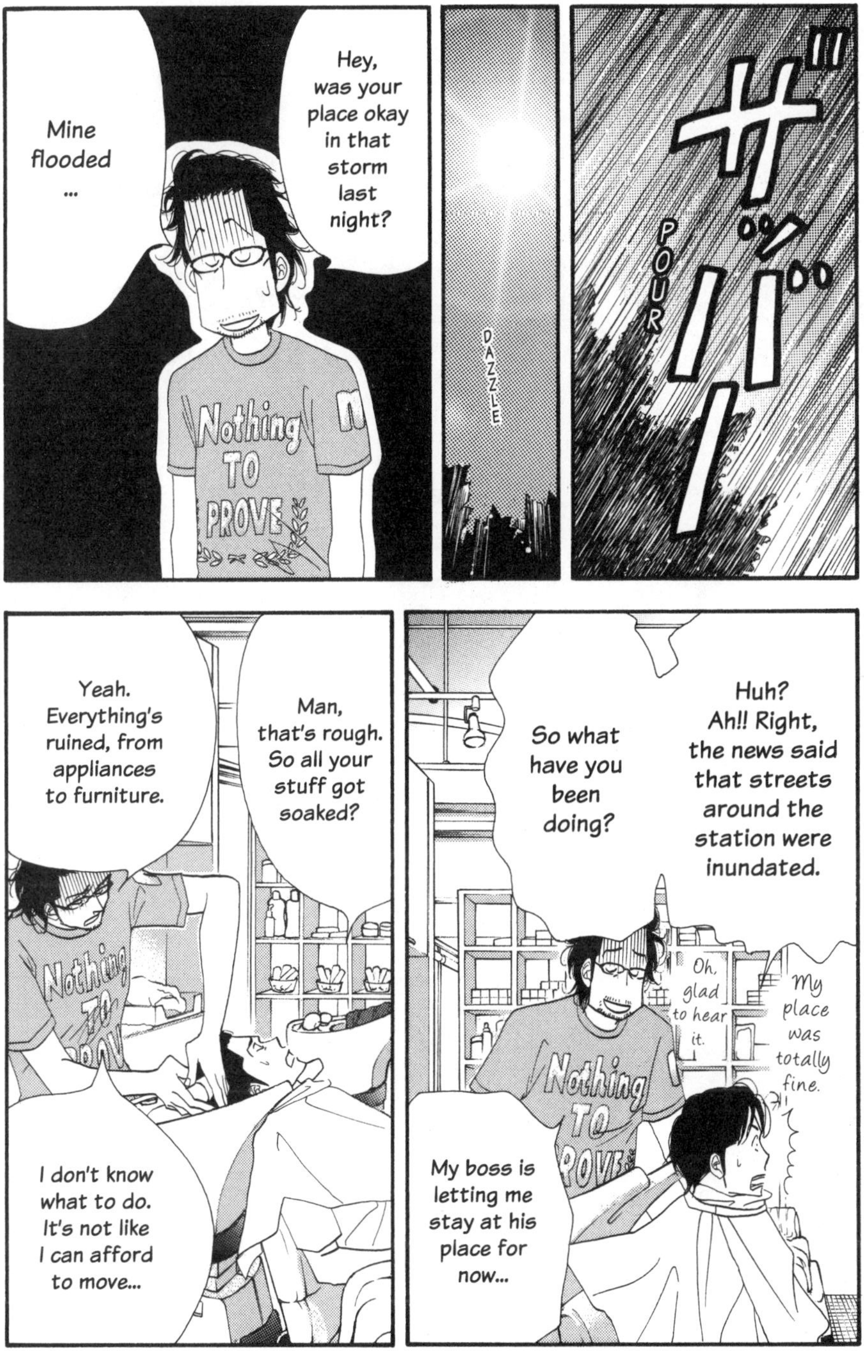
POUR
DAZZLE
Hey, was your place okay in that storm last night?
Mine flooded ...
Huh? Ah!! Right, the news said that streets around the station were inundated.
So what have you been doing?
My place was totally fine.
Oh, glad to hear it.
My boss is letting me stay at his place for now...
Man, that's rough. So all your stuff got soaked?
Yeah. Everything's ruined, from appliances to furniture.
I don't know what to do. It's not like I can afford to move...
Nothing TO PROVE

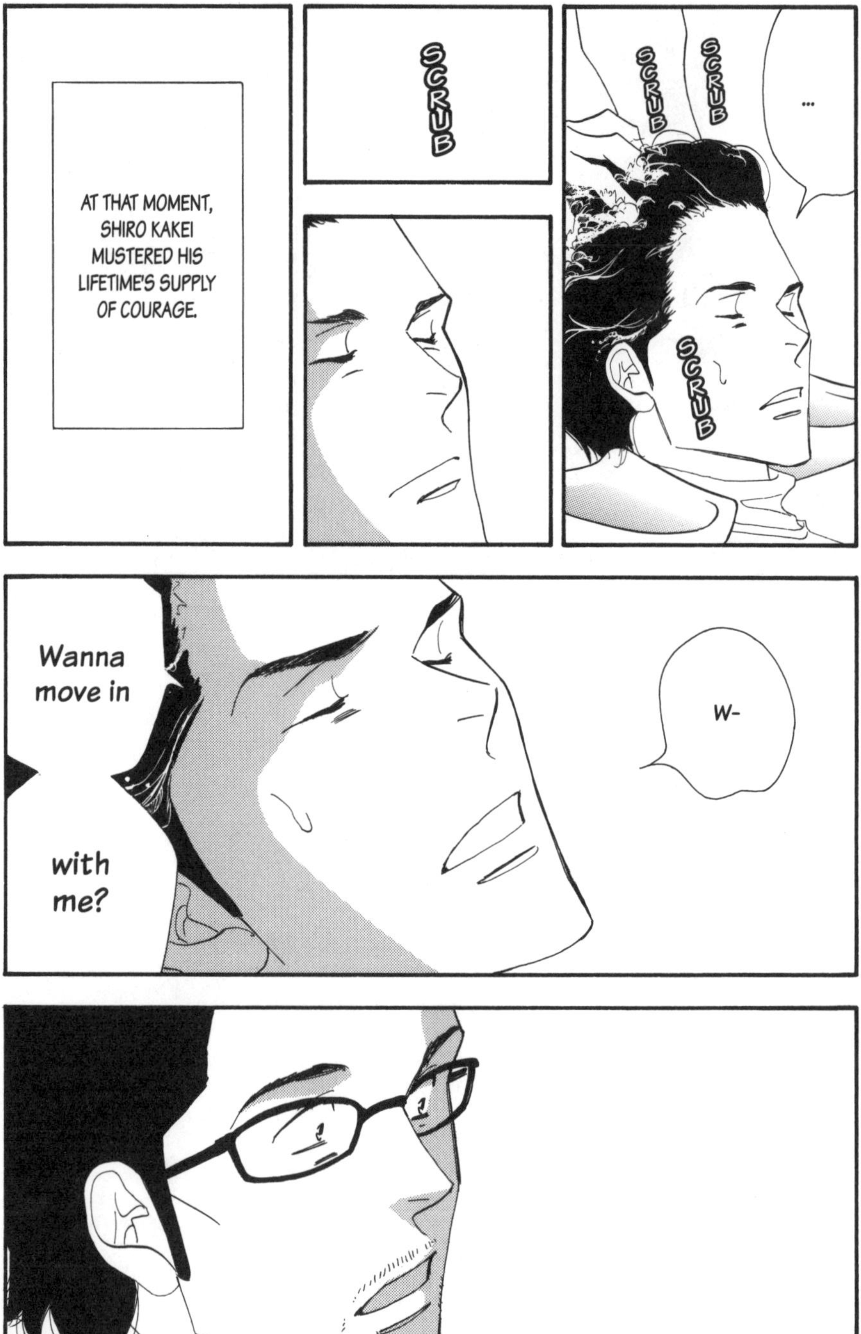
...
SCRUB
SCRUB
SCRUB
SCRUB
AT THAT MOMENT, SHIRO KAKEI MUSTERED HIS LIFETIME'S SUPPLY OF COURAGE.
W-
Wanna move in with me?

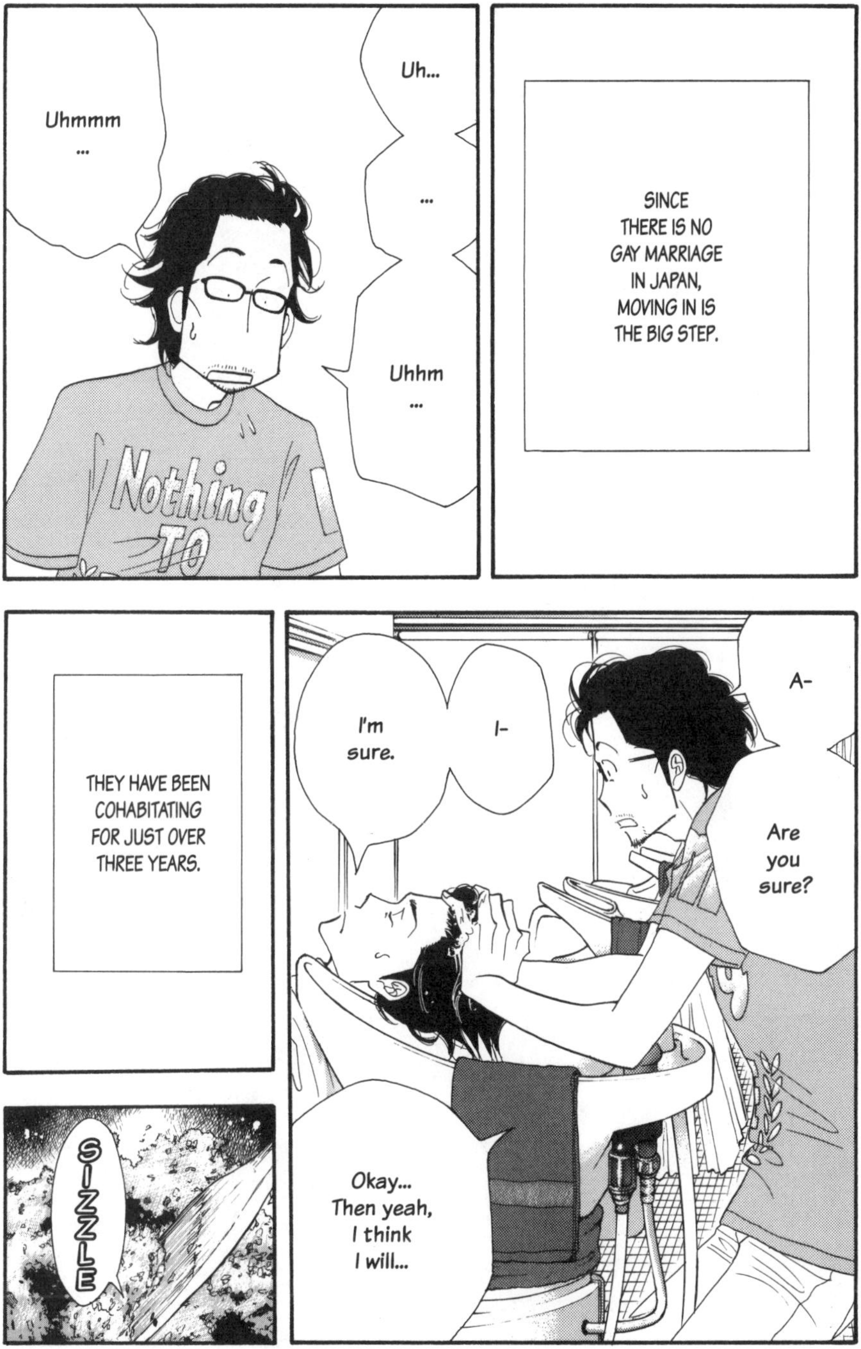
SINCE THERE IS NO GAY MARRIAGE IN JAPAN, MOVING IN IS THE BIG STEP.
Uh...
...
Uhhm ...
Uhmmm ...
Nothing TO
A-
Are you sure?
I-
I'm sure.
Okay... Then yeah, I think I will...
THEY HAVE BEEN COHABITATING FOR JUST OVER THREE YEARS.
SIZZLE

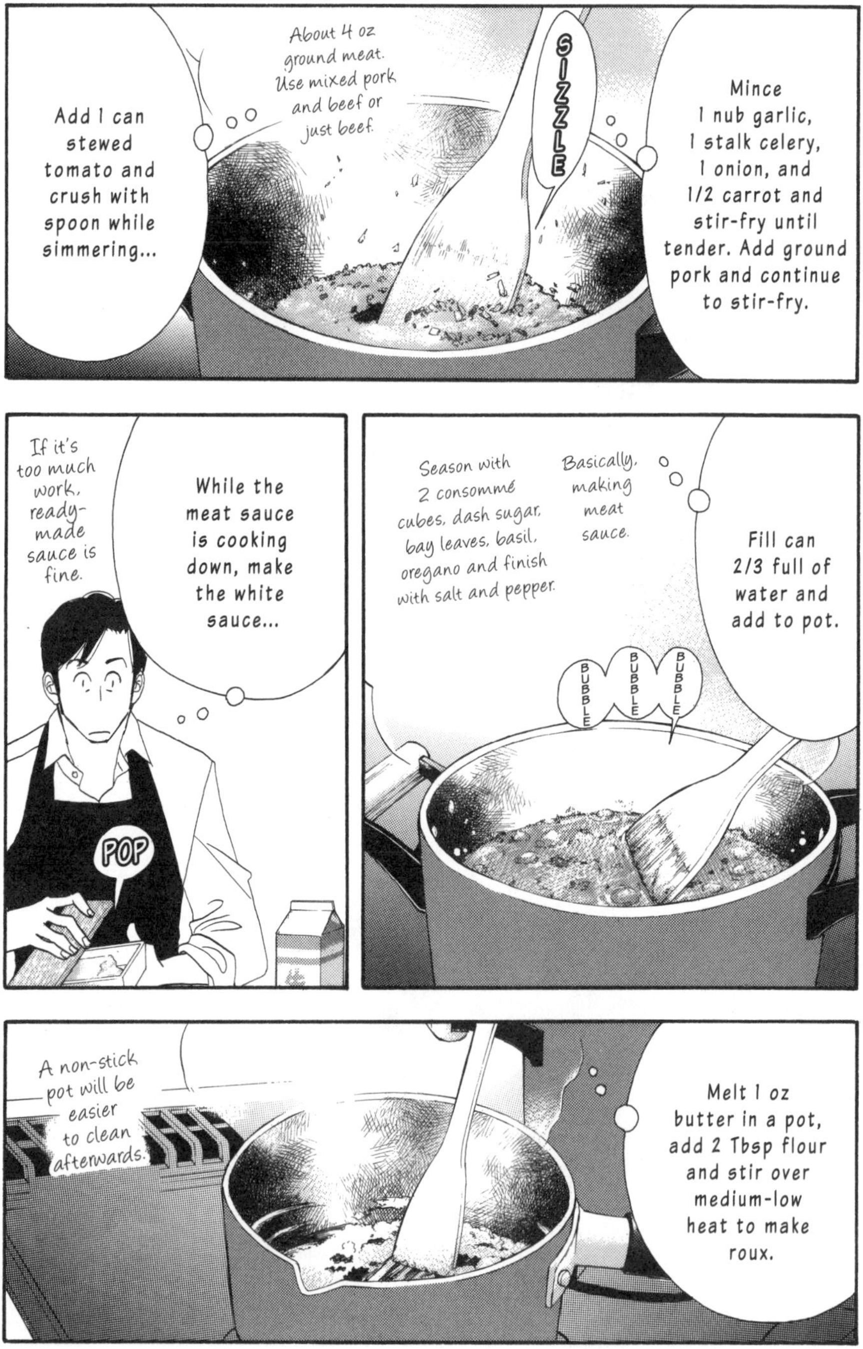
Mince 1 nub garlic, 1 stalk celery, 1 onion, and 1/2 carrot and stir-fry until tender. Add ground pork and continue to stir-fry.
SIZZLE
About 4 oz ground meat. Use mixed pork and beef or just beef.
Add 1 can stewed tomato and crush with spoon while simmering...
Fill can 2/3 full of water and add to pot.
Basically, making meat sauce.
Season with 2 consommé cubes, dash sugar, bay leaves, basil, oregano and finish with salt and pepper.
BUBBLE BUBBLE BUBBLE
While the meat sauce is cooking down, make the white sauce...
If it's too much work, ready-made sauce is fine.
POP
Melt 1 oz butter in a pot, add 2 Tbsp flour and stir over medium-low heat to make roux.
A non-stick pot will be easier to clean afterwards.

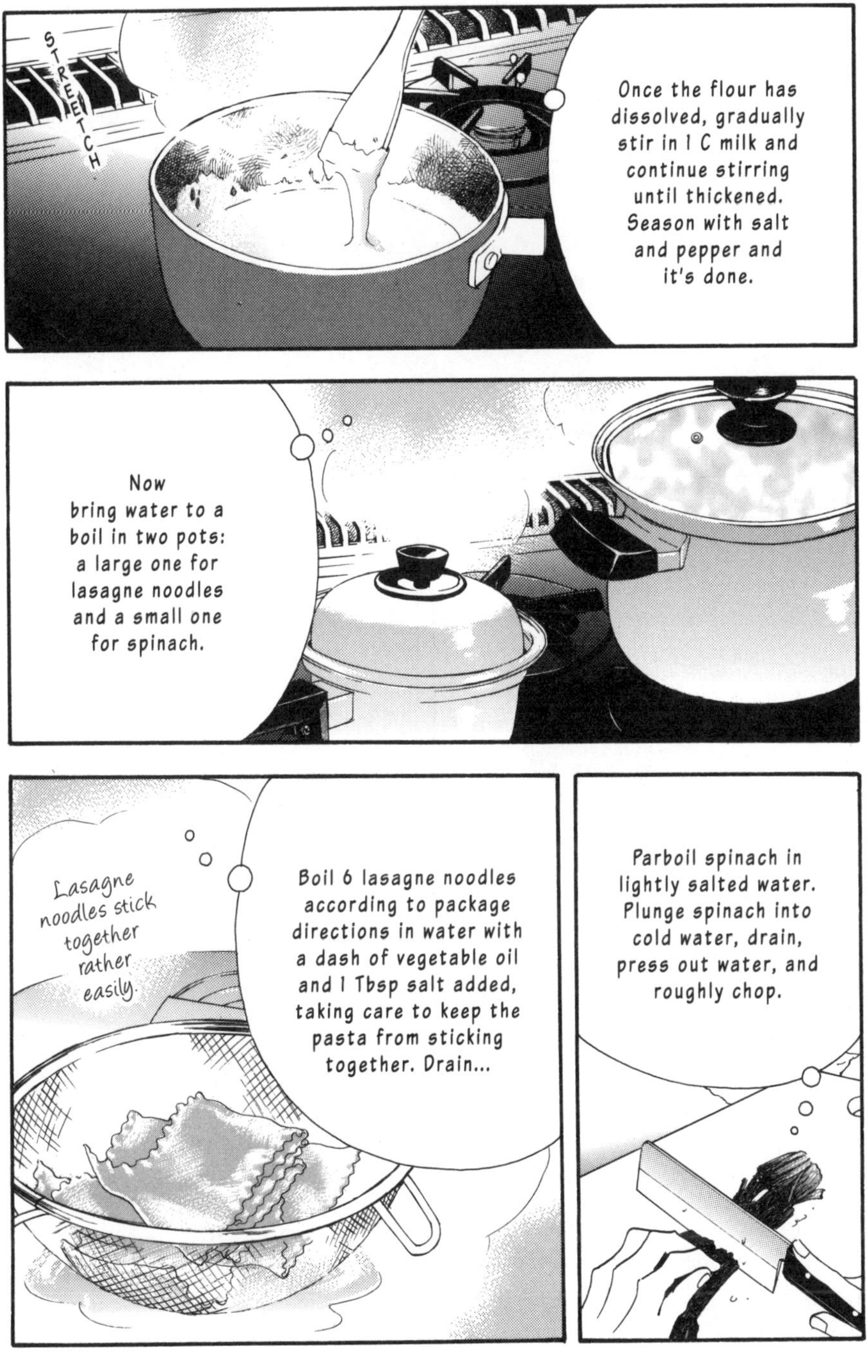
Once the flour has dissolved, gradually stir in 1 C milk and continue stirring until thickened. Season with salt and pepper and it's done.
STREETCH
Now bring water to a boil in two pots: a large one for lasagne noodles and a small one for spinach.
Parboil spinach in lightly salted water. Plunge spinach into cold water, drain, press out water, and roughly chop.
Boil 6 lasagne noodles according to package directions in water with a dash of vegetable oil and 1 Tbsp salt added, taking care to keep the pasta from sticking together. Drain...
Lasagne noodles stick together rather easily.

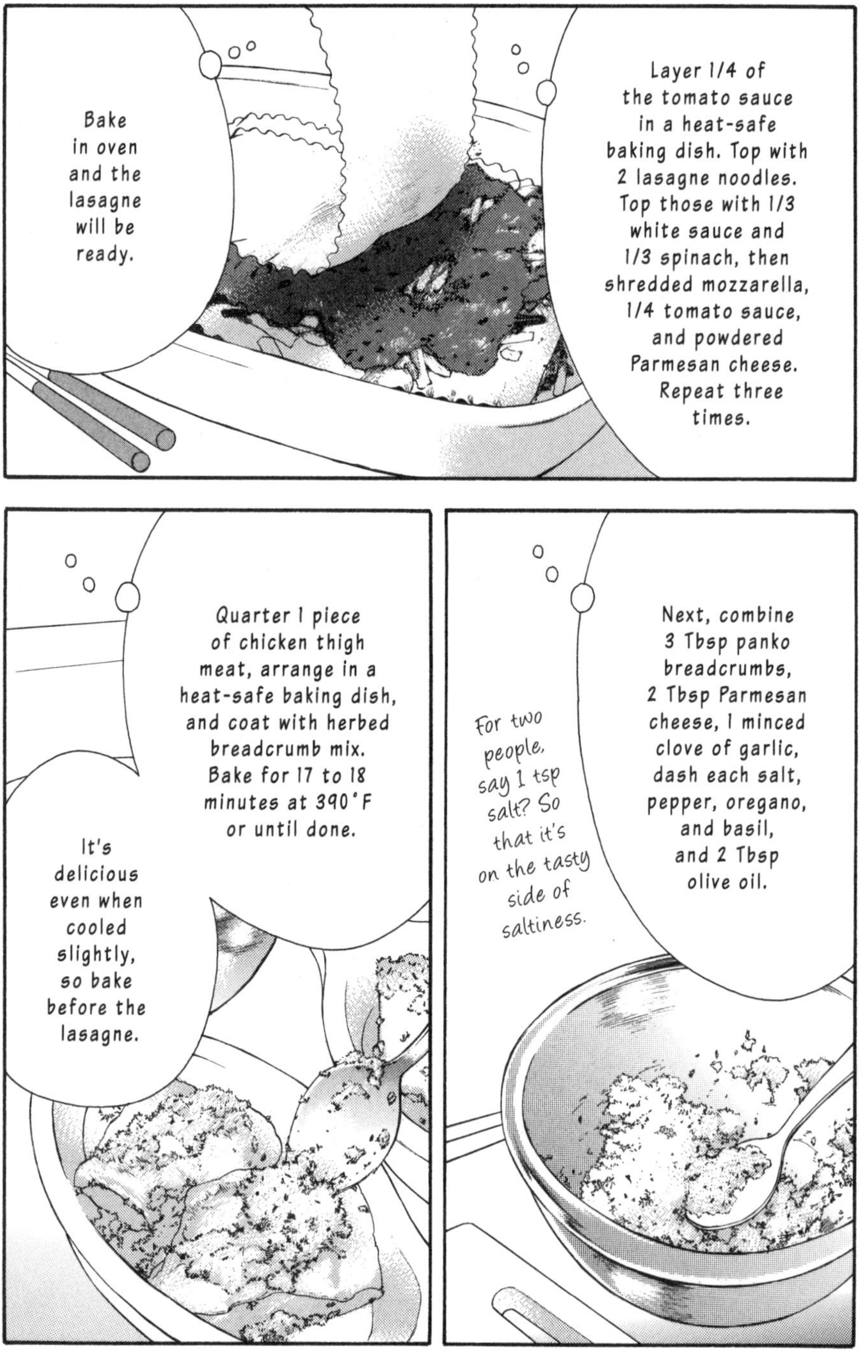
Layer 1/4 of the tomato sauce in a heat-safe baking dish. Top with 2 lasagne noodles. Top those with 1/3 white sauce and 1/3 spinach, then shredded mozzarella, 1/4 tomato sauce, and powdered Parmesan cheese. Repeat three times.
Bake in oven and the lasagne will be ready.
Next, combine 3 Tbsp panko breadcrumbs, 2 Tbsp Parmesan cheese, 1 minced clove of garlic, dash each salt, pepper, oregano, and basil, and 2 Tbsp olive oil.
For two people, say 1 tsp salt? So that it's on the tasty side of saltiness.
Quarter 1 piece of chicken thigh meat, arrange in a heat-safe baking dish, and coat with herbed breadcrumb mix. Bake for 17 to 18 minutes at 390°F or until done.
It's delicious even when cooled slightly, so bake before the lasagne.

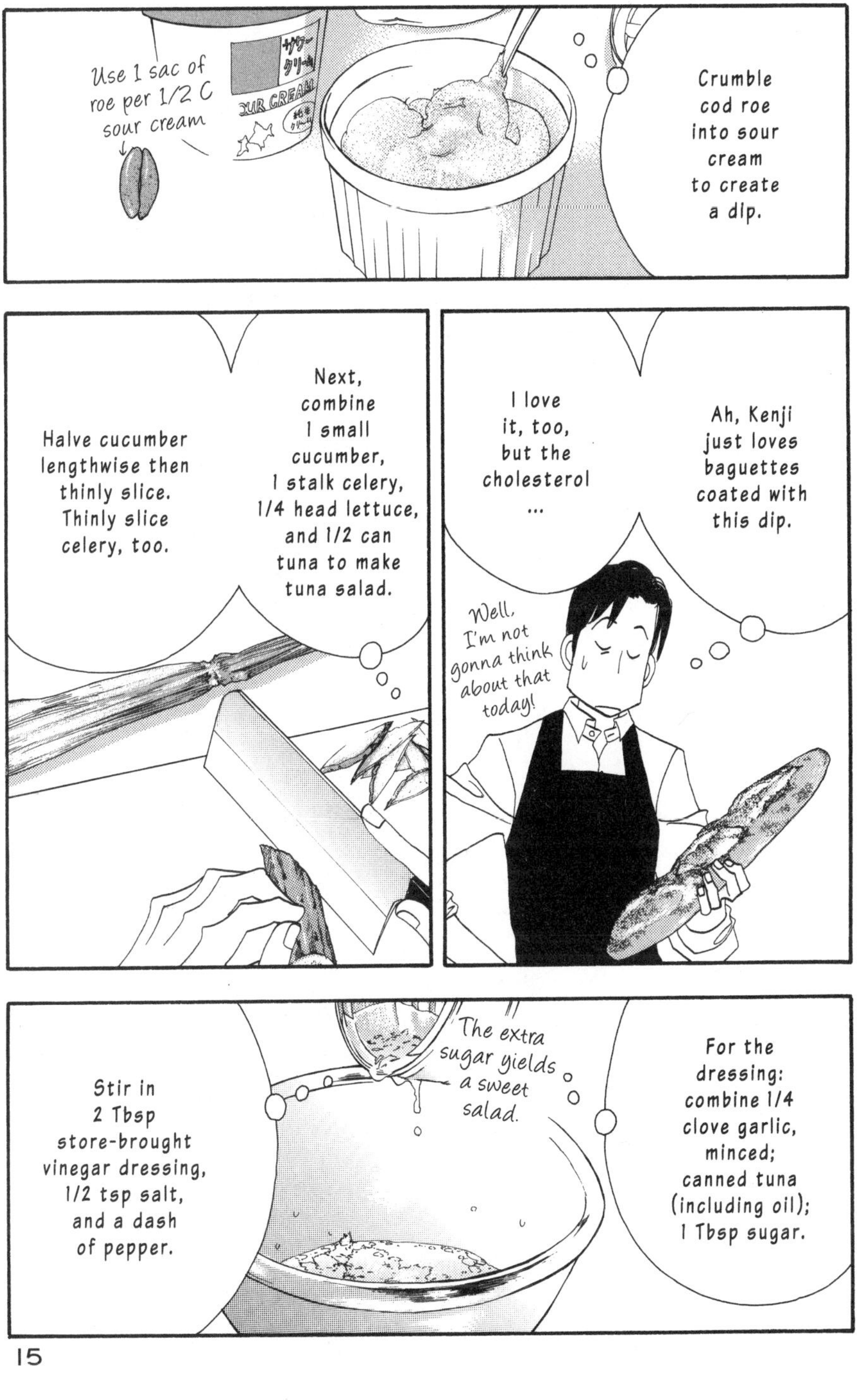
Crumble cod roe into sour cream to create a dip.
Use 1 sac of roe per 1/2 C sour cream
Ah, Kenji just loves baguettes coated with this dip.
I love it, too, but the cholesterol ...
Well, I'm not gonna think about that today!
Next, combine 1 small cucumber, 1 stalk celery, 1/4 head lettuce, and 1/2 can tuna to make tuna salad.
Halve cucumber lengthwise then thinly slice. Thinly slice celery, too.
For the dressing: combine 1/4 clove garlic, minced; canned tuna (including oil); 1 Tbsp sugar.
The extra sugar yields a sweet salad.
Stir in 2 Tbsp store-brought vinegar dressing, 1/2 tsp salt, and a dash of pepper.

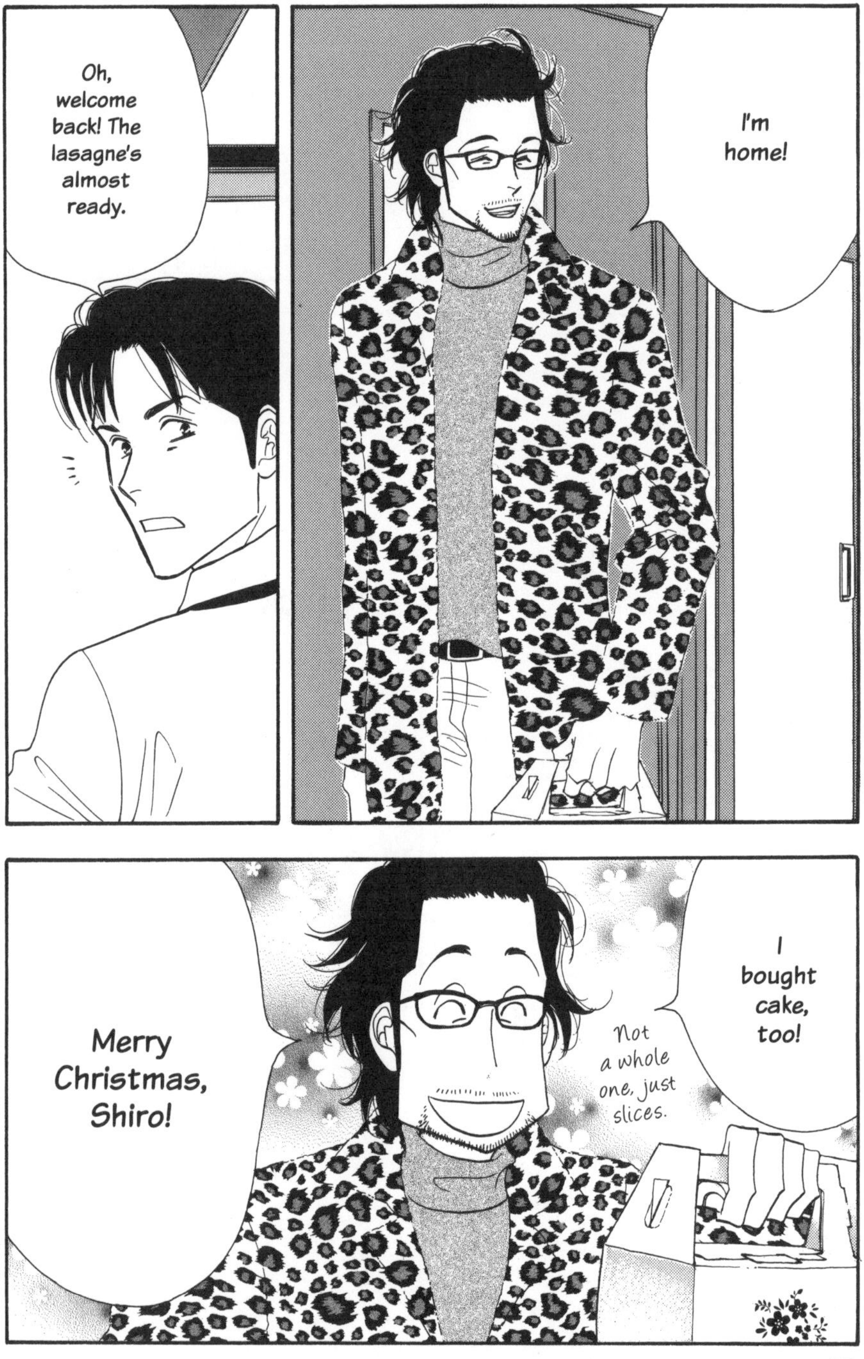
I'm home!
Oh, welcome back! The lasagne's almost ready.
I bought cake, too!
Not a whole one, just slices.
Merry Christmas, Shiro!

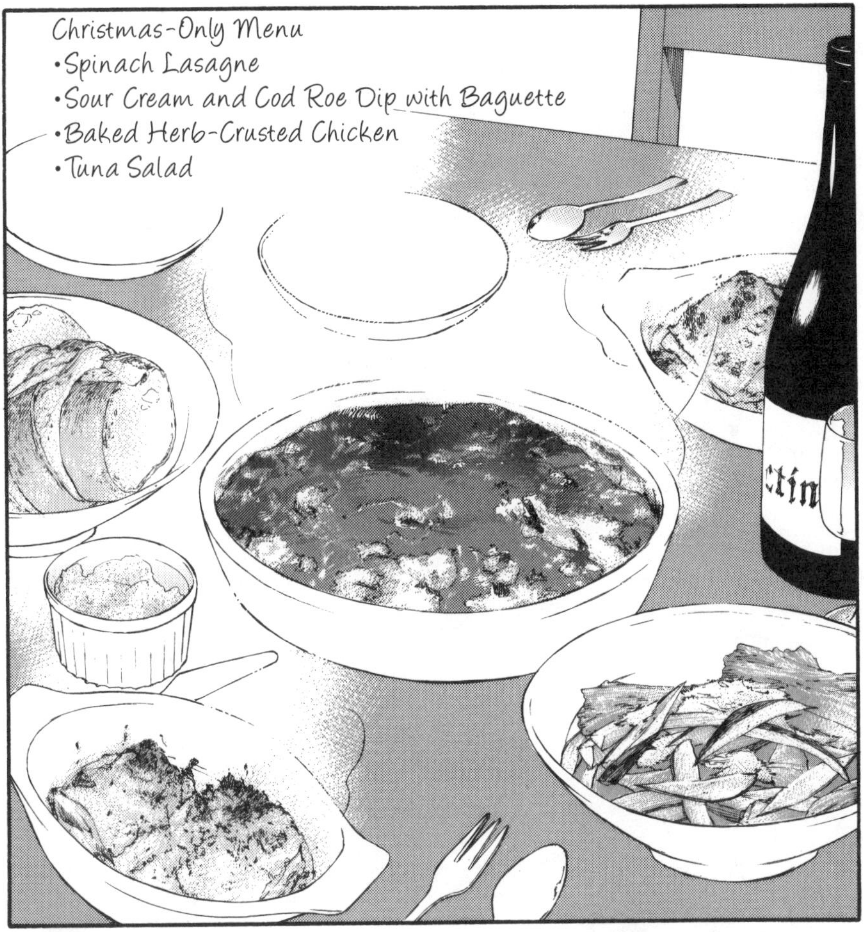
Christmas-Only Menu
•Spinach Lasagne
•Sour Cream and Cod Roe Dip with Baguette
•Baked Herb-Crusted Chicken
•Tuna Salad

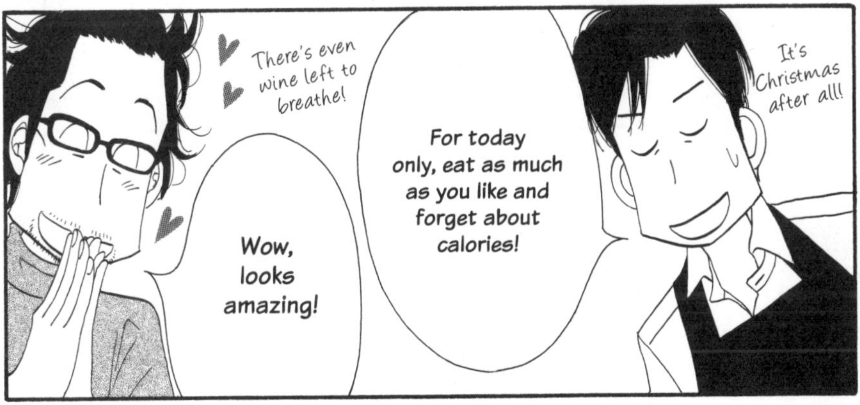
It's Christmas after all!
For today only, eat as much as you like and forget about calories!
There's even wine left to breathe!
Wow, looks amazing!

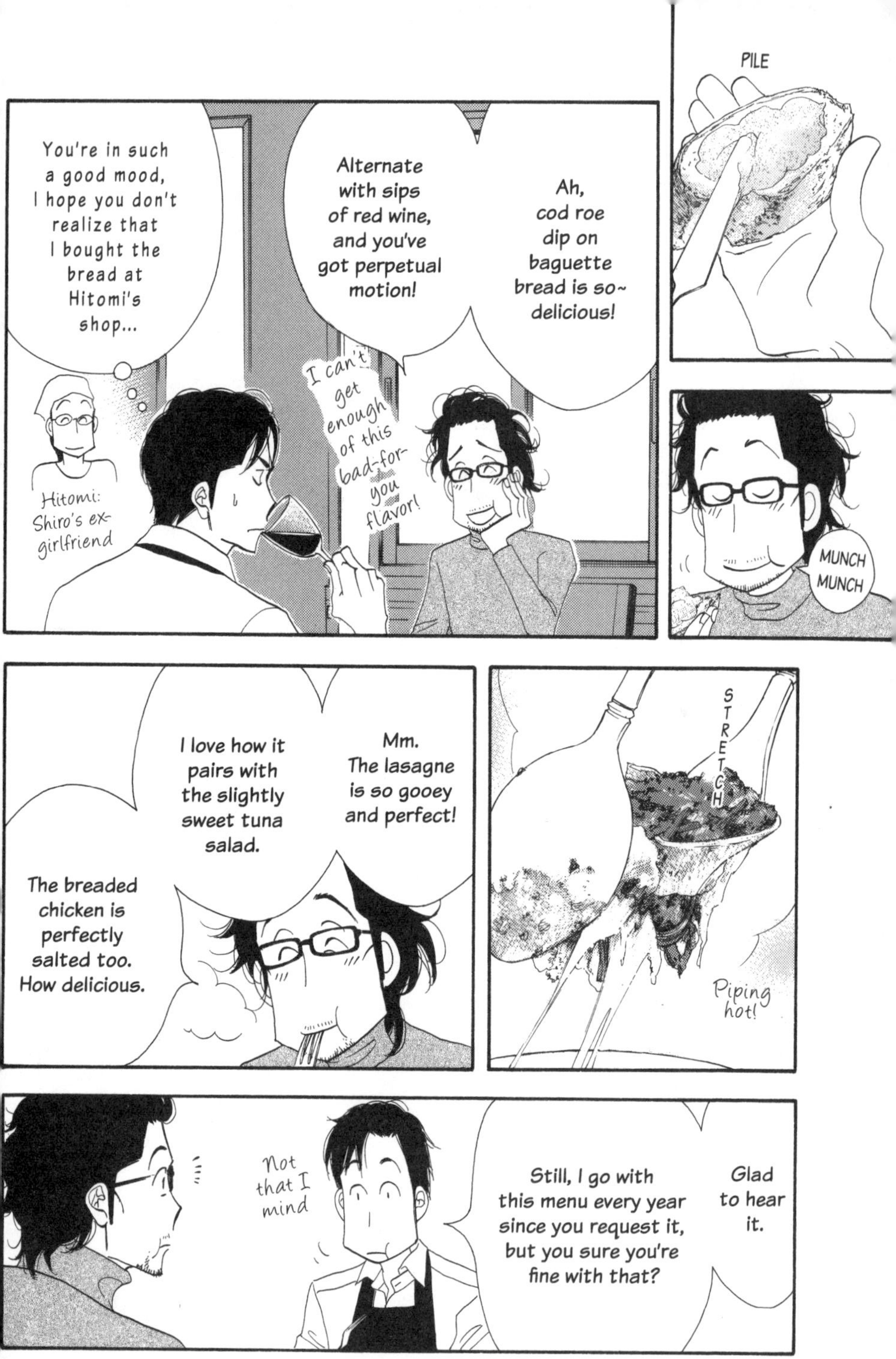
PILE
MUNCH MUNCH
Ah, cod roe dip on baguette bread is so~ delicious!
Alternate with sips of red wine, and you've got perpetual motion!
I can't get enough of this bad-for-you flavor!
You're in such a good mood, I hope you don't realize that I bought the bread at Hitomi's shop...
Hitomi: Shiro's ex-girlfriend
STRETCH
Piping hot!
Mm. The lasagne is so gooey and perfect!
I love how it pairs with the slightly sweet tuna salad.
The breaded chicken is perfectly salted too. How delicious.
Glad to hear it.
Still, I go with this menu every year since you request it, but you sure you're fine with that?
Not that I mind

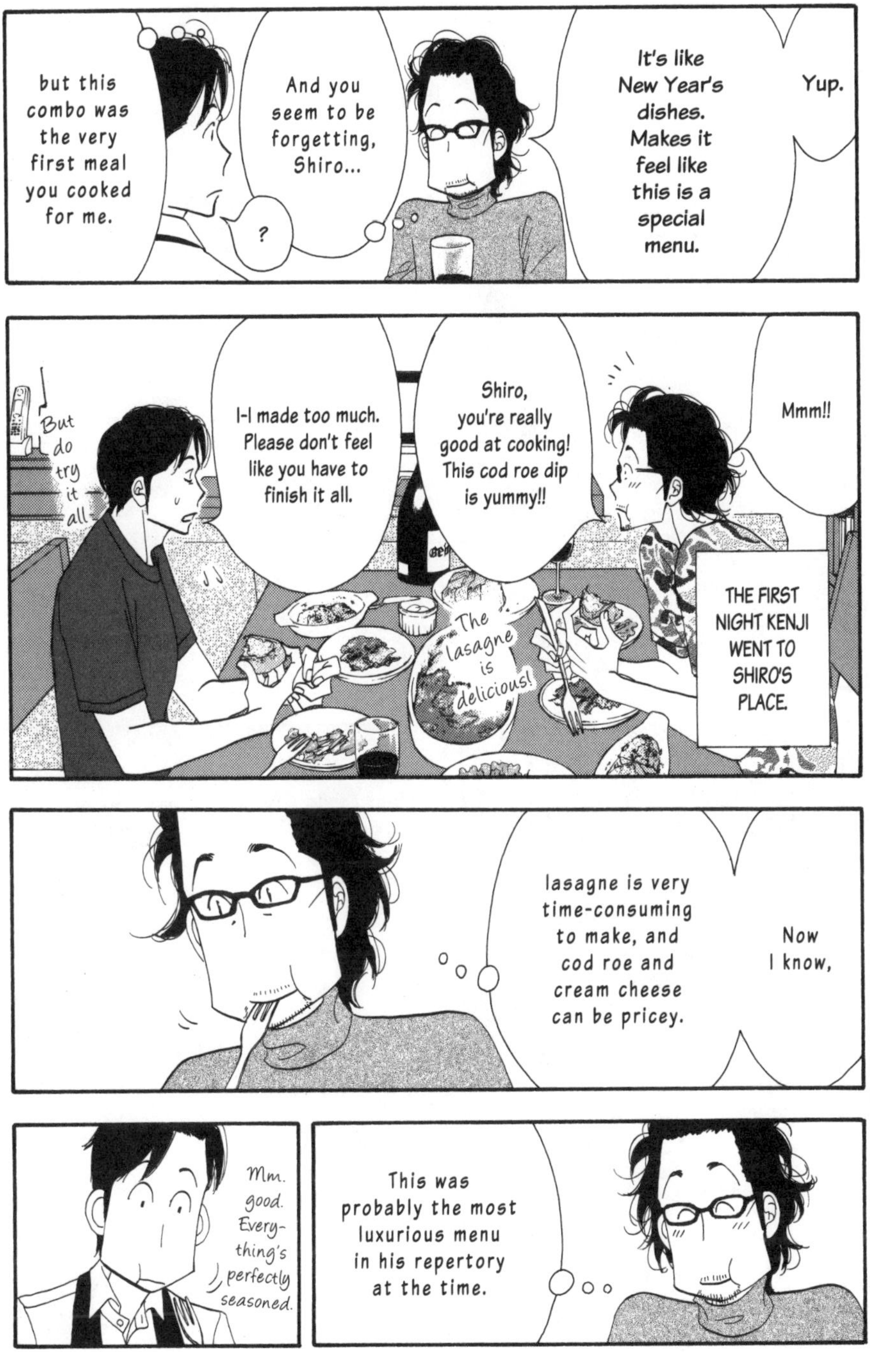
Yup.
It's like New Year's dishes. Makes it feel like this is a special menu.
And you seem to be forgetting, Shiro...
?
but this combo was the very first meal you cooked for me.
Mmm!!
Shiro, you're really good at cooking! This cod roe dip is yummy!!
THE FIRST NIGHT KENJI WENT TO SHIRO'S PLACE.
I-I made too much. Please don't feel like you have to finish it all.
The lasagne is delicious!
But do try it all
Now I know,
lasagne is very time-consuming to make, and cod roe and cream cheese can be pricey.
This was probably the most luxurious menu in his repertory at the time.
Mm. good. Every-thing's perfectly seasoned.

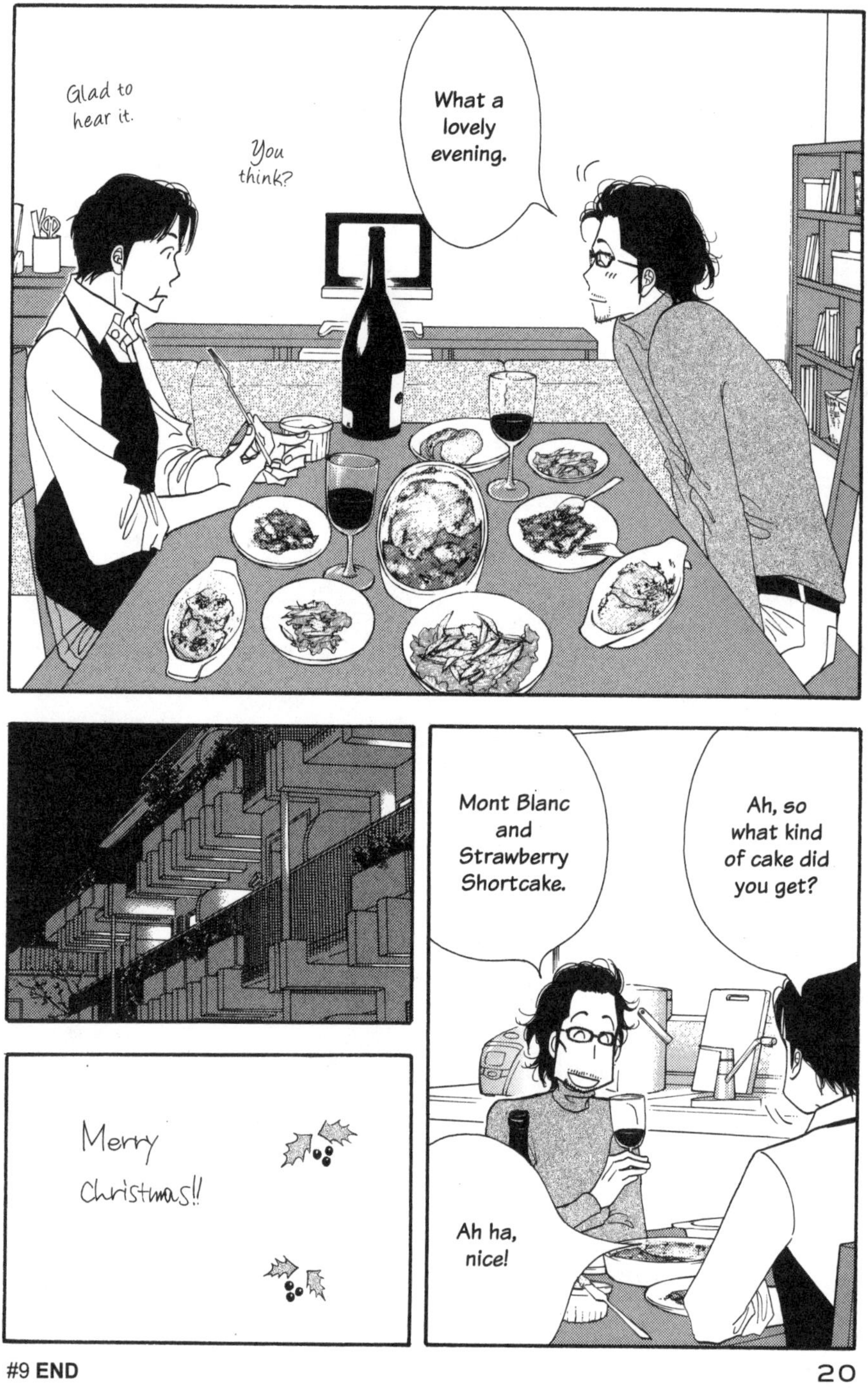
What a lovely evening.
You think?
Glad to hear it.
Ah, so what kind of cake did you get?
Mont Blanc and Strawberry Shortcake.
Ah ha, nice!
Merry Christmas!!

#9 END

The **tuna salad** used *Mitsukan*'s vinegar dressing, but feel free to substitute rice or wine vinegar, or any vinegar you have on hand. The trick is to season with enough sugar and garlic.

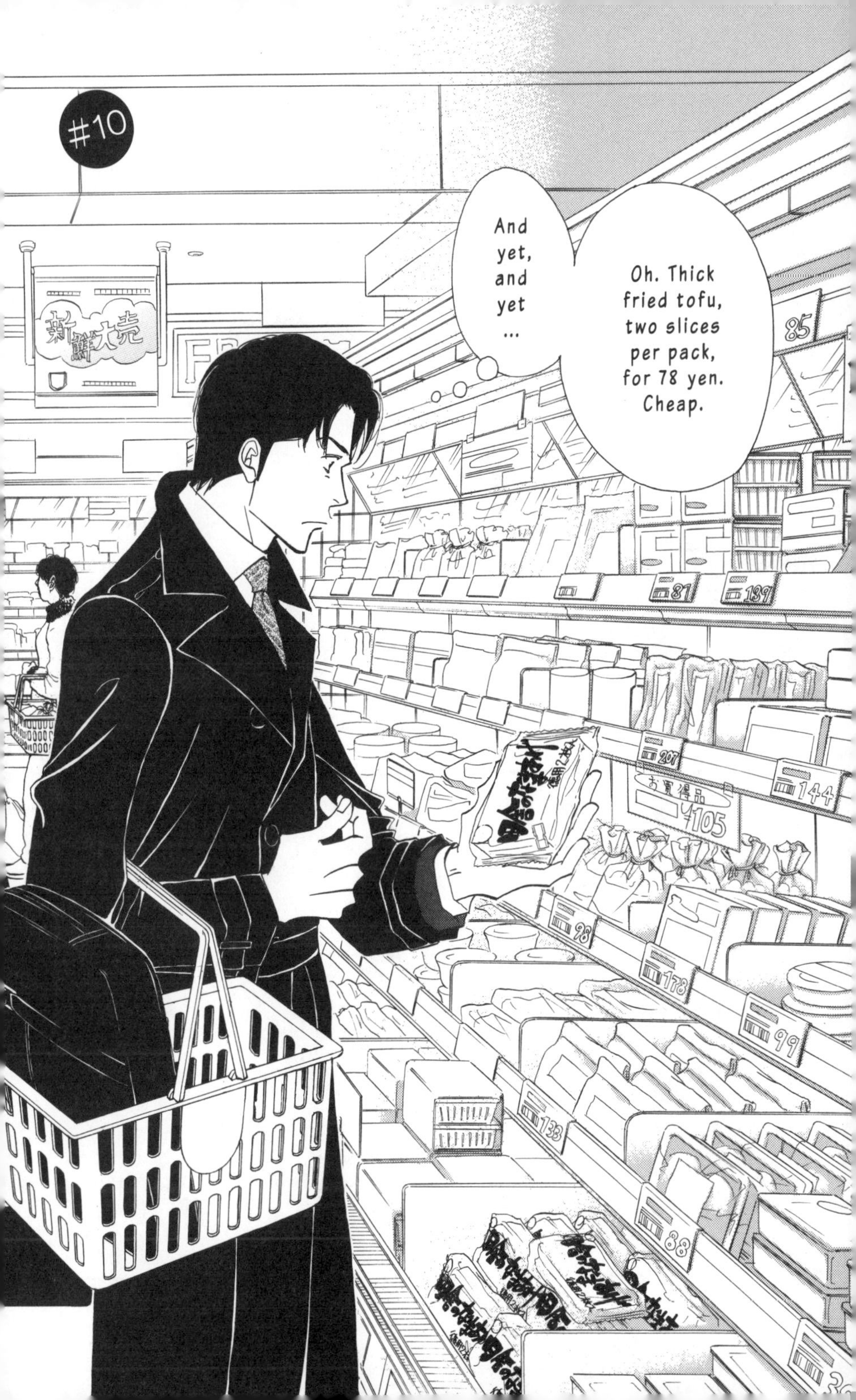
#10
Oh. Thick fried tofu, two slices per pack, for 78 yen. Cheap.
And yet, and yet ...
新鮮大売
お買得品

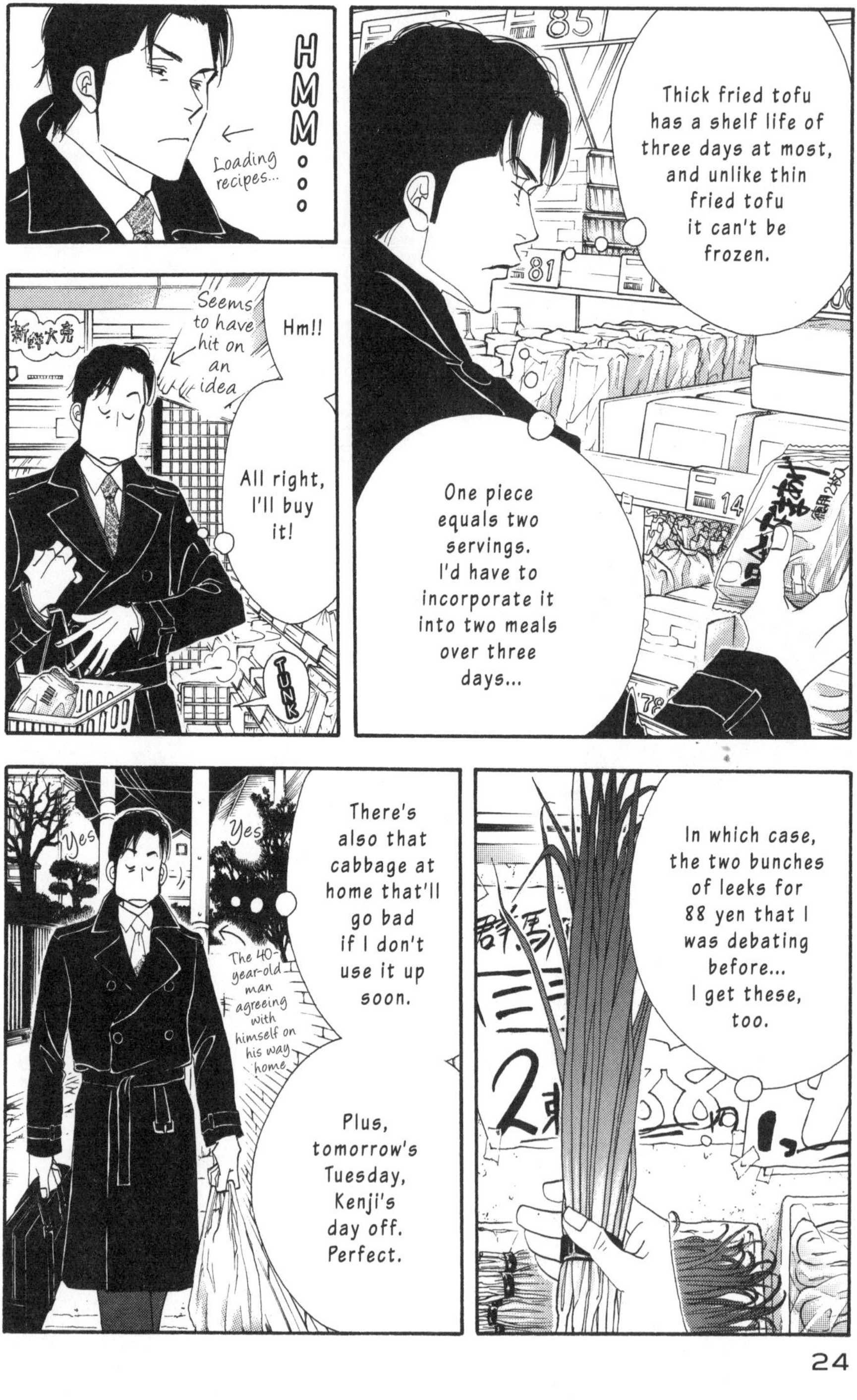
Thick fried tofu has a shelf life of three days at most, and unlike thin fried tofu it can't be frozen.
One piece equals two servings. I'd have to incorporate it into two meals over three days...
HMMooo
Loading recipes...
Hm!!
Seems to have hit on an idea
All right, I'll buy it!
TUNK
In which case, the two bunches of leeks for 88 yen that I was debating before... I get these, too.
There's also that cabbage at home that'll go bad if I don't use it up soon.
Yes
Yes
The 40-year-old man agreeing with himself on his way home
Plus, tomorrow's Tuesday, Kenji's day off. Perfect.

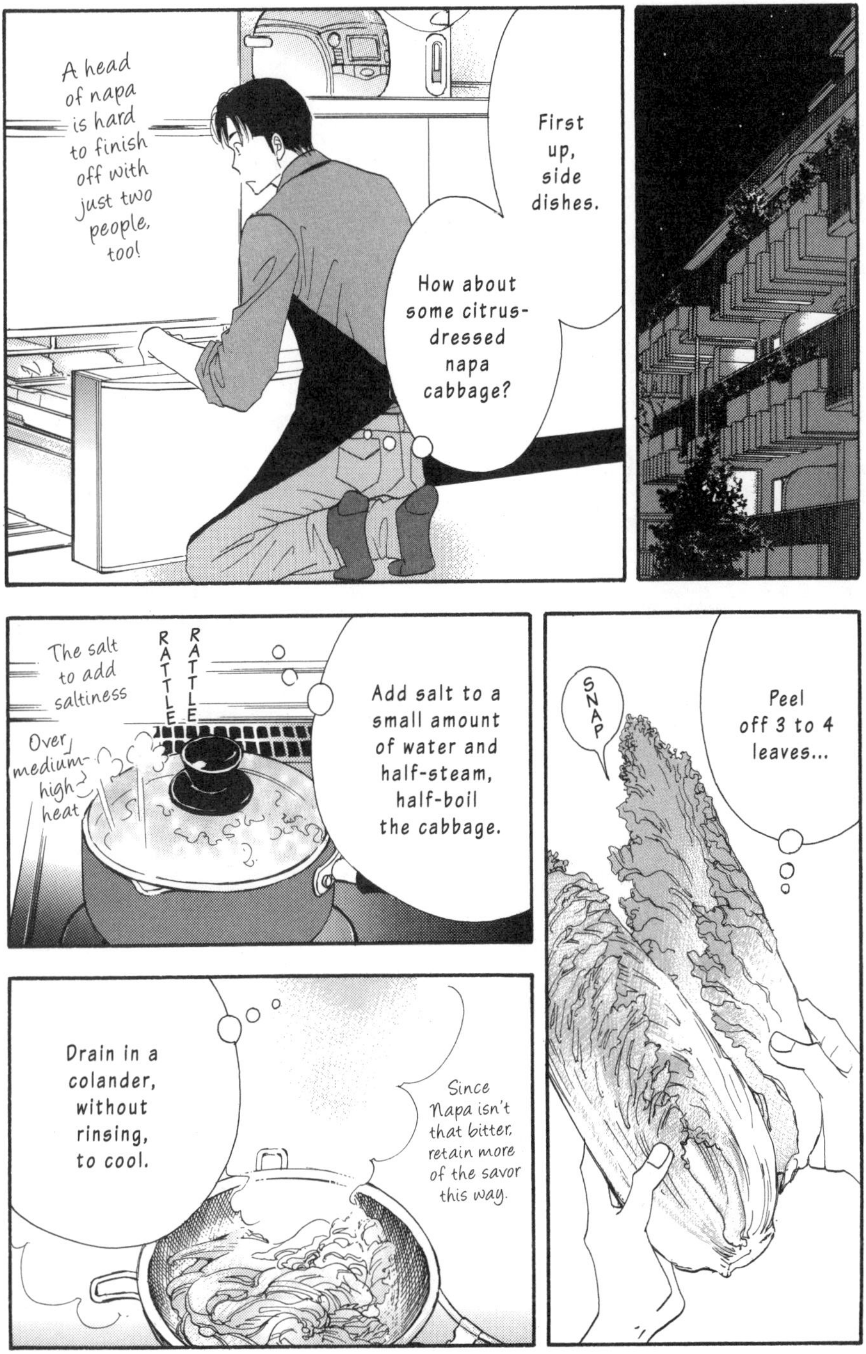
First up, side dishes.
How about some citrus-dressed napa cabbage?
A head of napa is hard to finish off with just two people, too!
Peel off 3 to 4 leaves...
SNAP
Add salt to a small amount of water and half-steam, half-boil the cabbage.
RATTLE
RATTLE
The salt to add saltiness
Over medium-high heat
Drain in a colander, without rinsing, to cool.
Since Napa isn't that bitter, retain more of the savor this way.

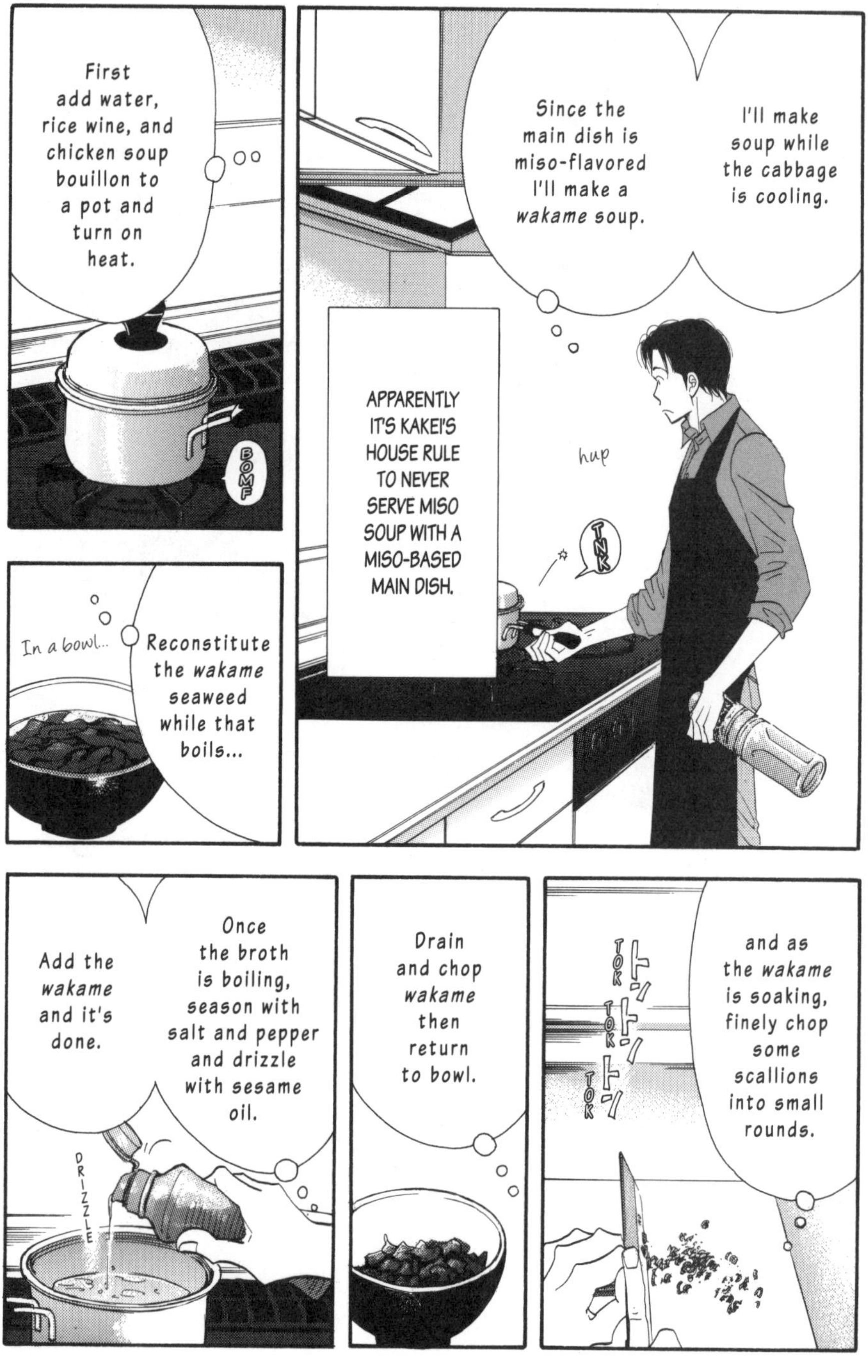
I'll make soup while the cabbage is cooling.
Since the main dish is miso-flavored I'll make a *wakame* soup.
APPARENTLY IT'S KAKEI'S HOUSE RULE TO NEVER SERVE MISO SOUP WITH A MISO-BASED MAIN DISH.
hup
TNK
First add water, rice wine, and chicken soup bouillon to a pot and turn on heat.
BOMF
In a bowl...
Reconstitute the *wakame* seaweed while that boils...
and as the *wakame* is soaking, finely chop some scallions into small rounds.
TOK
TOK
TOK
Drain and chop *wakame* then return to bowl.
Once the broth is boiling, season with salt and pepper and drizzle with sesame oil.
Add the *wakame* and it's done.
DRIZZLE

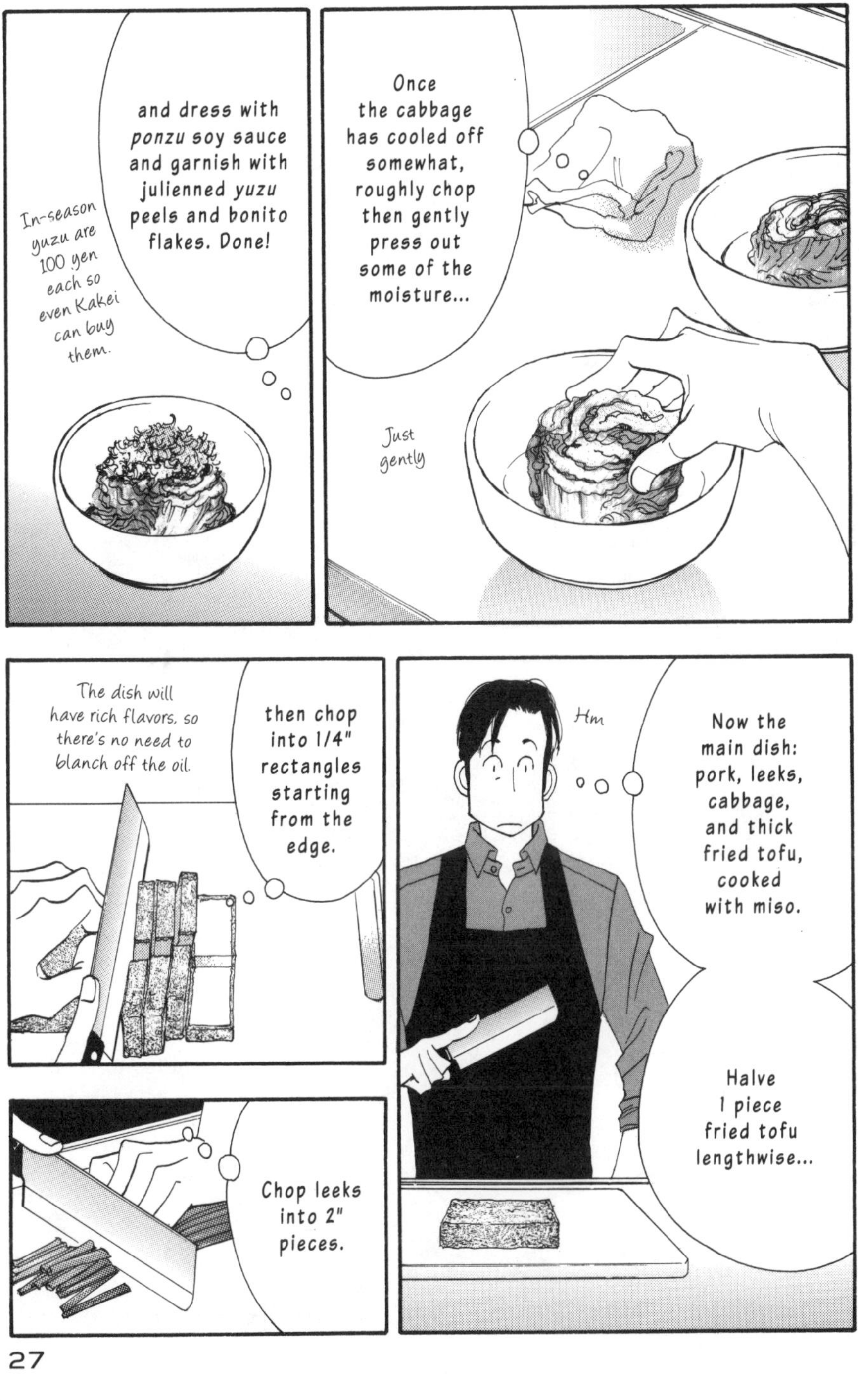
Once the cabbage has cooled off somewhat, roughly chop then gently press out some of the moisture...
Just gently
and dress with *ponzu* soy sauce and garnish with julienned *yuzu* peels and bonito flakes. Done!
In-season yuzu are 100 yen each so even Kakei can buy them.
Now the main dish: pork, leeks, cabbage, and thick fried tofu, cooked with miso.
Hm
Halve 1 piece fried tofu lengthwise...
then chop into 1/4" rectangles starting from the edge.
The dish will have rich flavors, so there's no need to blanch off the oil.
Chop leeks into 2" pieces.

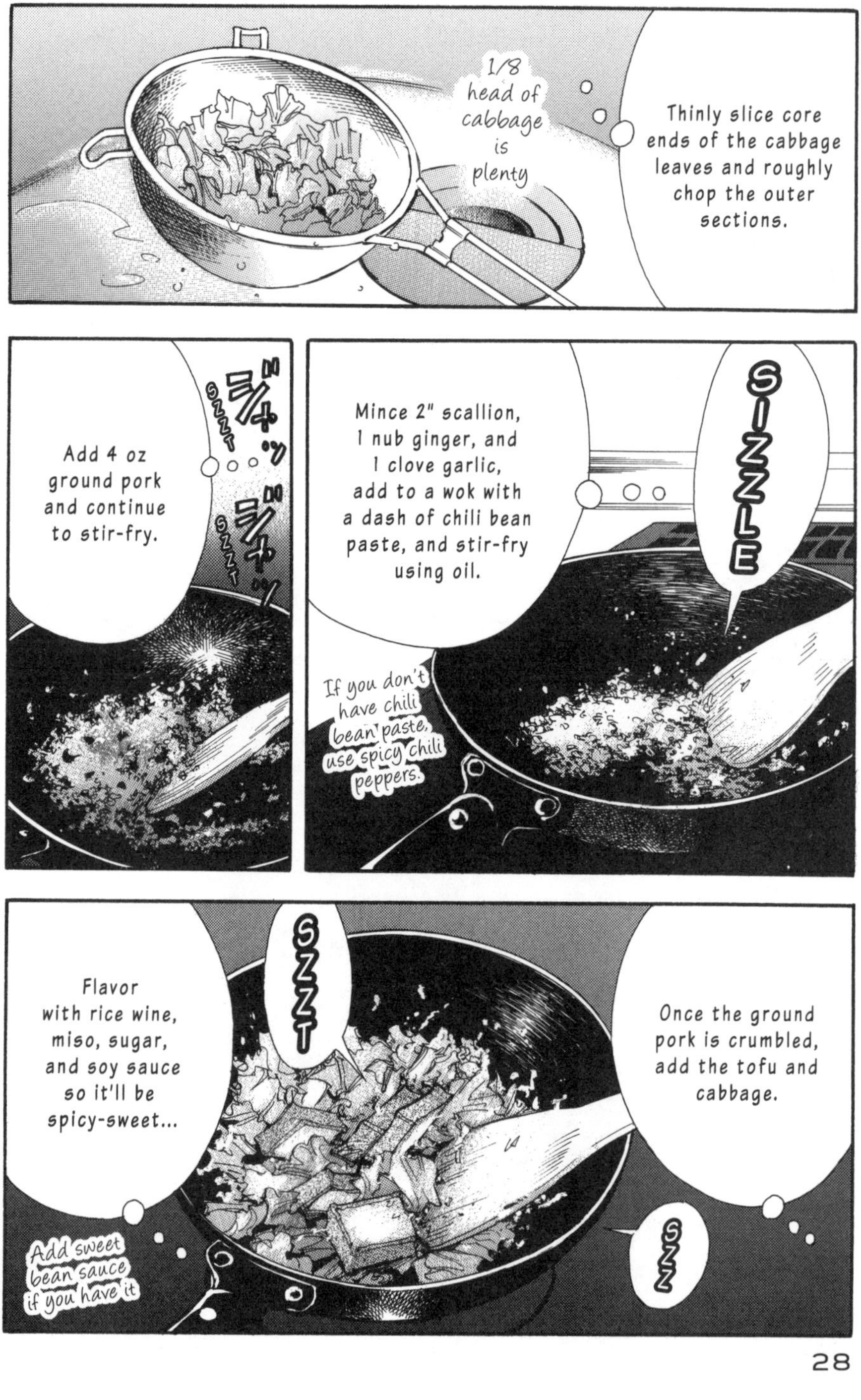
Thinly slice core ends of the cabbage leaves and roughly chop the outer sections.
1/8 head of cabbage is plenty
SIZZLE
Mince 2" scallion, 1 nub ginger, and 1 clove garlic, add to a wok with a dash of chili bean paste, and stir-fry using oil.
If you don't have chili bean paste, use spicy chili peppers.
SZZT
SZZT
Add 4 oz ground pork and continue to stir-fry.
Once the ground pork is crumbled, add the tofu and cabbage.
SZZ
SZZT
Flavor with rice wine, miso, sugar, and soy sauce so it'll be spicy-sweet...
Add sweet bean sauce if you have it

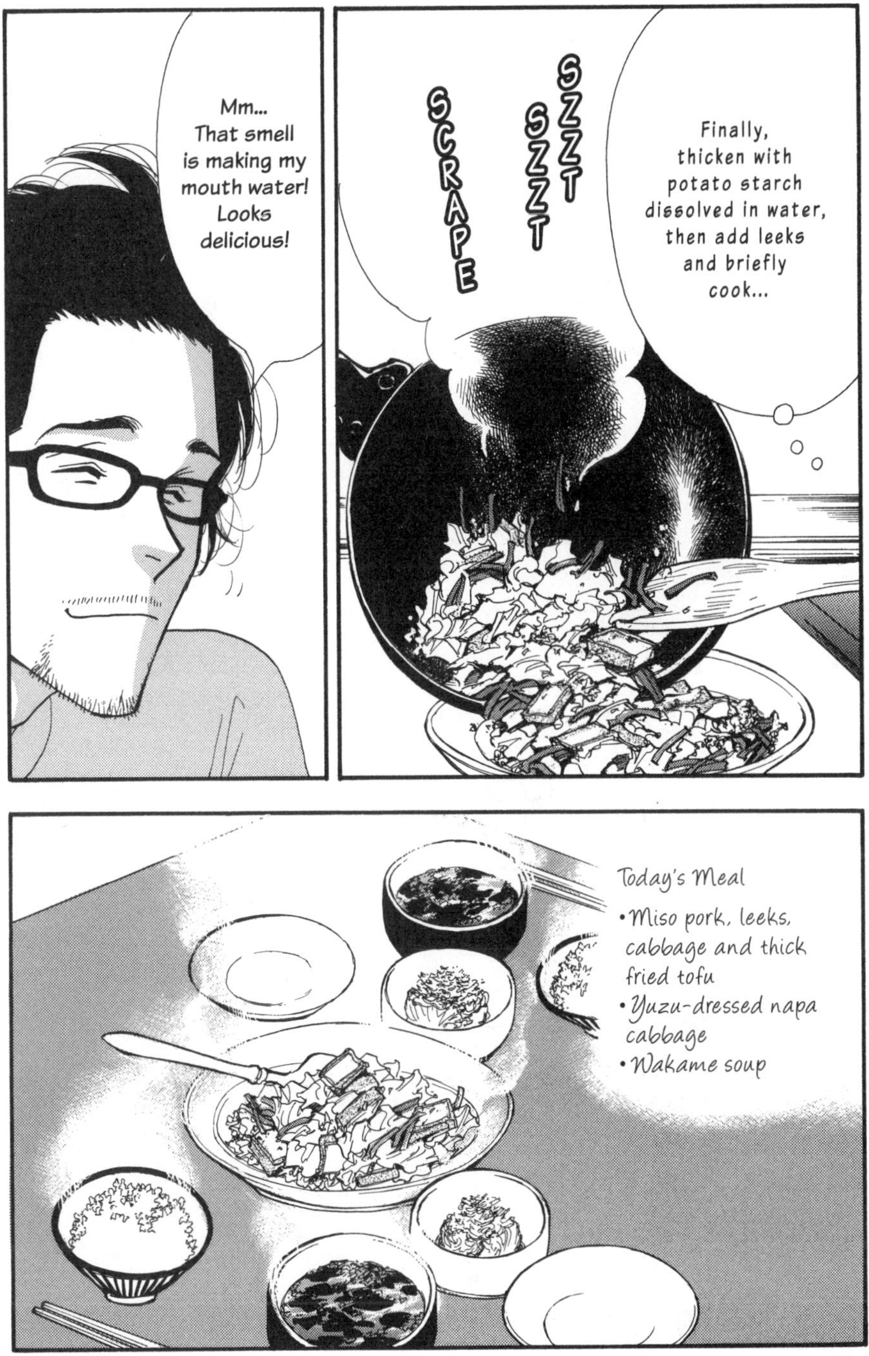
Finally, thicken with potato starch dissolved in water, then add leeks and briefly cook...
SZZT
SZZT
SCRAPE
Mm... That smell is making my mouth water! Looks delicious!
Today's Meal
•Miso pork, leeks, cabbage and thick fried tofu
•Yuzu-dressed napa cabbage
•Wakame soup

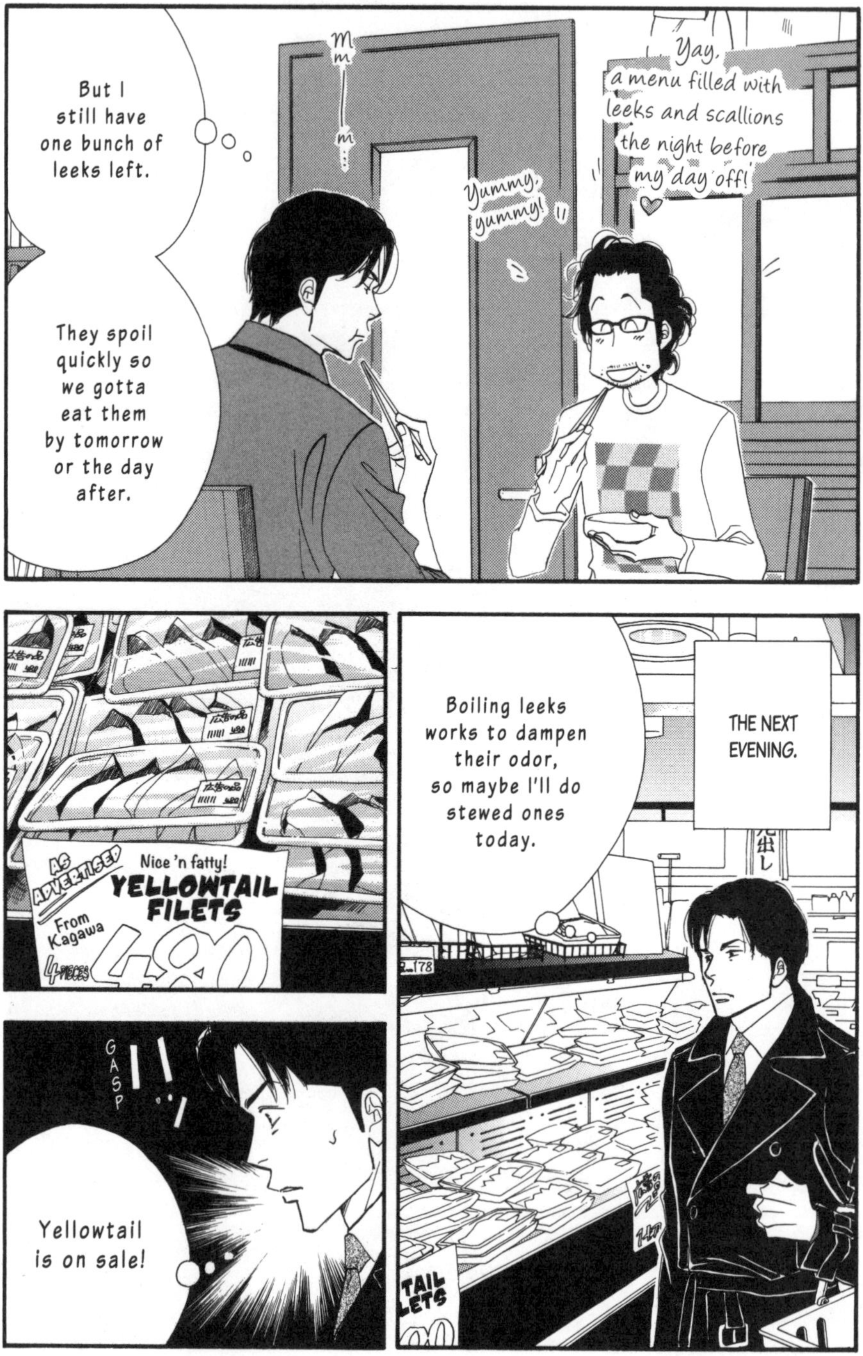
Mm—m...
Yay, a menu filled with leeks and scallions the night before my day off!
Yummy, yummy!
But I still have one bunch of leeks left.
They spoil quickly so we gotta eat them by tomorrow or the day after.
THE NEXT EVENING.
Boiling leeks works to dampen their odor, so maybe I'll do stewed ones today.
AS ADVERTISED
Nice 'n fatty!
YELLOWTAIL FILETS
From Kagawa
4 PIECES 480
GASP
Yellowtail is on sale!

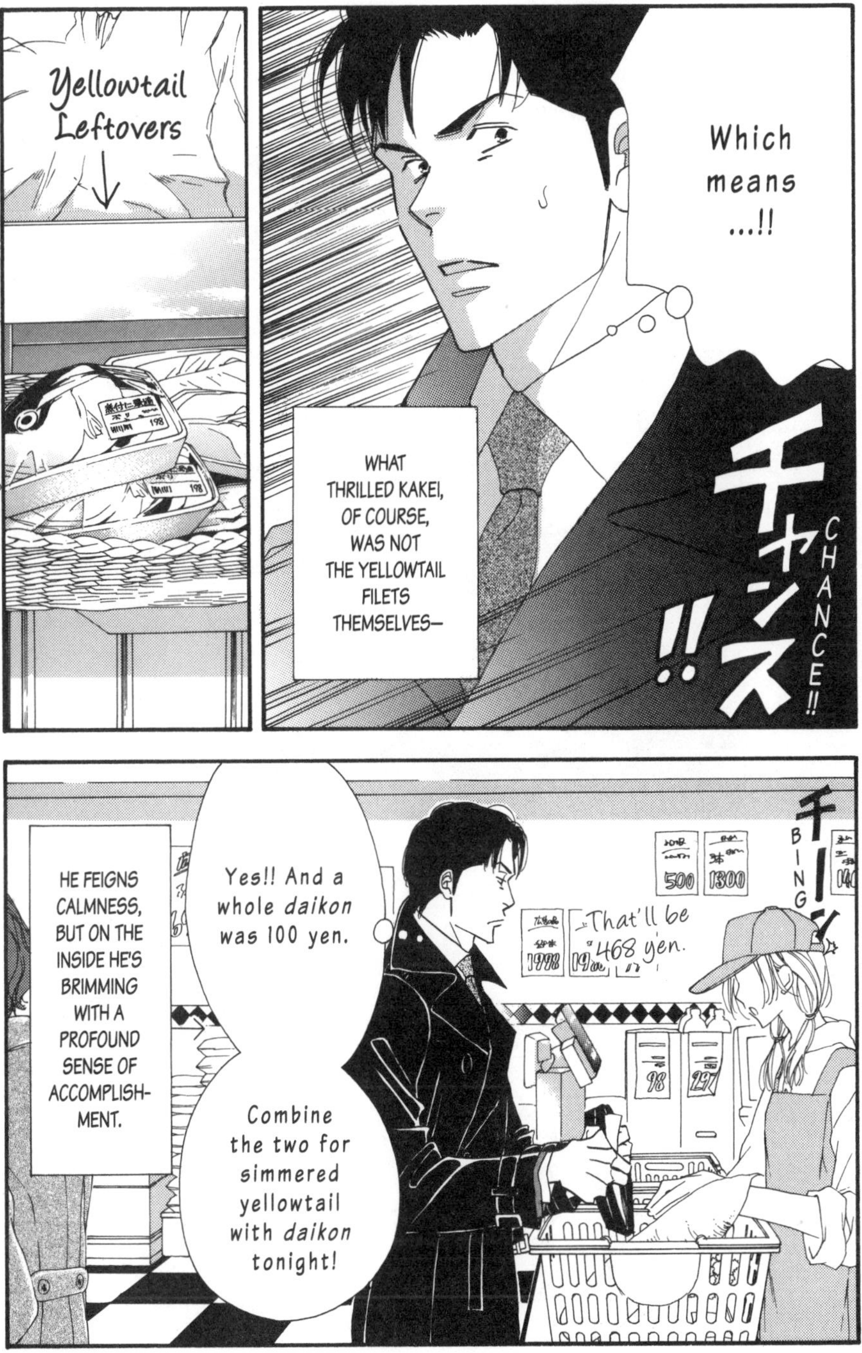
Which means ...!!
WHAT THRILLED KAKEI, OF COURSE, WAS NOT THE YELLOWTAIL FILETS THEMSELVES—
チャンス!!
CHANCE!!
Yellowtail Leftovers
チーン
BING
That'll be 468 yen.
Yes!! And a whole daikon was 100 yen.
Combine the two for simmered yellowtail with daikon tonight!
HE FEIGNS CALMNESS, BUT ON THE INSIDE HE'S BRIMMING WITH A PROFOUND SENSE OF ACCOMPLISHMENT.

Naturally, these are even cheaper than the filets.

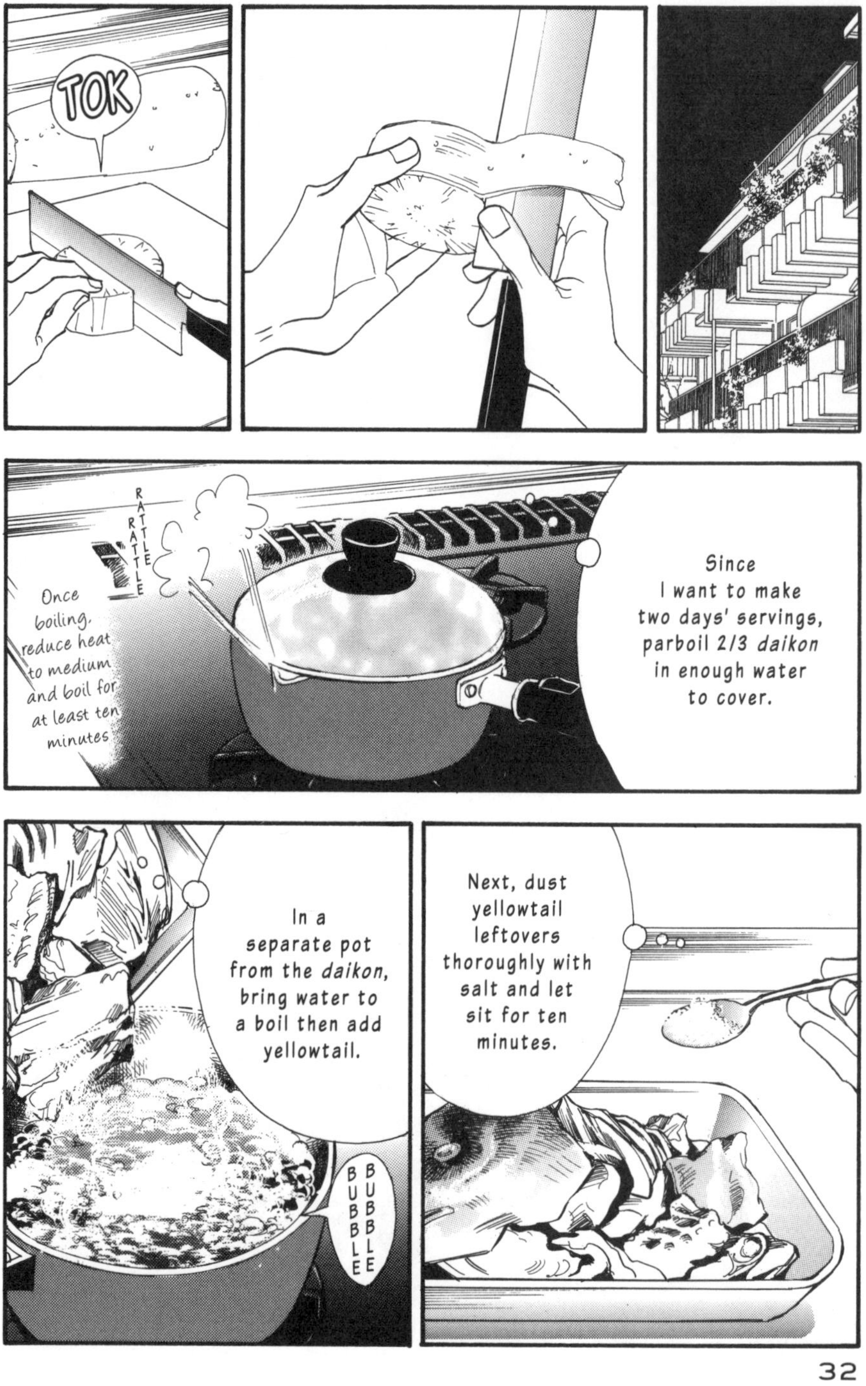
TOK
Since I want to make two days' servings, parboil 2/3 *daikon* in enough water to cover.
RATTLE RATTLE
Once boiling, reduce heat to medium and boil for at least ten minutes
Next, dust yellowtail leftovers thoroughly with salt and let sit for ten minutes.
In a separate pot from the *daikon*, bring water to a boil then add yellowtail.
BUBBLE BUBBLE

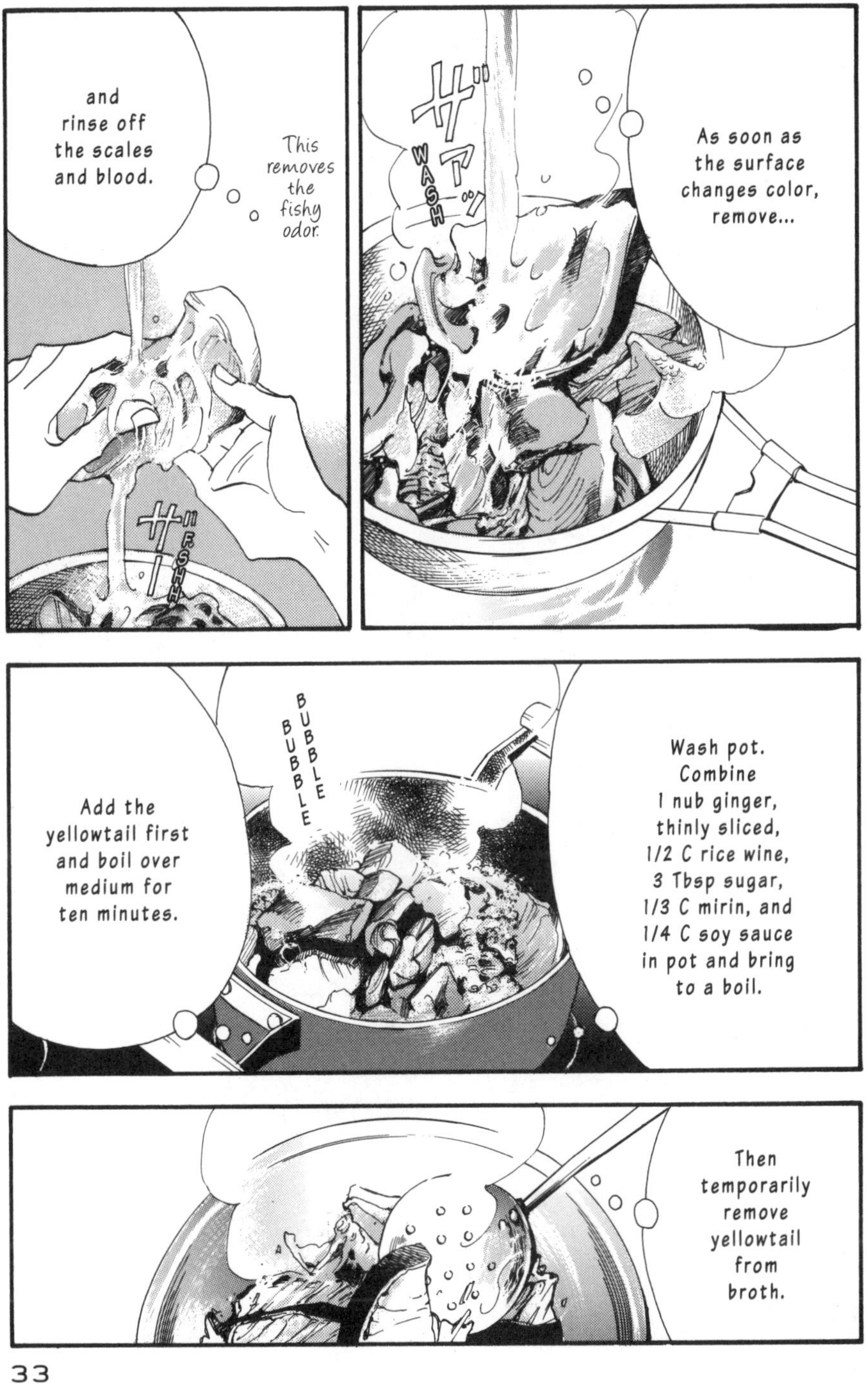
As soon as the surface changes color, remove...
ザァッ WASH
and rinse off the scales and blood.
This removes the fishy odor.
ザー FSHH
Wash pot. Combine 1 nub ginger, thinly sliced, 1/2 C rice wine, 3 Tbsp sugar, 1/3 C mirin, and 1/4 C soy sauce in pot and bring to a boil.
BUBBLE BUBBLE
Add the yellowtail first and boil over medium for ten minutes.
Then temporarily remove yellowtail from broth.

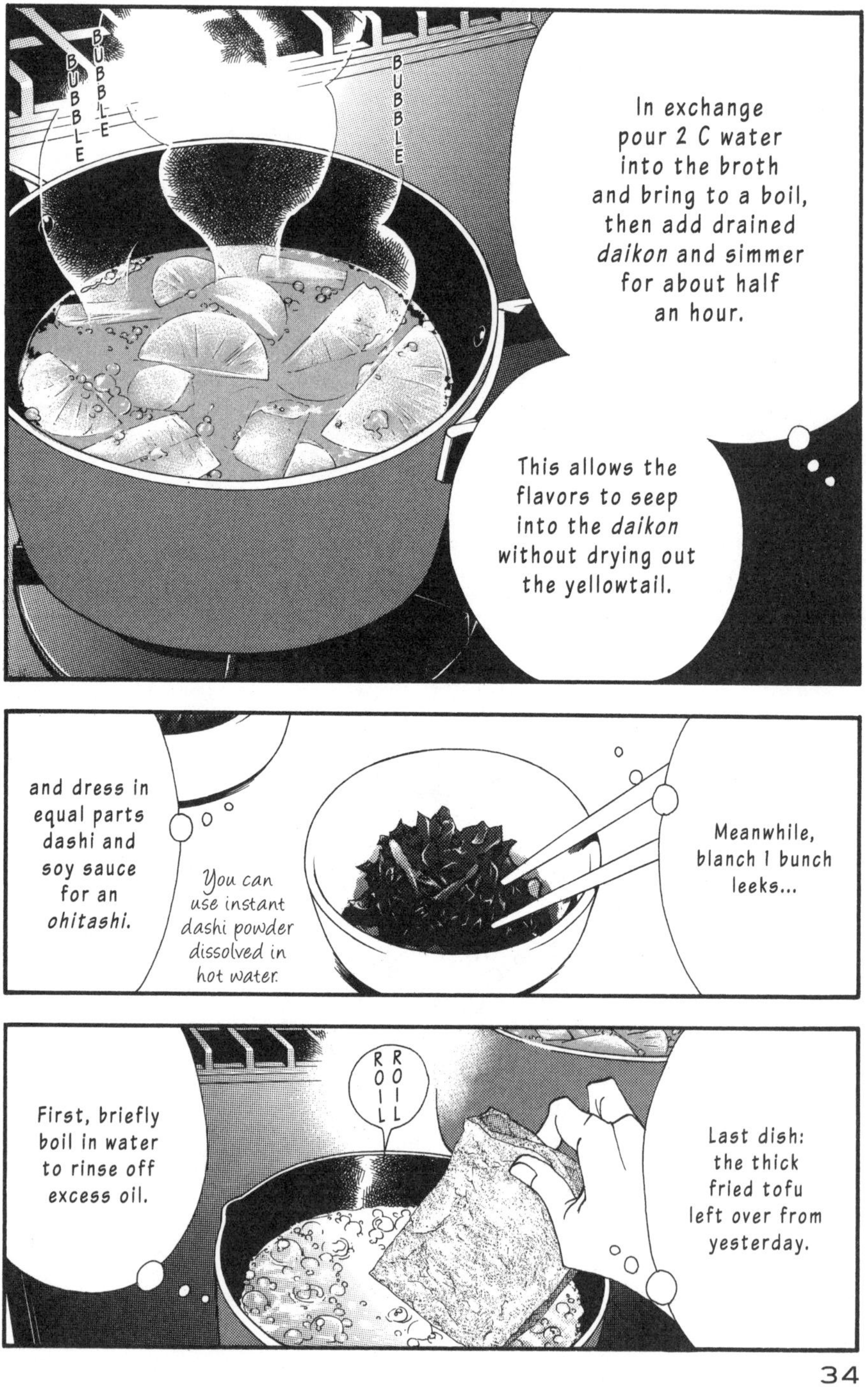
In exchange pour 2 C water into the broth and bring to a boil, then add drained *daikon* and simmer for about half an hour.
BUBBLE
BUBBLE
BUBBLE
This allows the flavors to seep into the *daikon* without drying out the yellowtail.
Meanwhile, blanch 1 bunch leeks...
You can use instant dashi powder dissolved in hot water.
and dress in equal parts dashi and soy sauce for an *ohitashi.*
Last dish: the thick fried tofu left over from yesterday.
ROLL ROLL
First, briefly boil in water to rinse off excess oil.

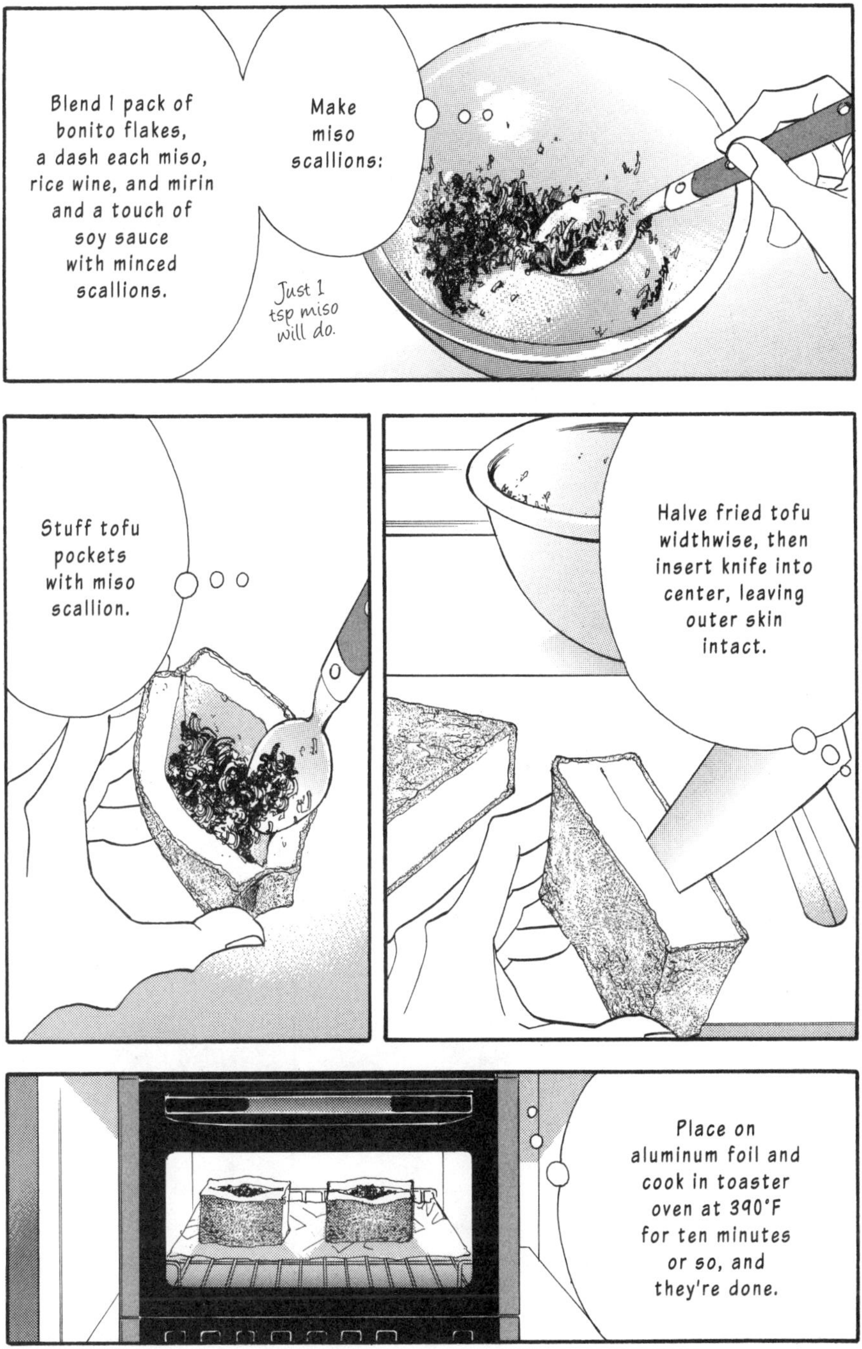
Make miso scallions:
Blend 1 pack of bonito flakes, a dash each miso, rice wine, and mirin and a touch of soy sauce with minced scallions.
Just 1 tsp miso will do.
Halve fried tofu widthwise, then insert knife into center, leaving outer skin intact.
Stuff tofu pockets with miso scallion.
Place on aluminum foil and cook in toaster oven at 390°F for ten minutes or so, and they're done.

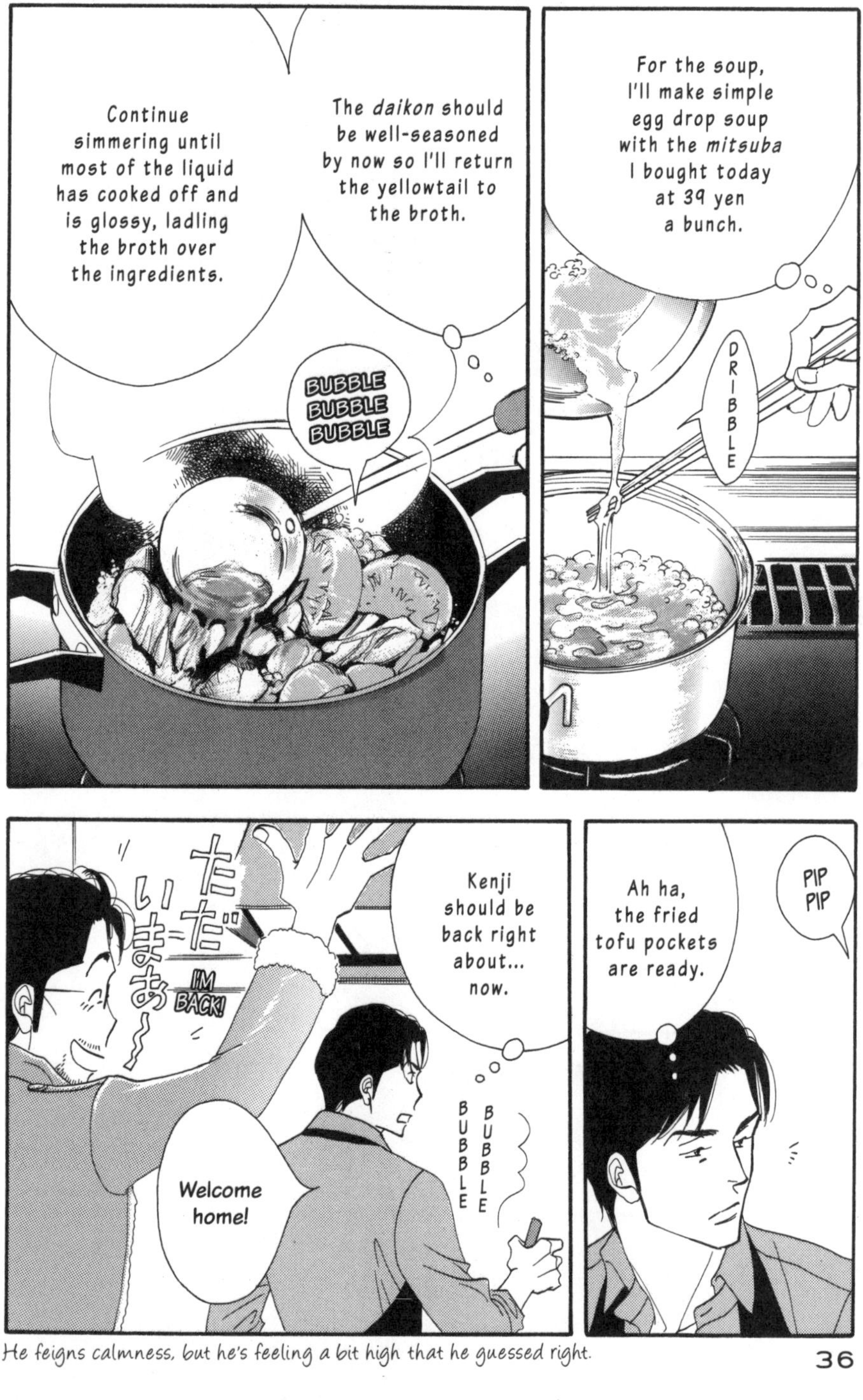
For the soup, I'll make simple egg drop soup with the *mitsuba* I bought today at 39 yen a bunch.
DRIBBLE
The *daikon* should be well-seasoned by now so I'll return the yellowtail to the broth.
Continue simmering until most of the liquid has cooked off and is glossy, ladling the broth over the ingredients.
BUBBLE BUBBLE BUBBLE
PIP PIP
Ah ha, the fried tofu pockets are ready.
Kenji should be back right about... now.
ただいまあ～
I'M BACK!
BUBBLE BUBBLE
Welcome home!

He feigns calmness, but he's feeling a bit high that he guessed right.

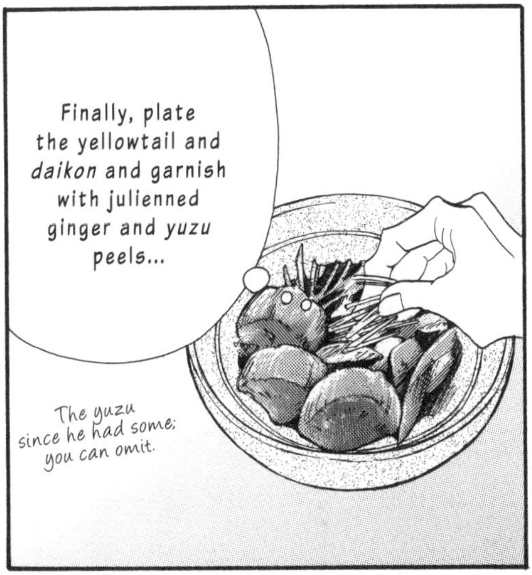
Finally, plate the yellowtail and daikon and garnish with julienned ginger and yuzu peels...
The yuzu since he had some; you can omit.

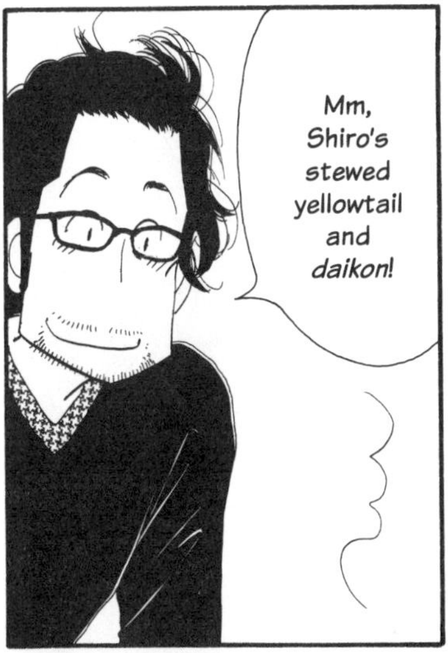
Mm, Shiro's stewed yellowtail and daikon!

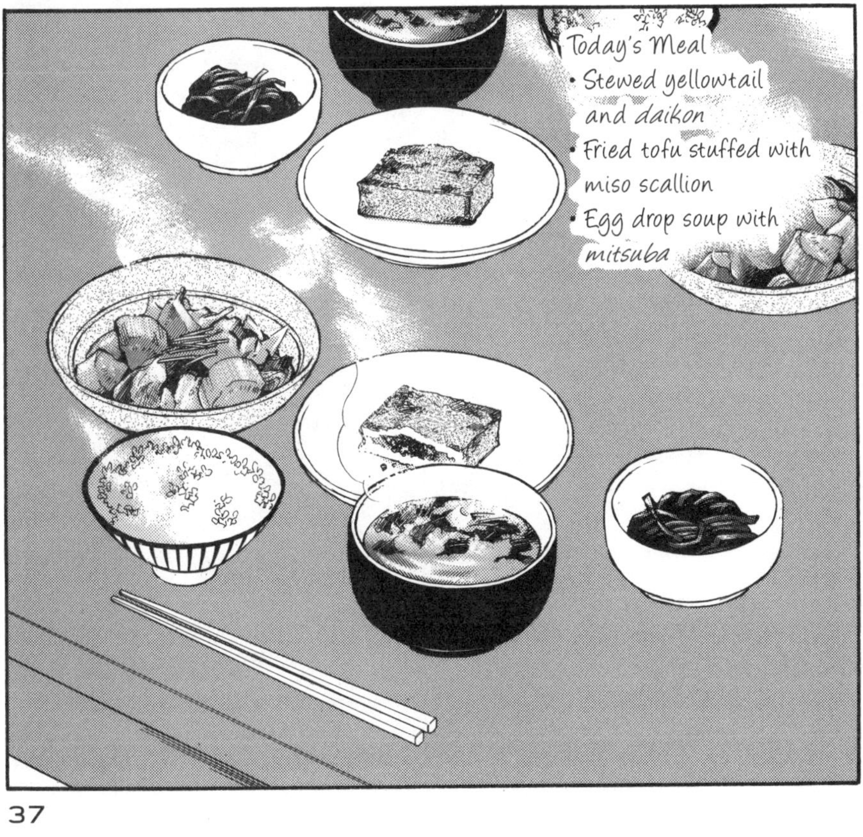
Today's Meal
• Stewed yellowtail and daikon
• Fried tofu stuffed with miso scallion
• Egg drop soup with mitsuba

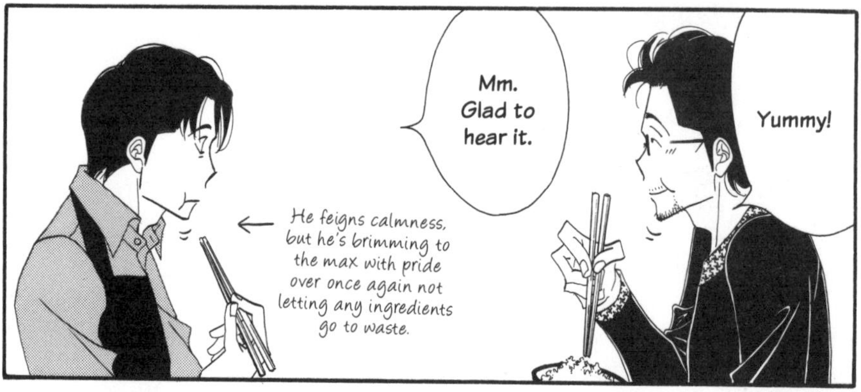
Yummy!
Mm. Glad to hear it.
He feigns calmness, but he's brimming to the max with pride over once again not letting any ingredients go to waste.

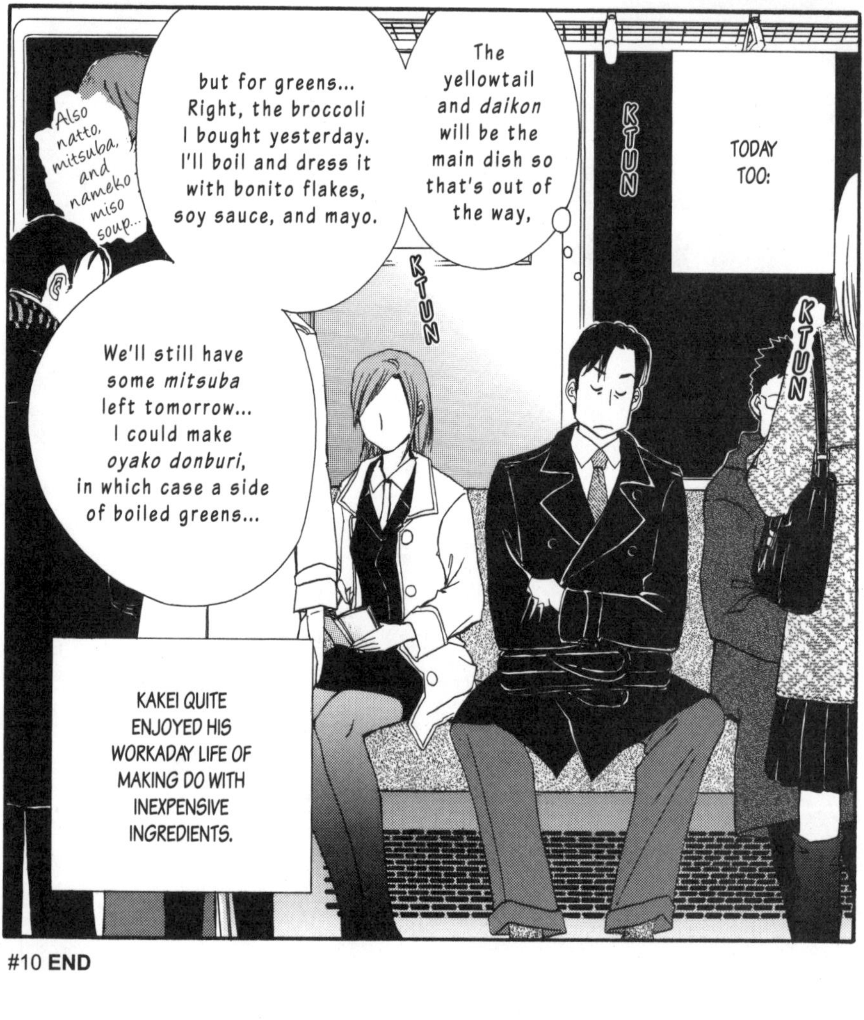
TODAY TOO:
KTUN
The yellowtail and *daikon* will be the main dish so that's out of the way,
but for greens... Right, the broccoli I bought yesterday. I'll boil and dress it with bonito flakes, soy sauce, and mayo.
Also natto, mitsuba, and nameko miso soup...
KTUN
KTUN
We'll still have some *mitsuba* left tomorrow... I could make *oyako donburi*, in which case a side of boiled greens...
KAKEI QUITE ENJOYED HIS WORKADAY LIFE OF MAKING DO WITH INEXPENSIVE INGREDIENTS.

#10 **END**

You can also toss in **chopped leeks** to complete
a **mapo tofu** dish (1 bunch for four servings mapo tofu).

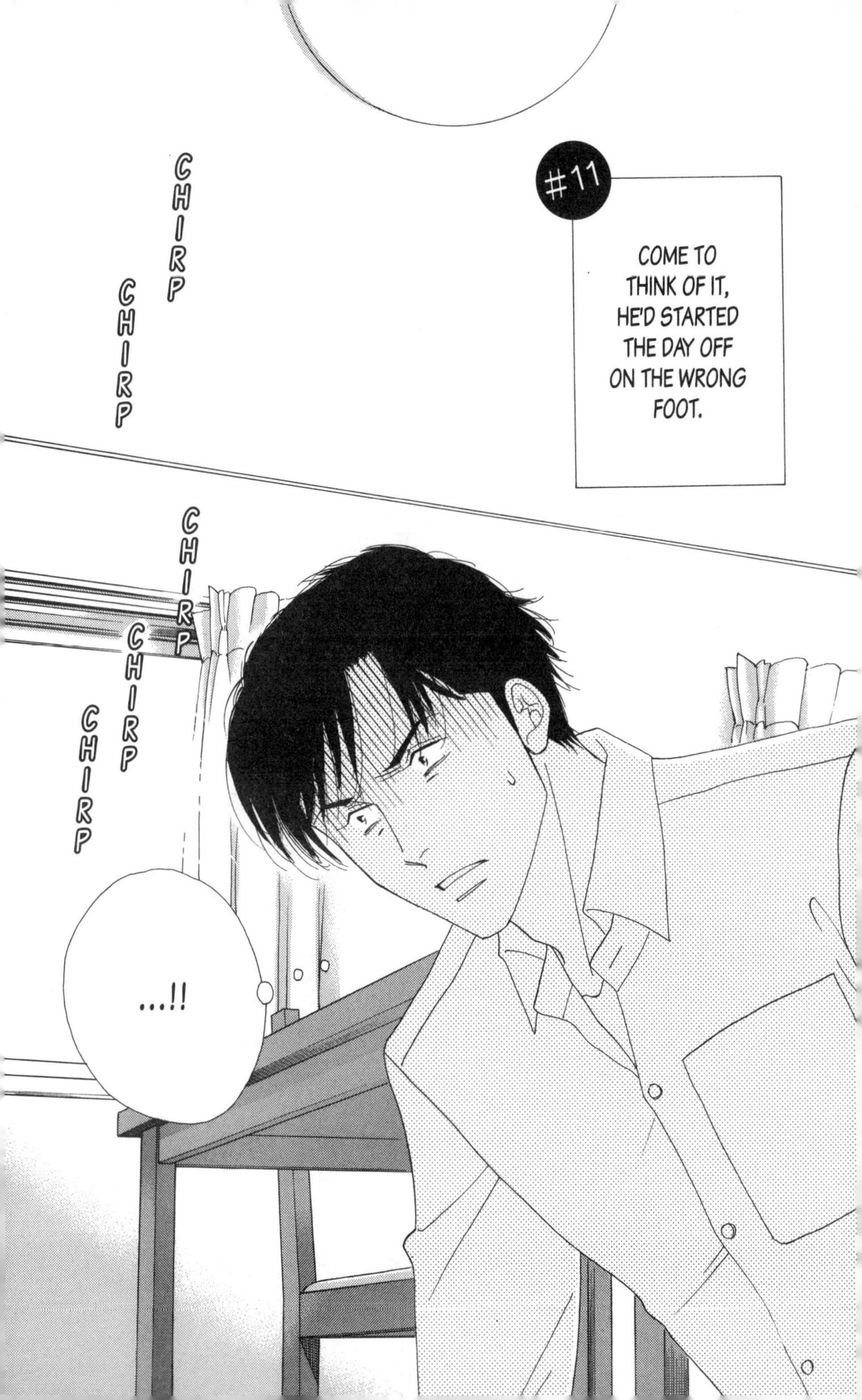
#11
COME TO THINK OF IT, HE'D STARTED THE DAY OFF ON THE WRONG FOOT.
CHIRP
CHIRP
CHIRP
CHIRP
CHIRP
...!!

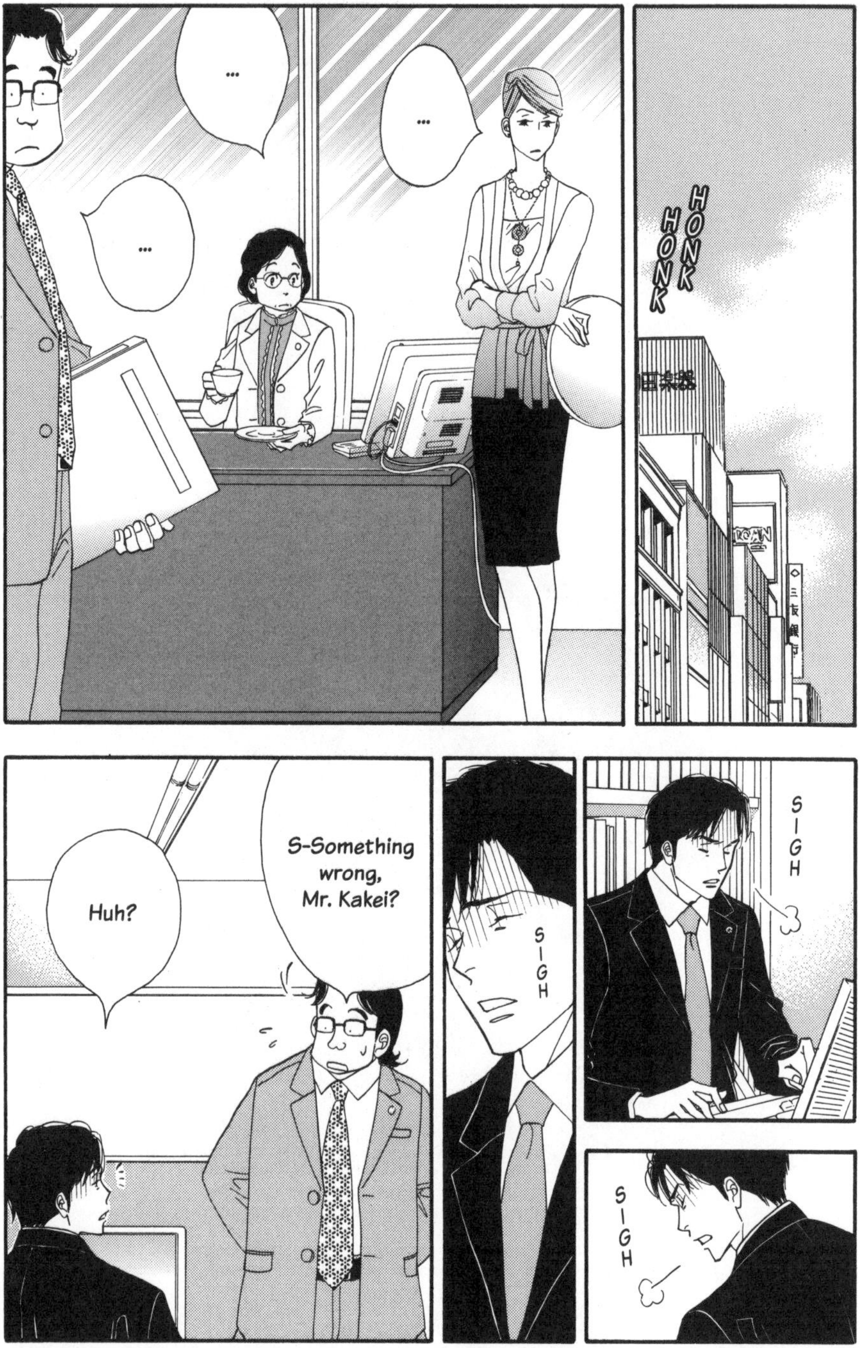
HONK
HONK
...
...
...
SIGH
SIGH
SIGH
S-Something wrong, Mr. Kakei?
Huh?

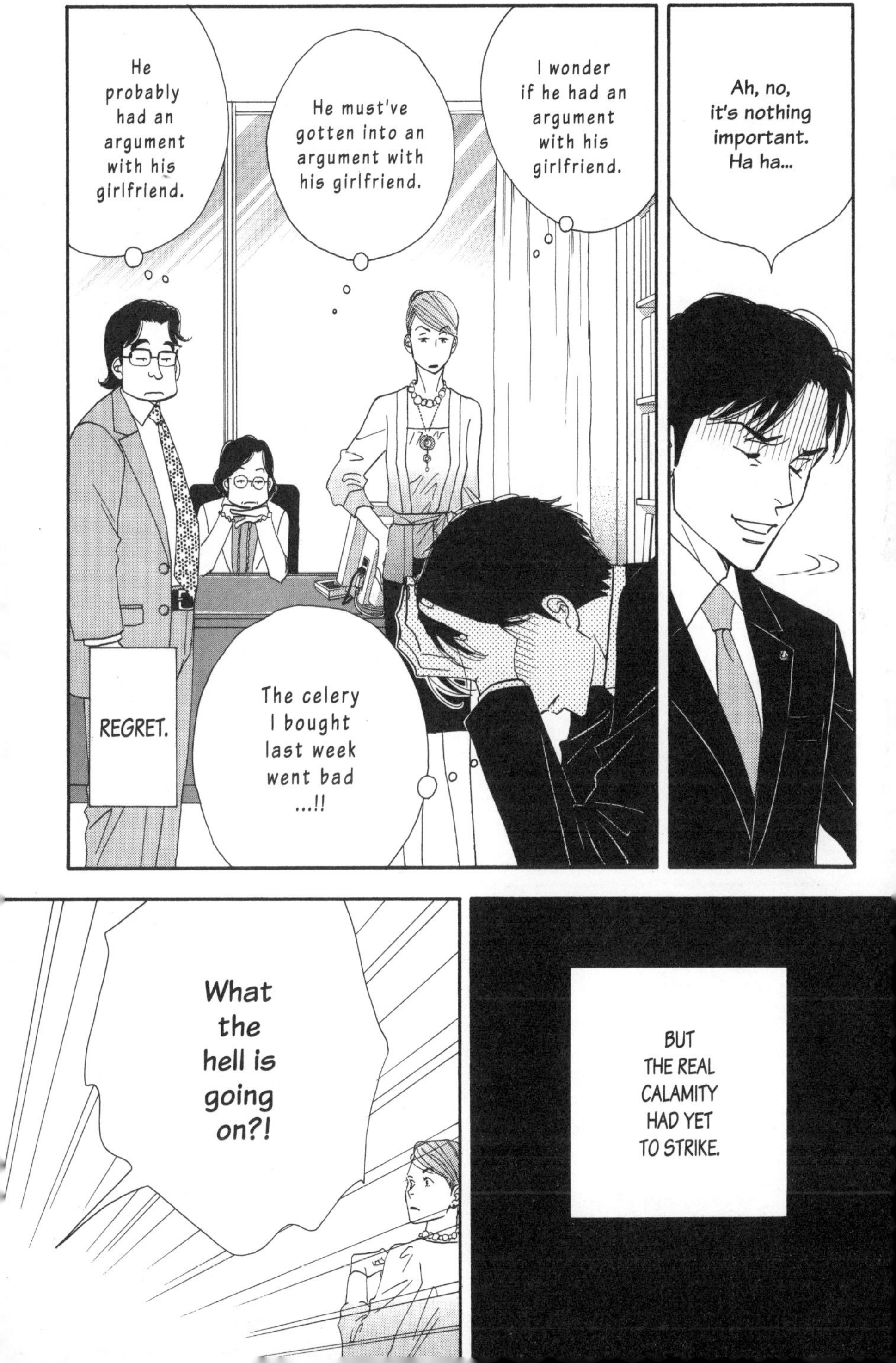
Ah, no, it's nothing important. Ha ha...
I wonder if he had an argument with his girlfriend.
He must've gotten into an argument with his girlfriend.
He probably had an argument with his girlfriend.
The celery I bought last week went bad ...!!
REGRET.
BUT THE REAL CALAMITY HAD YET TO STRIKE.
What the hell is going on?!

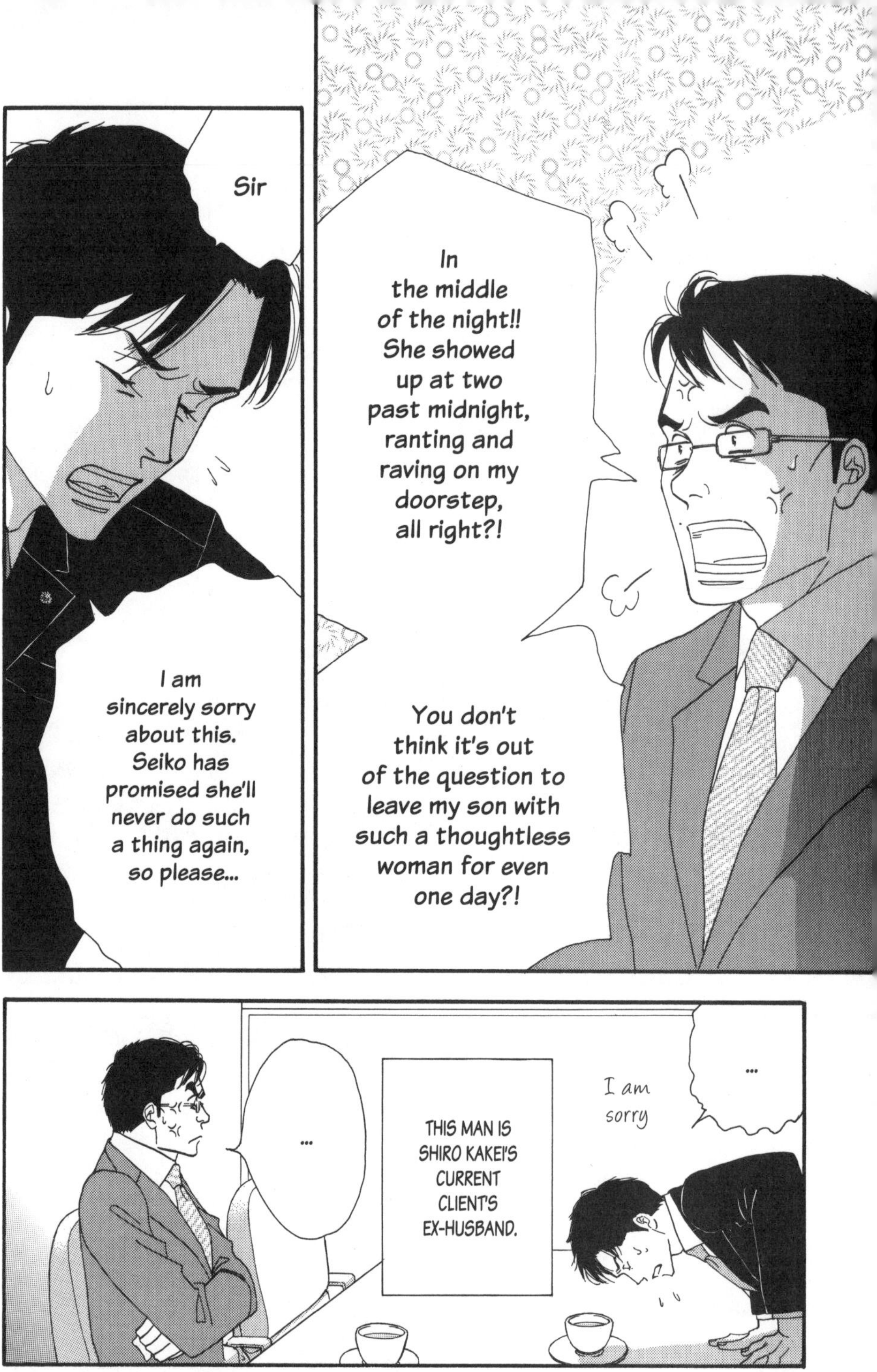
In the middle of the night!! She showed up at two past midnight, ranting and raving on my doorstep, all right?!
You don't think it's out of the question to leave my son with such a thoughtless woman for even one day?!
Sir
I am sincerely sorry about this. Seiko has promised she'll never do such a thing again, so please...
...
I am sorry
THIS MAN IS SHIRO KAKEI'S CURRENT CLIENT'S EX-HUSBAND.
...

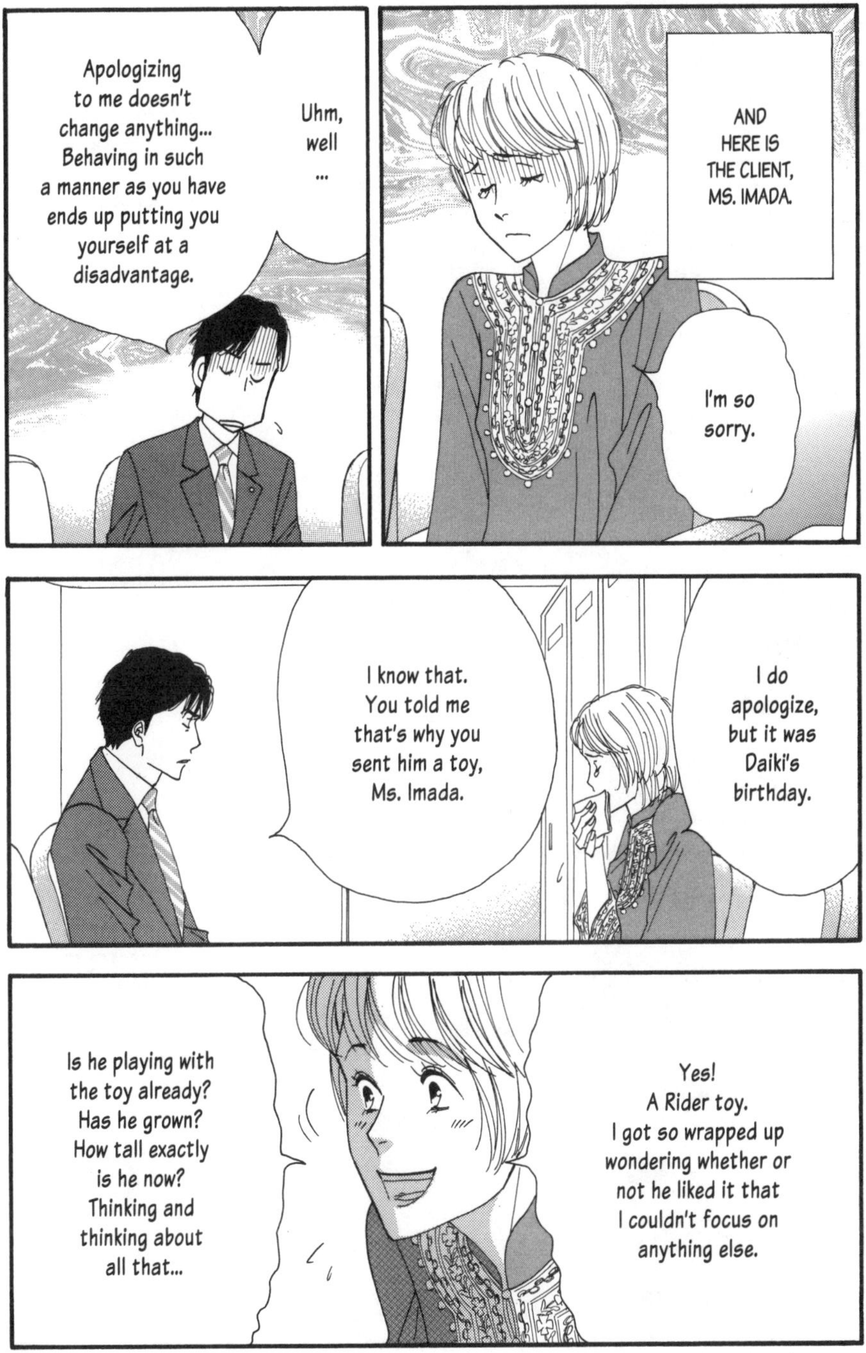
AND HERE IS THE CLIENT, MS. IMADA.
I'm so sorry.
Uhm, well ...
Apologizing to me doesn't change anything... Behaving in such a manner as you have ends up putting you yourself at a disadvantage.
I do apologize, but it was Daiki's birthday.
I know that. You told me that's why you sent him a toy, Ms. Imada.
Yes! A Rider toy. I got so wrapped up wondering whether or not he liked it that I couldn't focus on anything else.
Is he playing with the toy already? Has he grown? How tall exactly is he now? Thinking and thinking about all that...

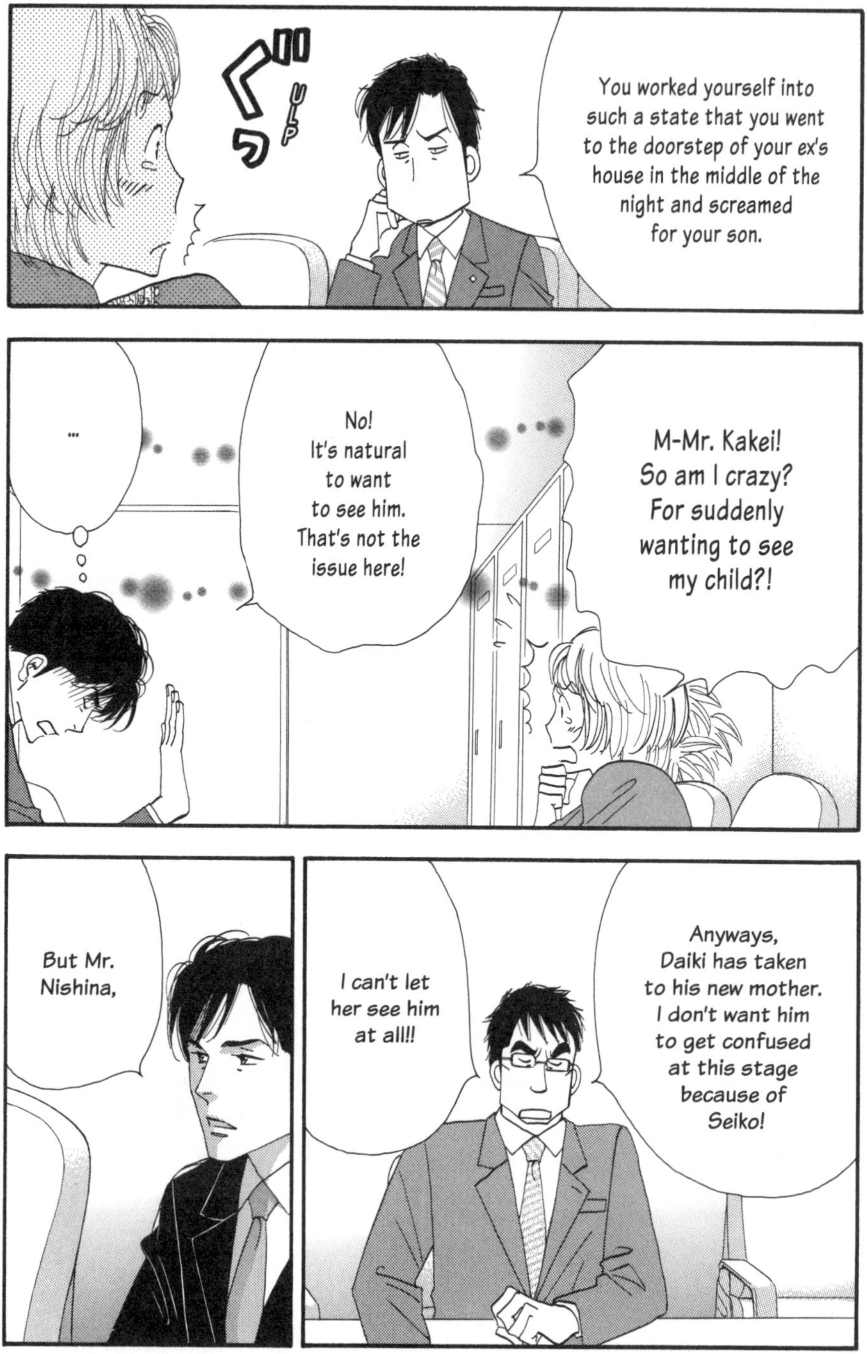
You worked yourself into such a state that you went to the doorstep of your ex's house in the middle of the night and screamed for your son.
ULP
M-Mr. Kakei! So am I crazy? For suddenly wanting to see my child?!
No! It's natural to want to see him. That's not the issue here!
...
Anyways, Daiki has taken to his new mother. I don't want him to get confused at this stage because of Seiko!
I can't let her see him at all!!
But Mr. Nishina,

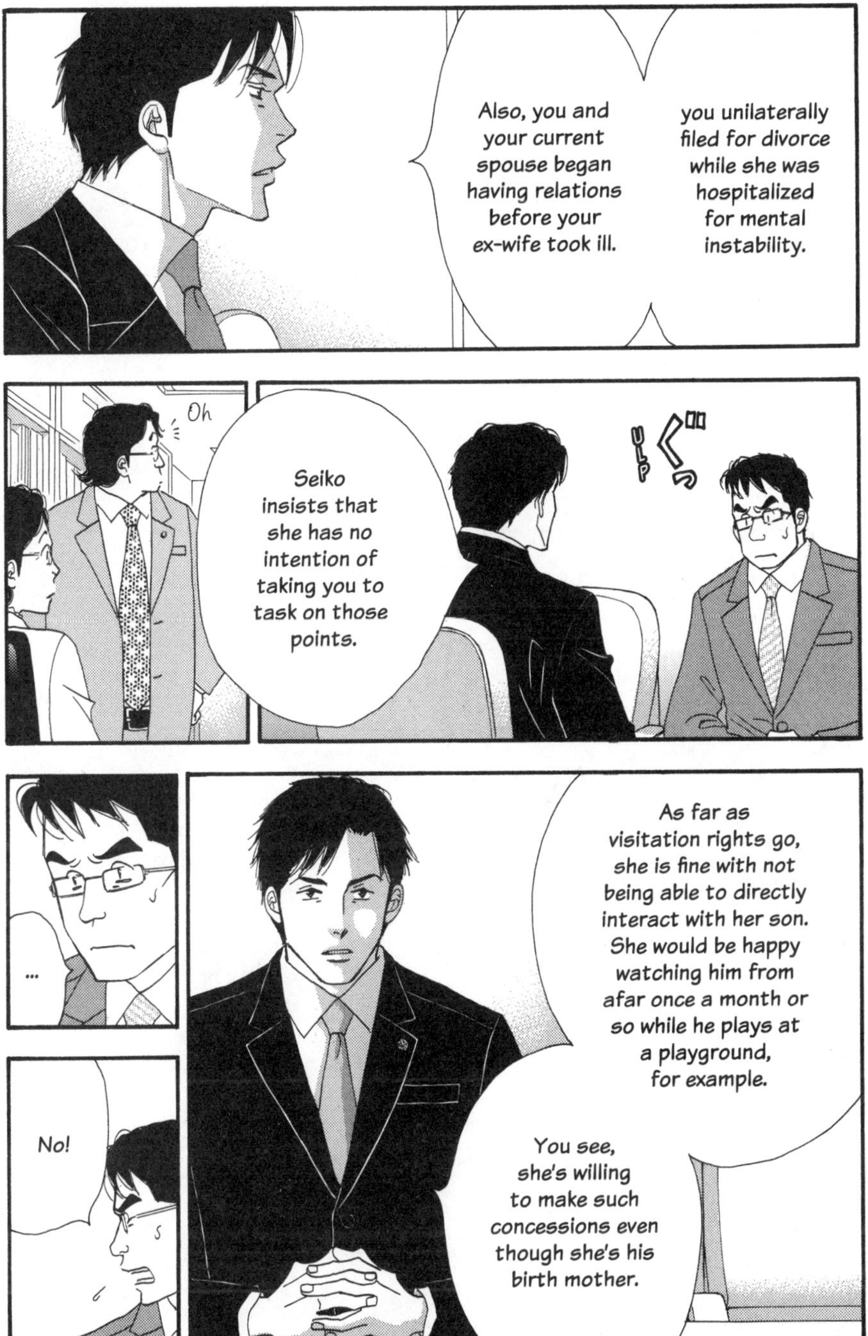
Also, you and your current spouse began having relations before your ex-wife took ill.
you unilaterally filed for divorce while she was hospitalized for mental instability.
ULP
ぐっ
Seiko insists that she has no intention of taking you to task on those points.
Oh
As far as visitation rights go, she is fine with not being able to directly interact with her son. She would be happy watching him from afar once a month or so while he plays at a playground, for example.
You see, she's willing to make such concessions even though she's his birth mother.
...
No!

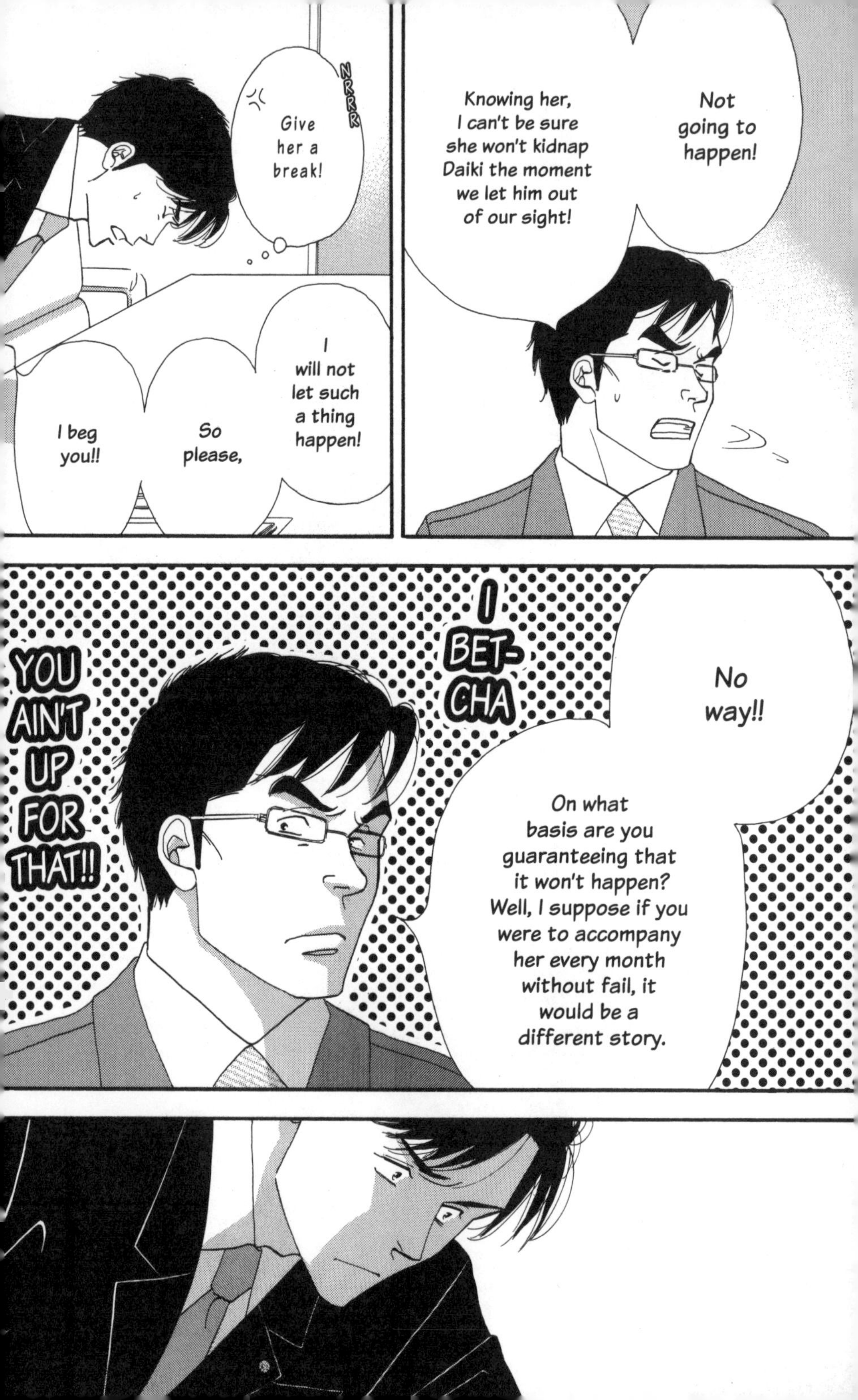
Not going to happen!
Knowing her, I can't be sure she won't kidnap Daiki the moment we let him out of our sight!
NRRR
Give her a break!
I will not let such a thing happen!
So please,
I beg you!!
No way!!
On what basis are you guaranteeing that it won't happen? Well, I suppose if you were to accompany her every month without fail, it would be a different story.
I BET-CHA
YOU AIN'T UP FOR THAT!!

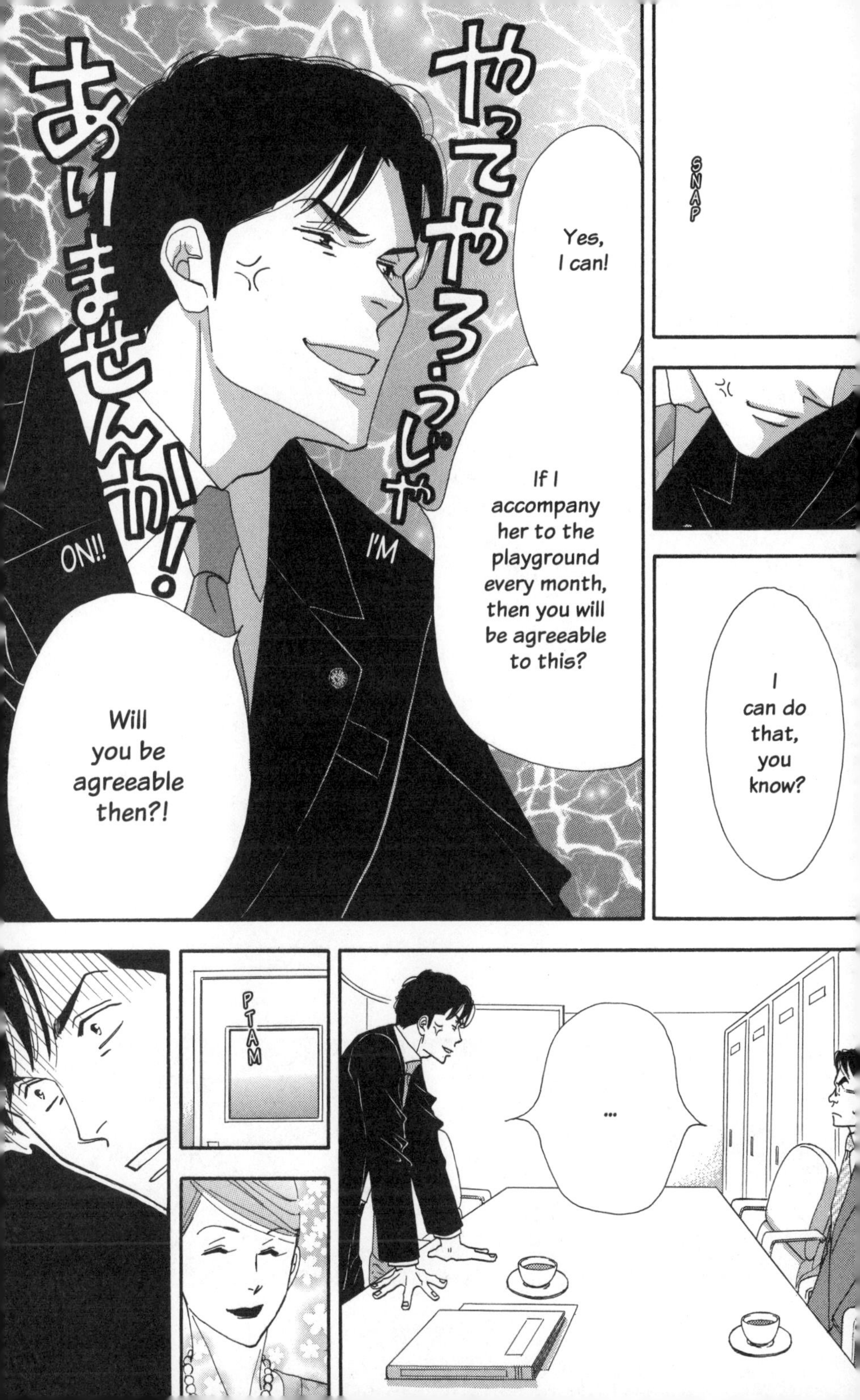
SNAP
I can do that, you know?
Yes, I can!
If I accompany her to the playground every month, then you will be agreeable to this?
やってやろうじゃ
ありませんか!
I'M
ON!!
Will you be agreeable then?!
...
PTAM

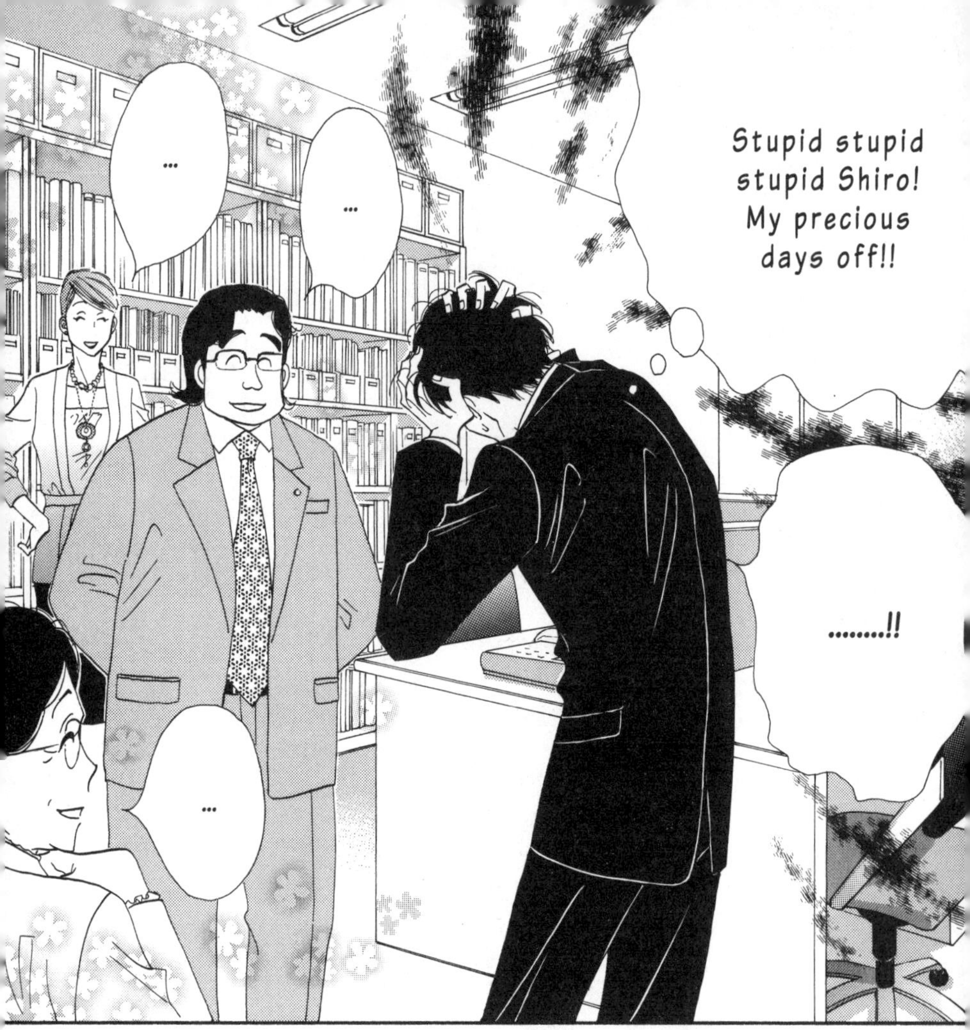
Stupid stupid stupid Shiro! My precious days off!!
.........!!
...
...
...

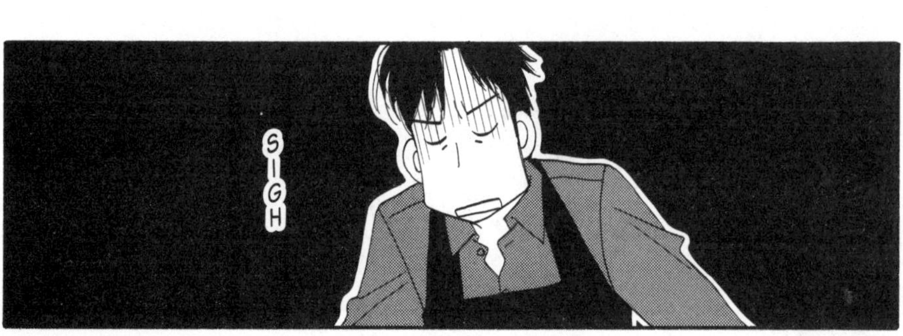
SIGH

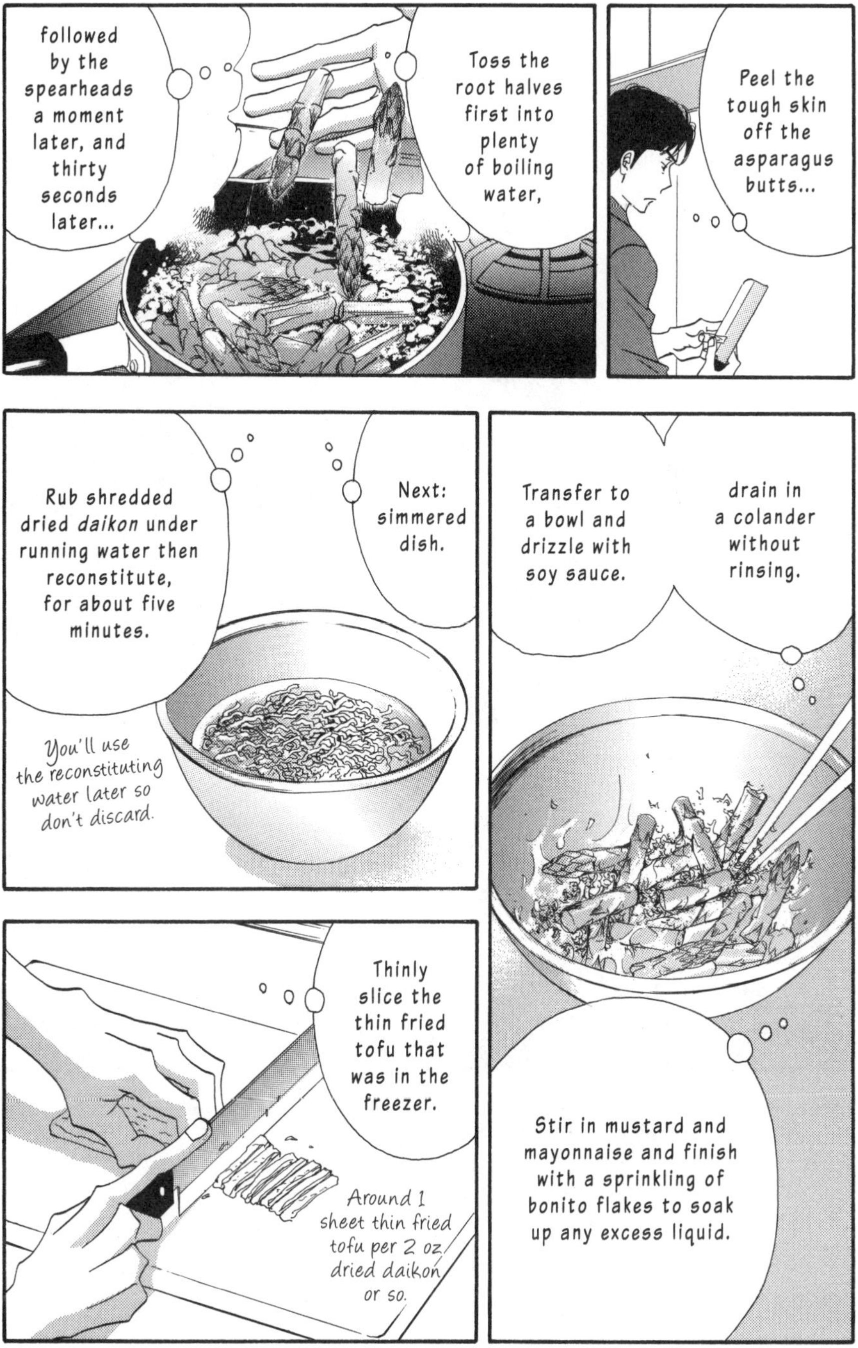
Peel the tough skin off the asparagus butts...
Toss the root halves first into plenty of boiling water,
followed by the spearheads a moment later, and thirty seconds later...
drain in a colander without rinsing.
Transfer to a bowl and drizzle with soy sauce.
Stir in mustard and mayonnaise and finish with a sprinkling of bonito flakes to soak up any excess liquid.
Next: simmered dish.
Rub shredded dried *daikon* under running water then reconstitute, for about five minutes.
You'll use the reconstituting water later so don't discard.
Thinly slice the thin fried tofu that was in the freezer.
Around 1 sheet thin fried tofu per 2 oz dried daikon or so.

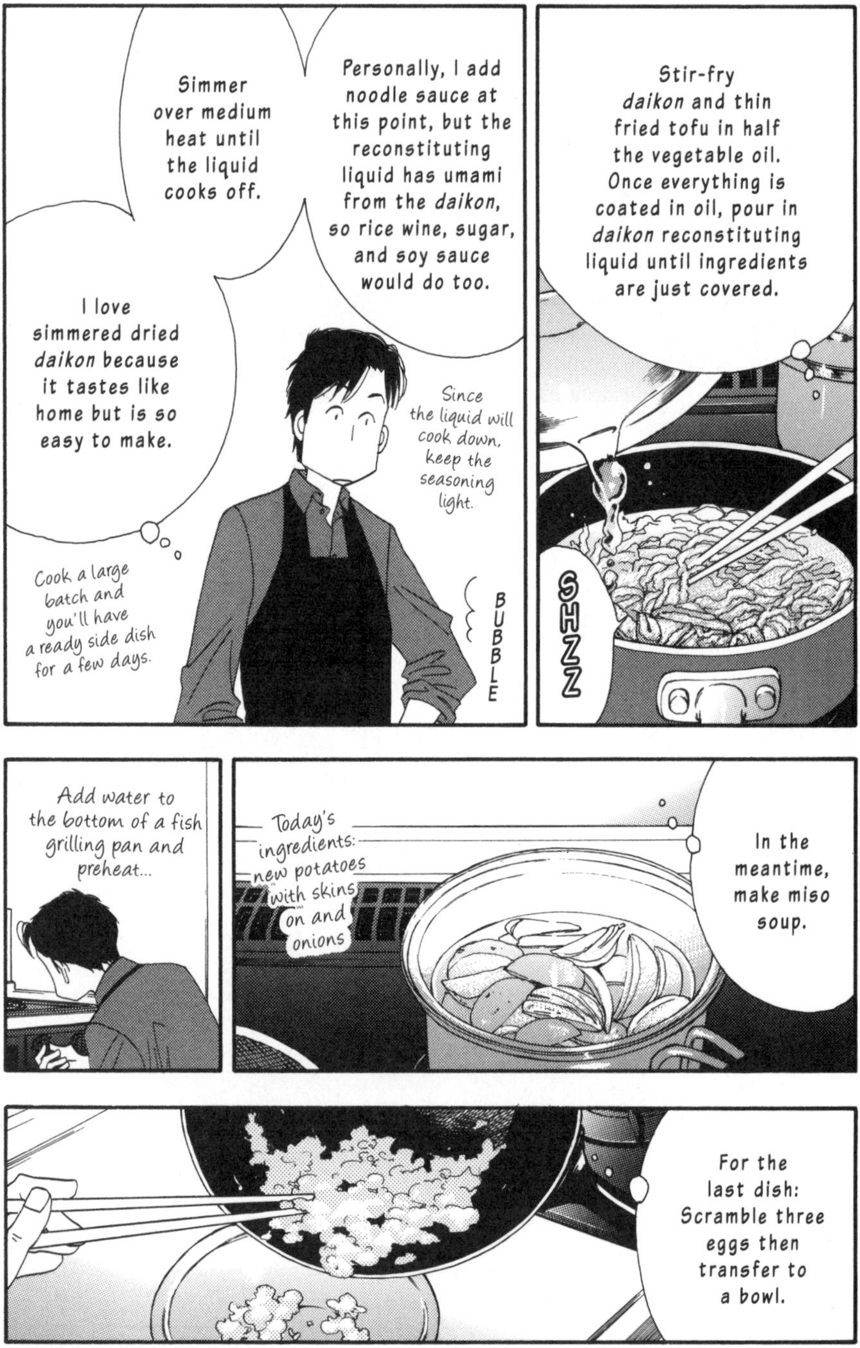
Stir-fry daikon and thin fried tofu in half the vegetable oil. Once everything is coated in oil, pour in daikon reconstituting liquid until ingredients are just covered.
SHZZ
Personally, I add noodle sauce at this point, but the reconstituting liquid has umami from the daikon, so rice wine, sugar, and soy sauce would do too.
Simmer over medium heat until the liquid cooks off.
Since the liquid will cook down, keep the seasoning light.
I love simmered dried daikon because it tastes like home but is so easy to make.
BUBBLE
Cook a large batch and you'll have a ready side dish for a few days.
In the meantime, make miso soup.
Today's ingredients: new potatoes with skins on and onions
Add water to the bottom of a fish grilling pan and preheat...
For the last dish: Scramble three eggs then transfer to a bowl.

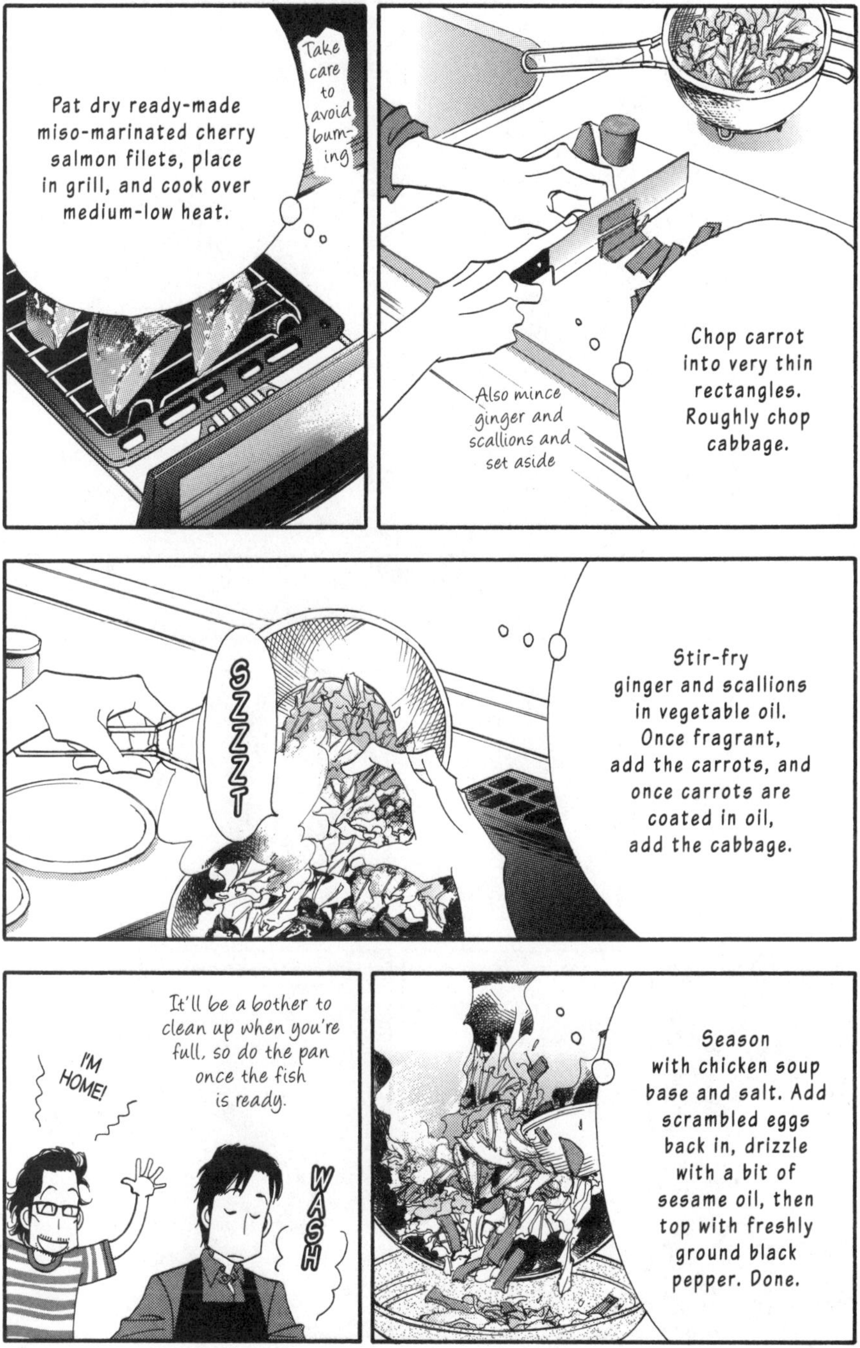
Chop carrot into very thin rectangles. Roughly chop cabbage.
Also mince ginger and scallions and set aside
Take care to avoid burn-ing
Pat dry ready-made miso-marinated cherry salmon filets, place in grill, and cook over medium-low heat.
Stir-fry ginger and scallions in vegetable oil. Once fragrant, add the carrots, and once carrots are coated in oil, add the cabbage.
SZZZZT
Season with chicken soup base and salt. Add scrambled eggs back in, drizzle with a bit of sesame oil, then top with freshly ground black pepper. Done.
It'll be a bother to clean up when you're full, so do the pan once the fish is ready.
I'M HOME!
WASH

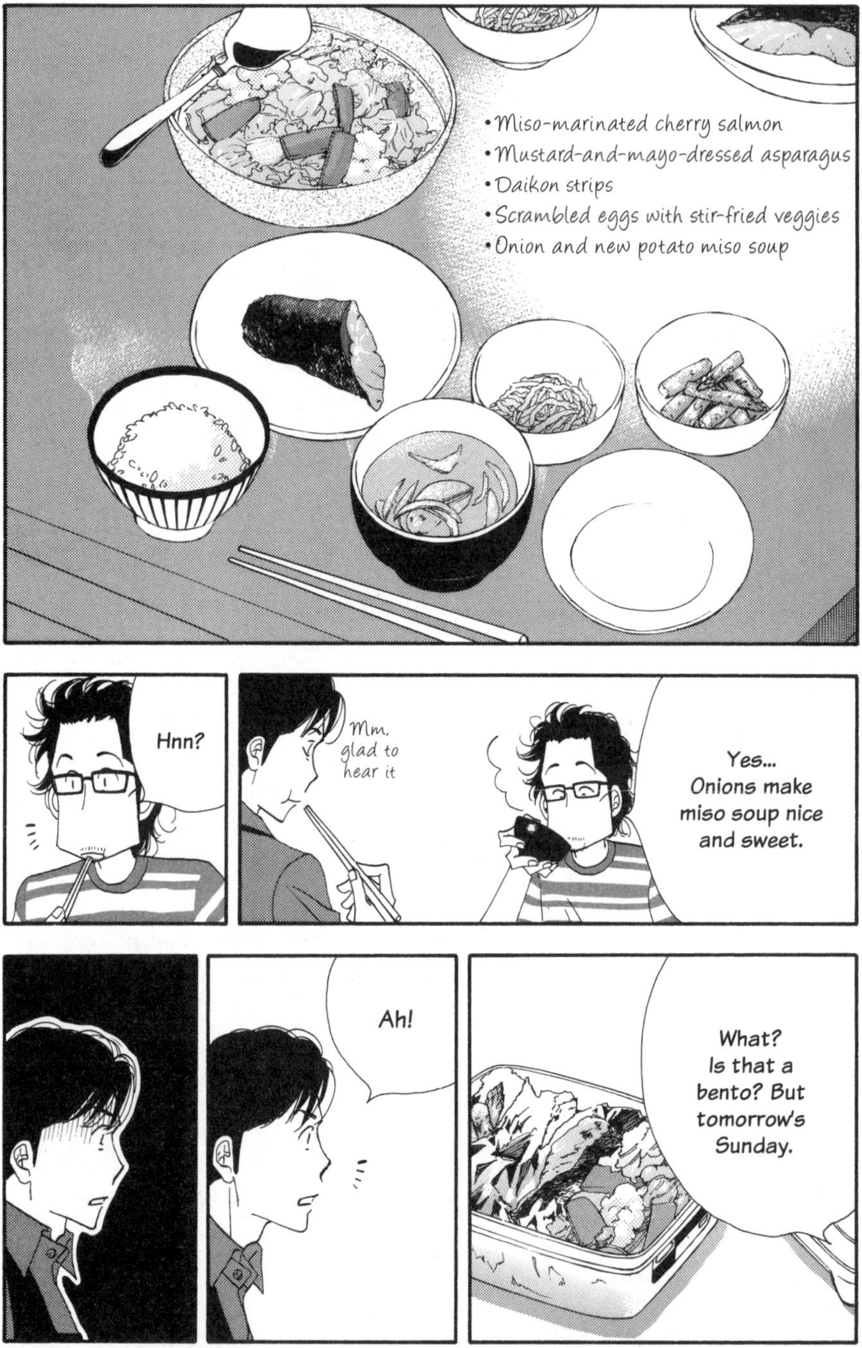
•Miso-marinated cherry salmon
•Mustard-and-mayo-dressed asparagus
•Daikon strips
•Scrambled eggs with stir-fried veggies
•Onion and new potato miso soup
Yes... Onions make miso soup nice and sweet.
Mm, glad to hear it
Hnn?
What? Is that a bento? But tomorrow's Sunday.
Ah!

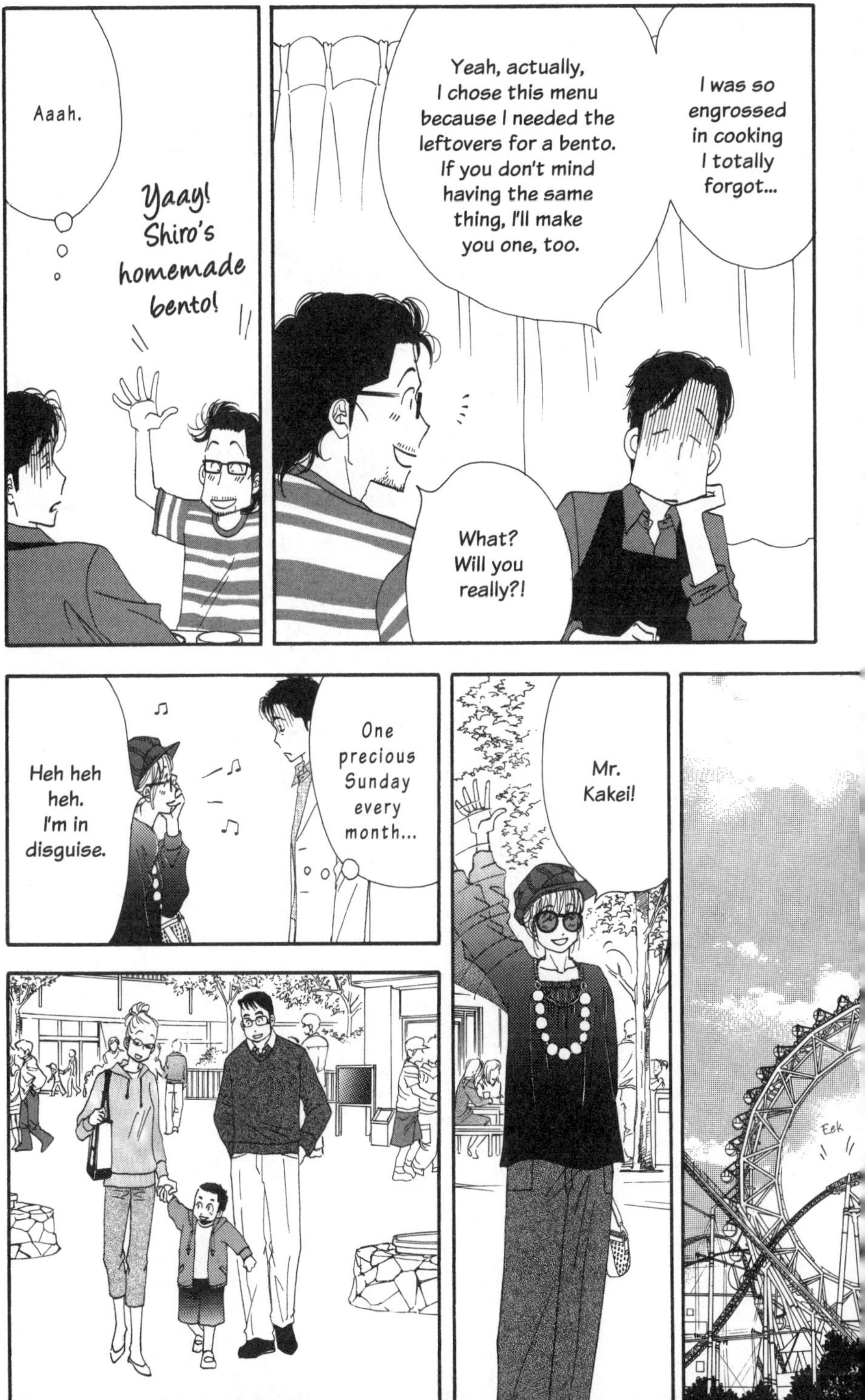
I was so engrossed in cooking I totally forgot...
Yeah, actually, I chose this menu because I needed the leftovers for a bento. If you don't mind having the same thing, I'll make you one, too.
What? Will you really?!
Aaah.
Yaay! Shiro's homemade bento!
Eek
Mr. Kakei!
One precious Sunday every month...
Heh heh heh. I'm in disguise.

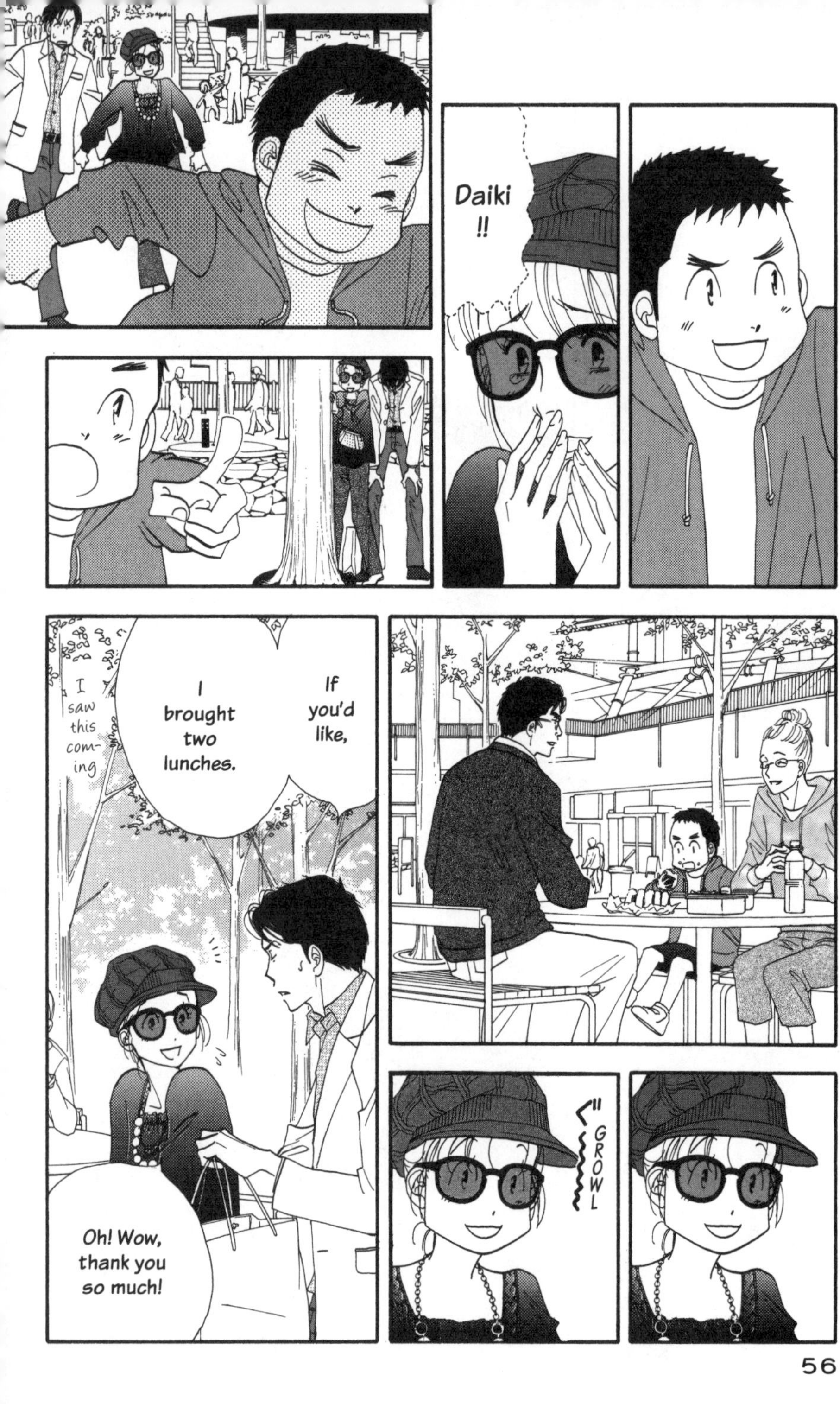
Daiki !!
GROWL
If you'd like,
I brought two lunches.
I saw this coming
Oh! Wow, thank you so much!

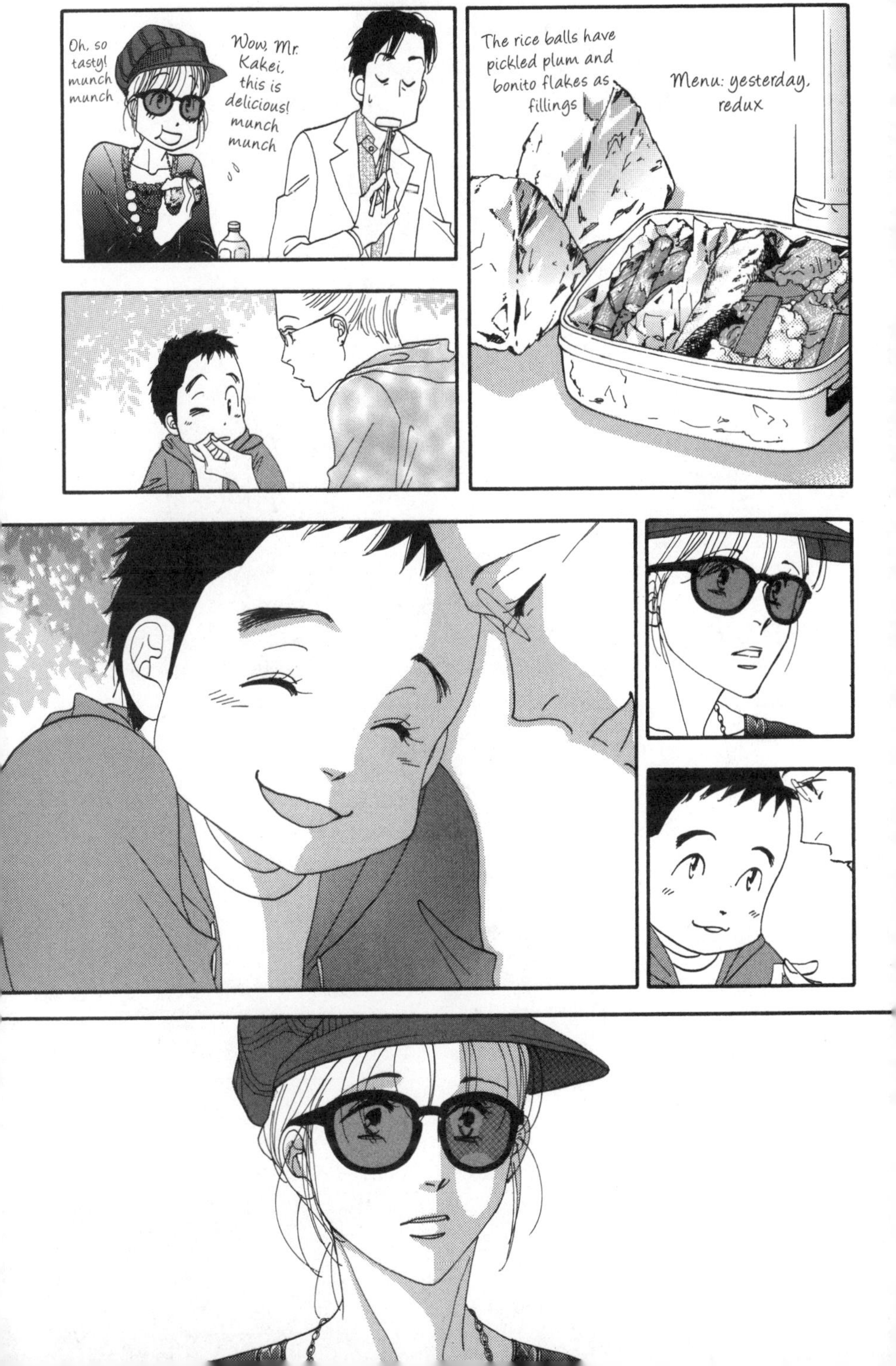
Menu: yesterday, redux
The rice balls have pickled plum and bonito flakes as fillings
Wow, Mr. Kakei, this is delicious! munch munch
Oh, so tasty! munch munch

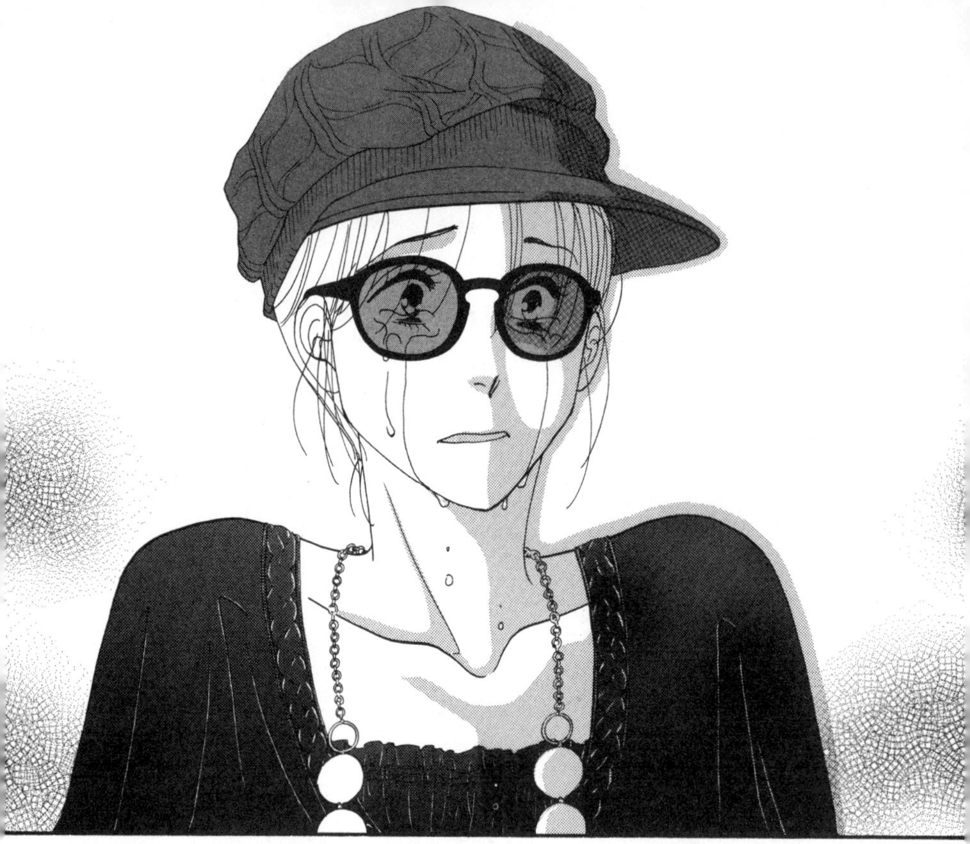

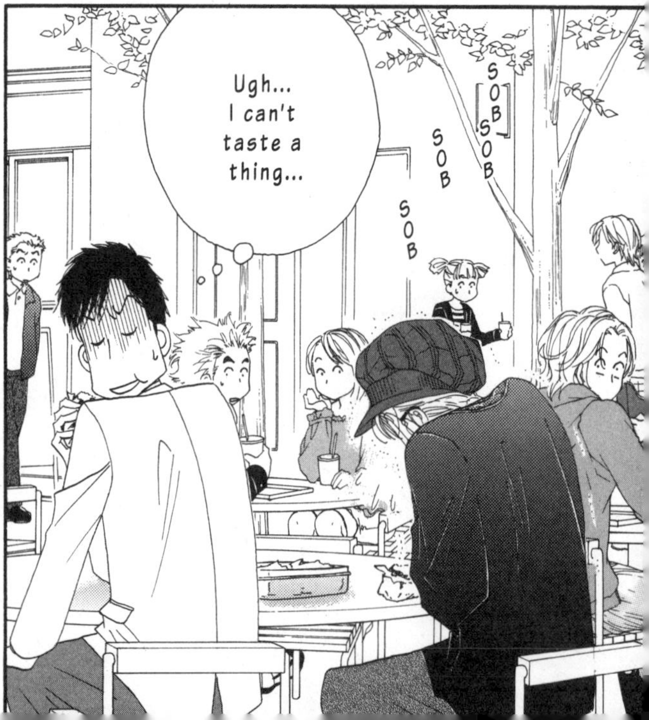
SOB SOB
SOB
SOB
Ugh... I can't taste a thing...

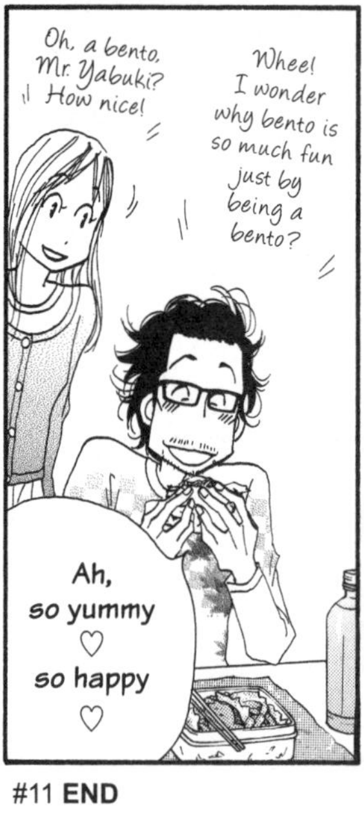
Whee! I wonder why bento is so much fun just by being a bento?
Oh, a bento, Mr. Yabuki? How nice!
Ah, so yummy ♡ so happy ♡

#11 **END**

This time, I wanted more vegetables
so I added carrots, but just cabbage and
scrambled eggs are plenty delicious.
Also, fish marinated in sake lees or miso
can burn really easily, so be careful...

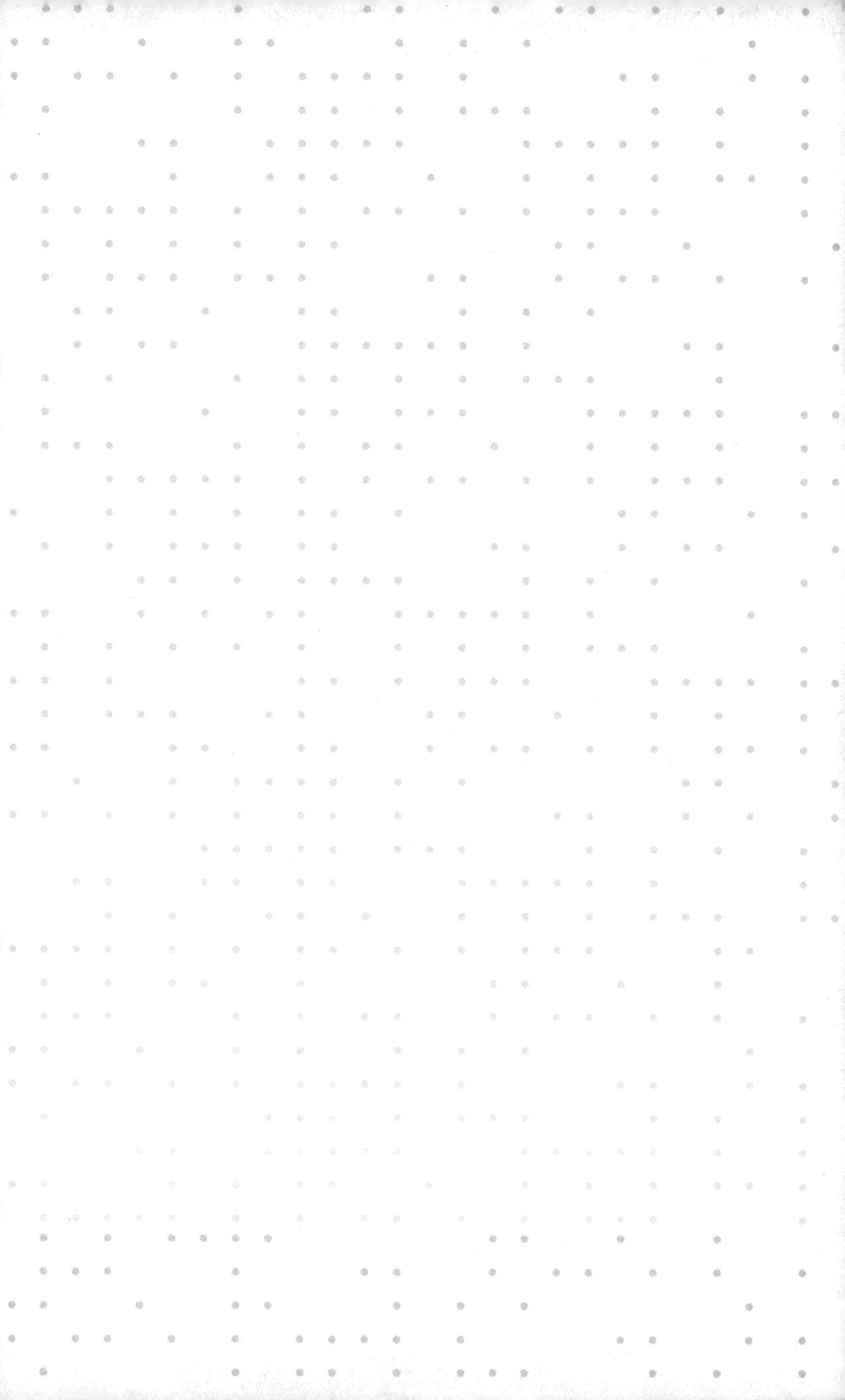

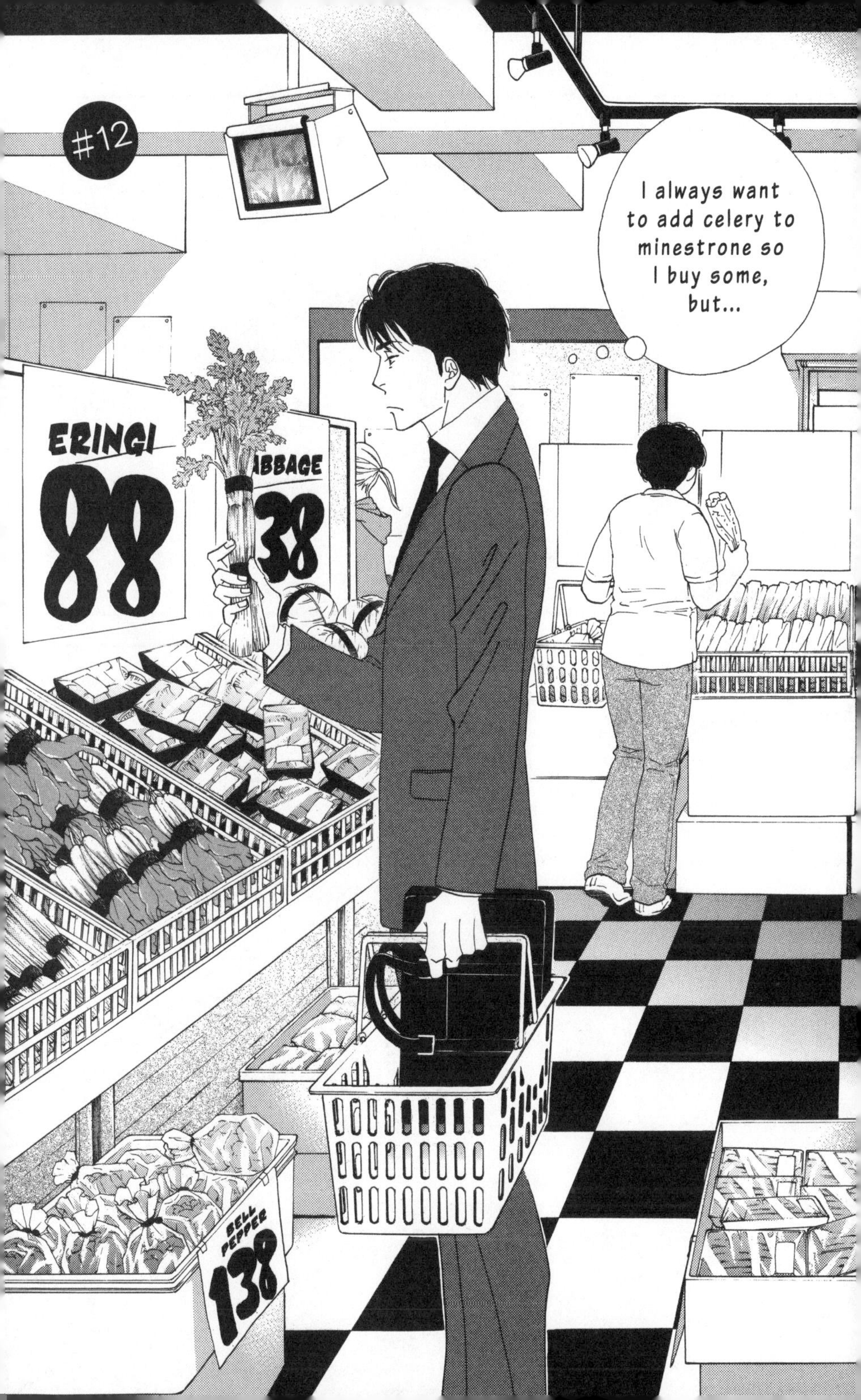
#12
I always want to add celery to minestrone so I buy some, but...
ERINGI 88
ABBAGE 38
BELL PEPPER 138

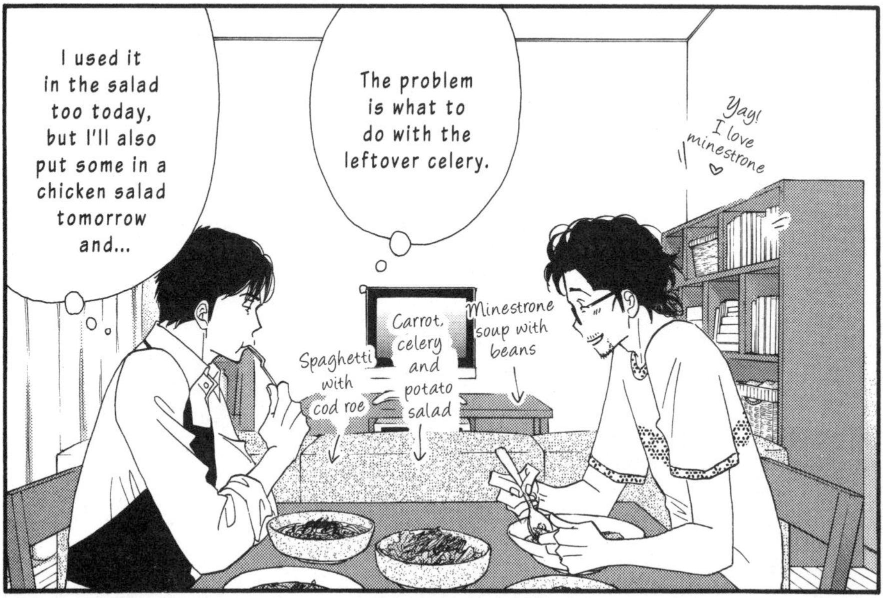
Yay! I love minestrone
The problem is what to do with the leftover celery.
I used it in the salad too today, but I'll also put some in a chicken salad tomorrow and...
Minestrone soup with beans
Carrot, celery and potato salad
Spaghetti with cod roe

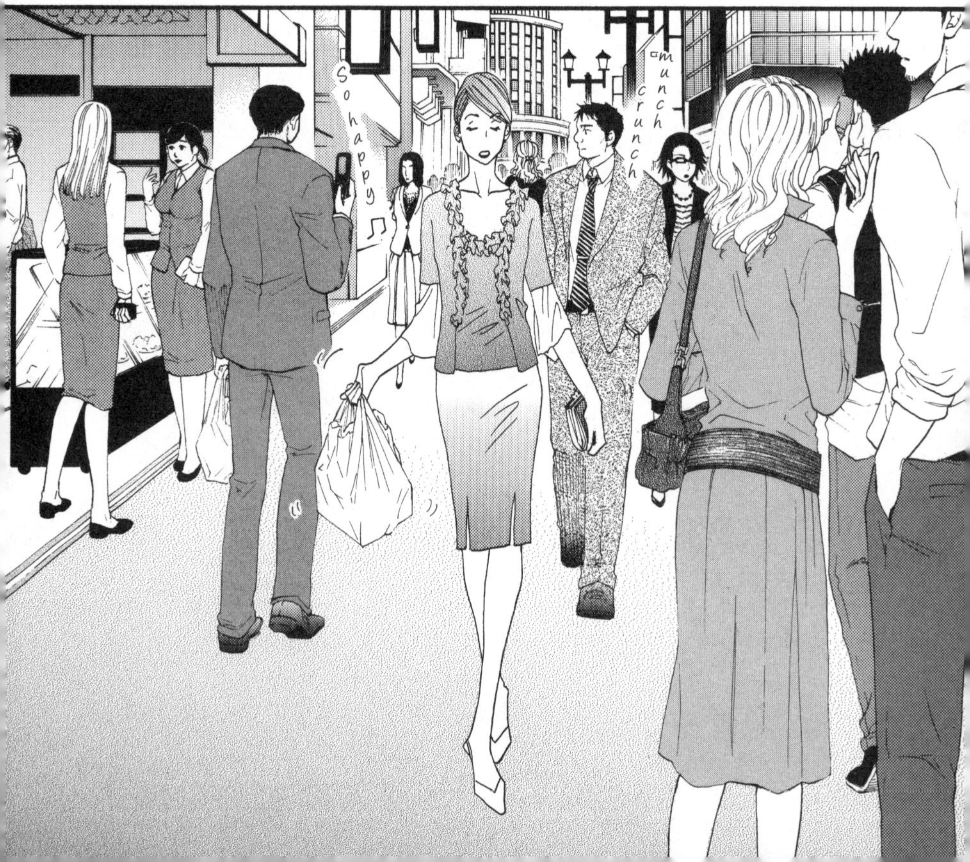
munch crunch
So happy

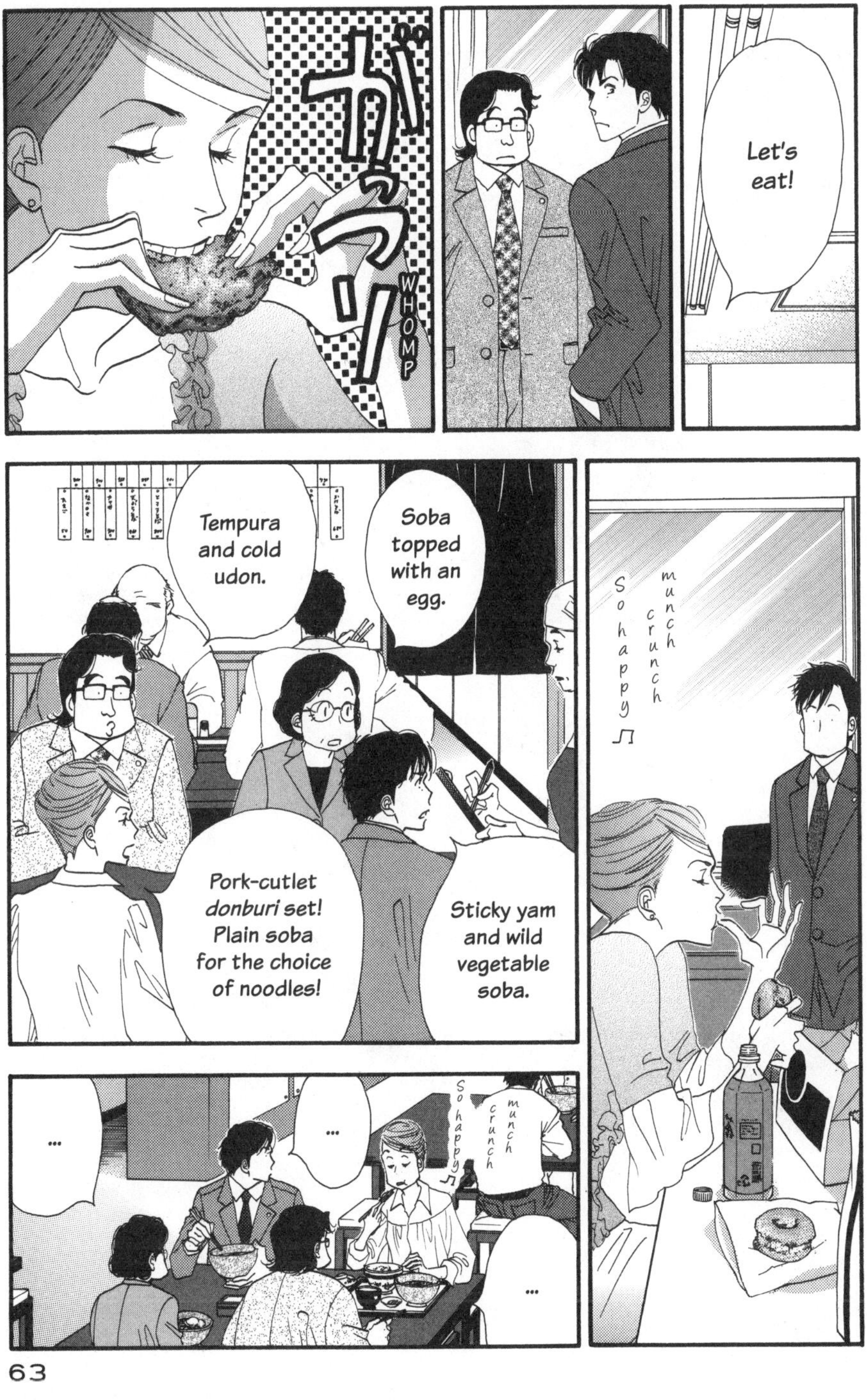
Let's eat!
WHOMP
munch crunch
So happy ♫
Soba topped with an egg.
Tempura and cold udon.
Sticky yam and wild vegetable soba.
Pork-cutlet *donburi* set! Plain soba for the choice of noodles!
...
munch crunch
So happy ♫
...
...

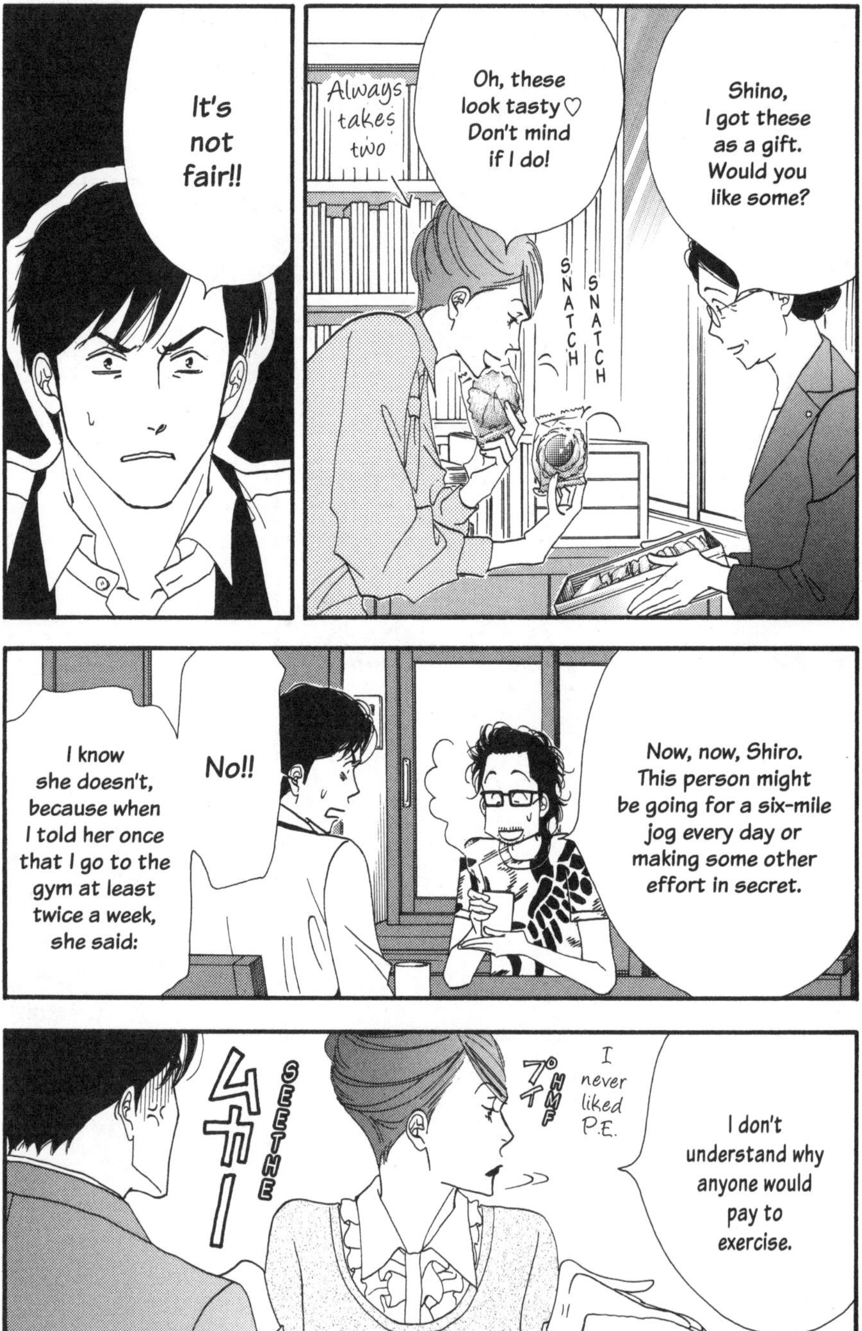
Shino, I got these as a gift. Would you like some?
Oh, these look tasty♡ Don't mind if I do!
Always takes two
SNATCH SNATCH
It's not fair!!
Now, now, Shiro. This person might be going for a six-mile jog every day or making some other effort in secret.
No!!
I know she doesn't, because when I told her once that I go to the gym at least twice a week, she said:
I don't understand why anyone would pay to exercise.
I never liked P.E.
プイ HMF
ムカー SEETHE

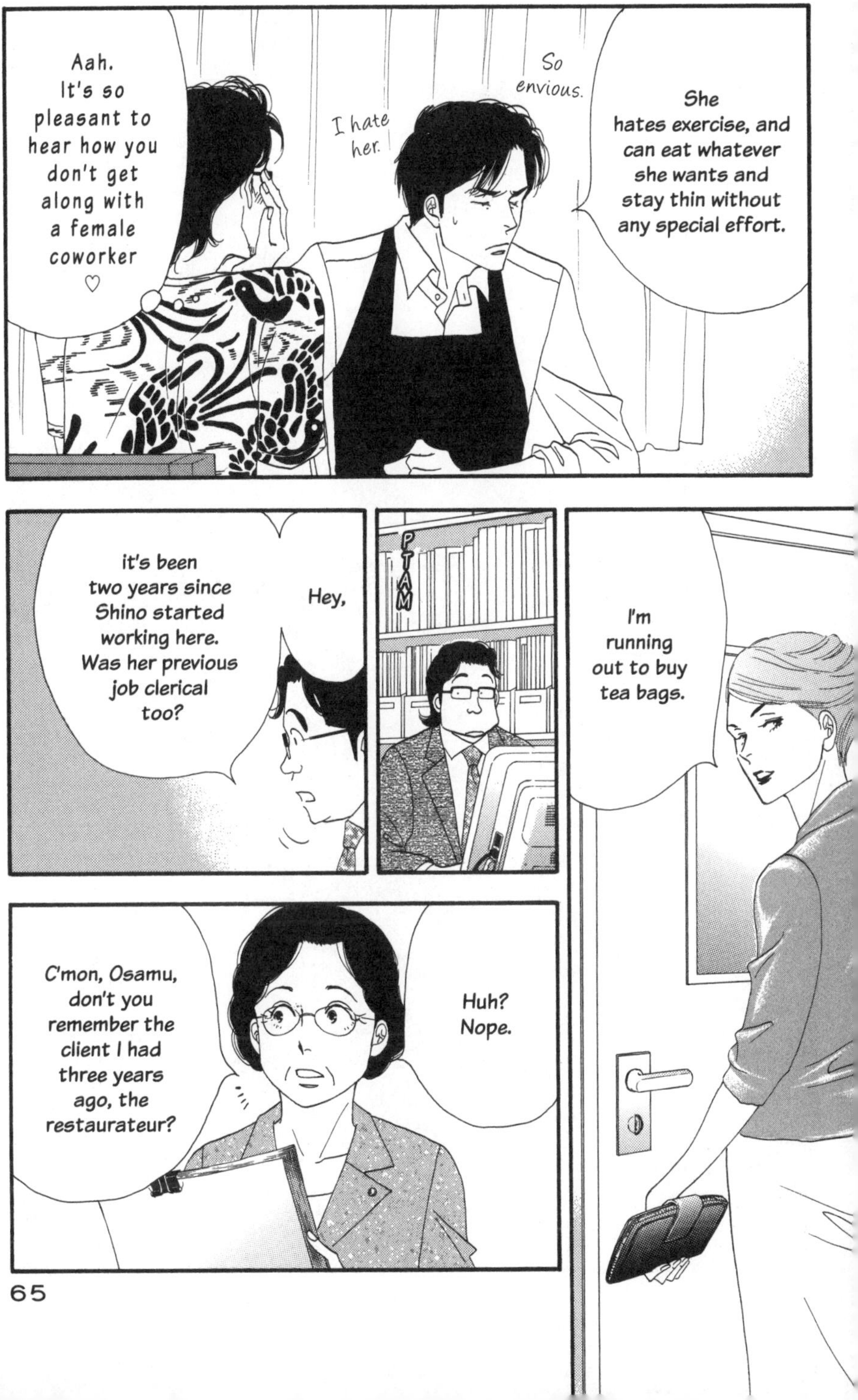

She hates exercise, and can eat whatever she wants and stay thin without any special effort.
So envious.
I hate her.
Aah. It's so pleasant to hear how you don't get along with a female coworker ♡
I'm running out to buy tea bags.
PTTAM
Hey,
it's been two years since Shino started working here. Was her previous job clerical too?
Huh? Nope.
C'mon, Osamu, don't you remember the client I had three years ago, the restaurateur?

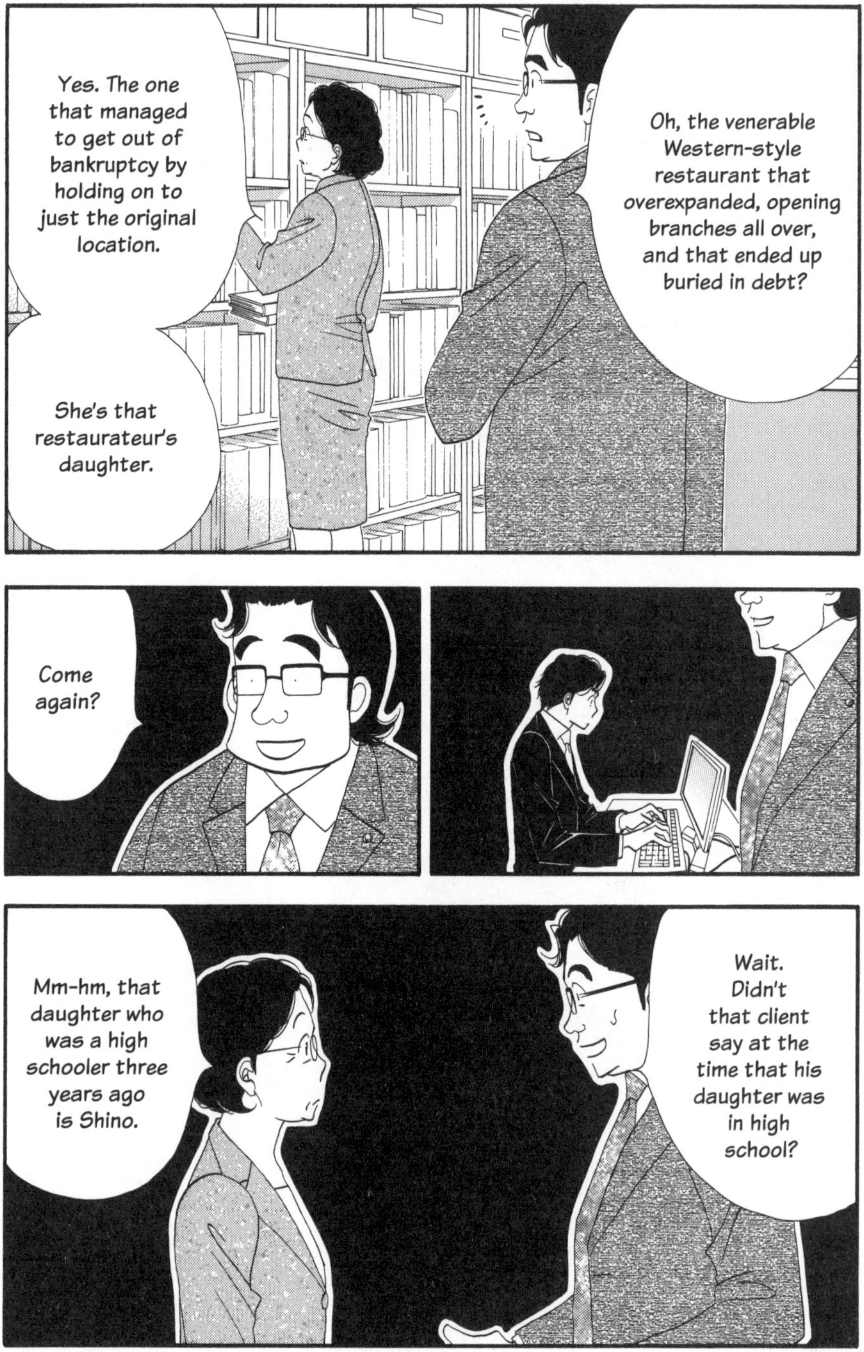
Oh, the venerable Western-style restaurant that overexpanded, opening branches all over, and that ended up buried in debt?
Yes. The one that managed to get out of bankruptcy by holding on to just the original location.
She's that restaurateur's daughter.
Come again?
Wait. Didn't that client say at the time that his daughter was in high school?
Mm-hm, that daughter who was a high schooler three years ago is Shino.

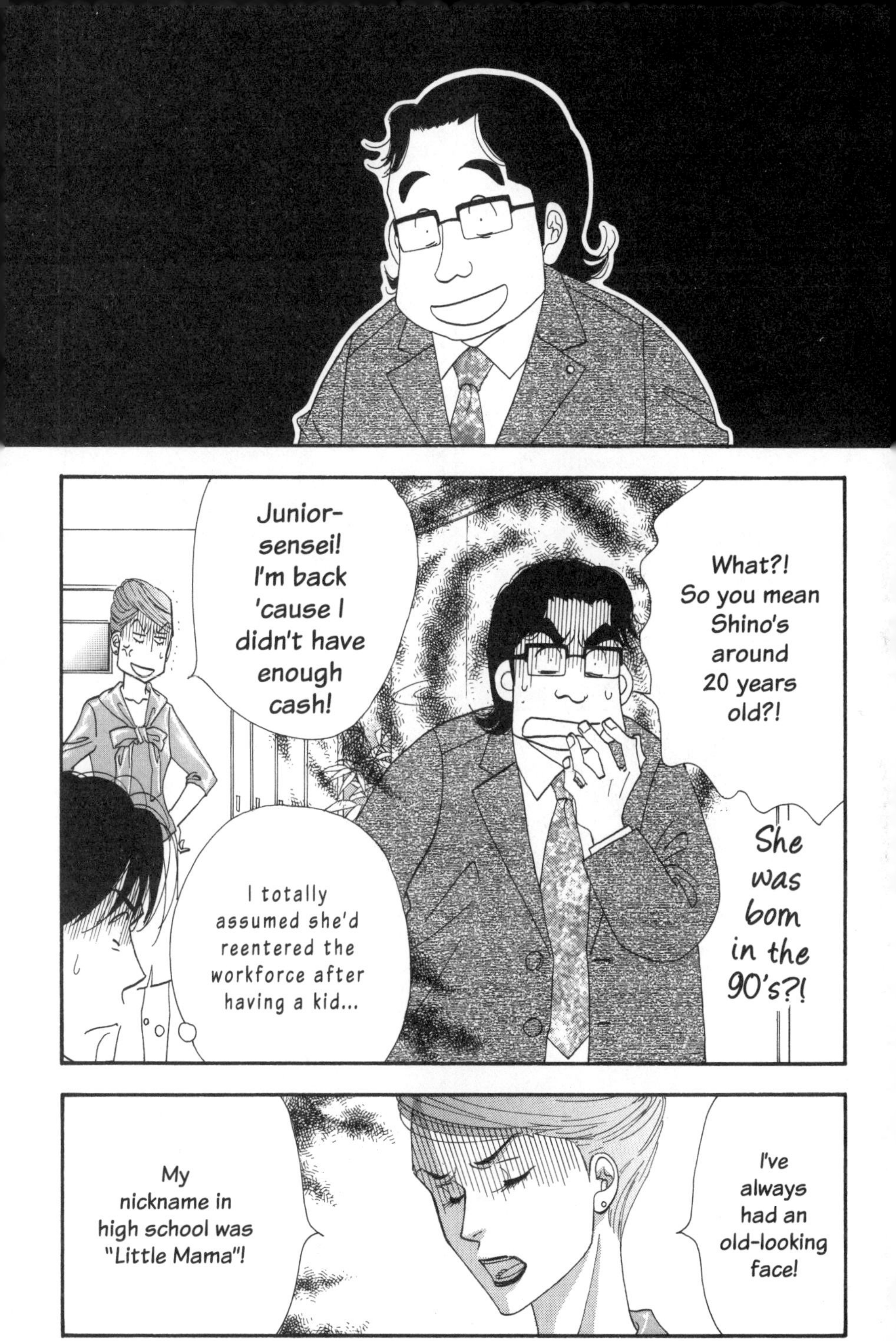
What?! So you mean Shino's around 20 years old?!
She was born in the 90's?!
Junior-sensei! I'm back 'cause I didn't have enough cash!
I totally assumed she'd reentered the workforce after having a kid...
I've always had an old-looking face!
My nickname in high school was "Little Mama"!

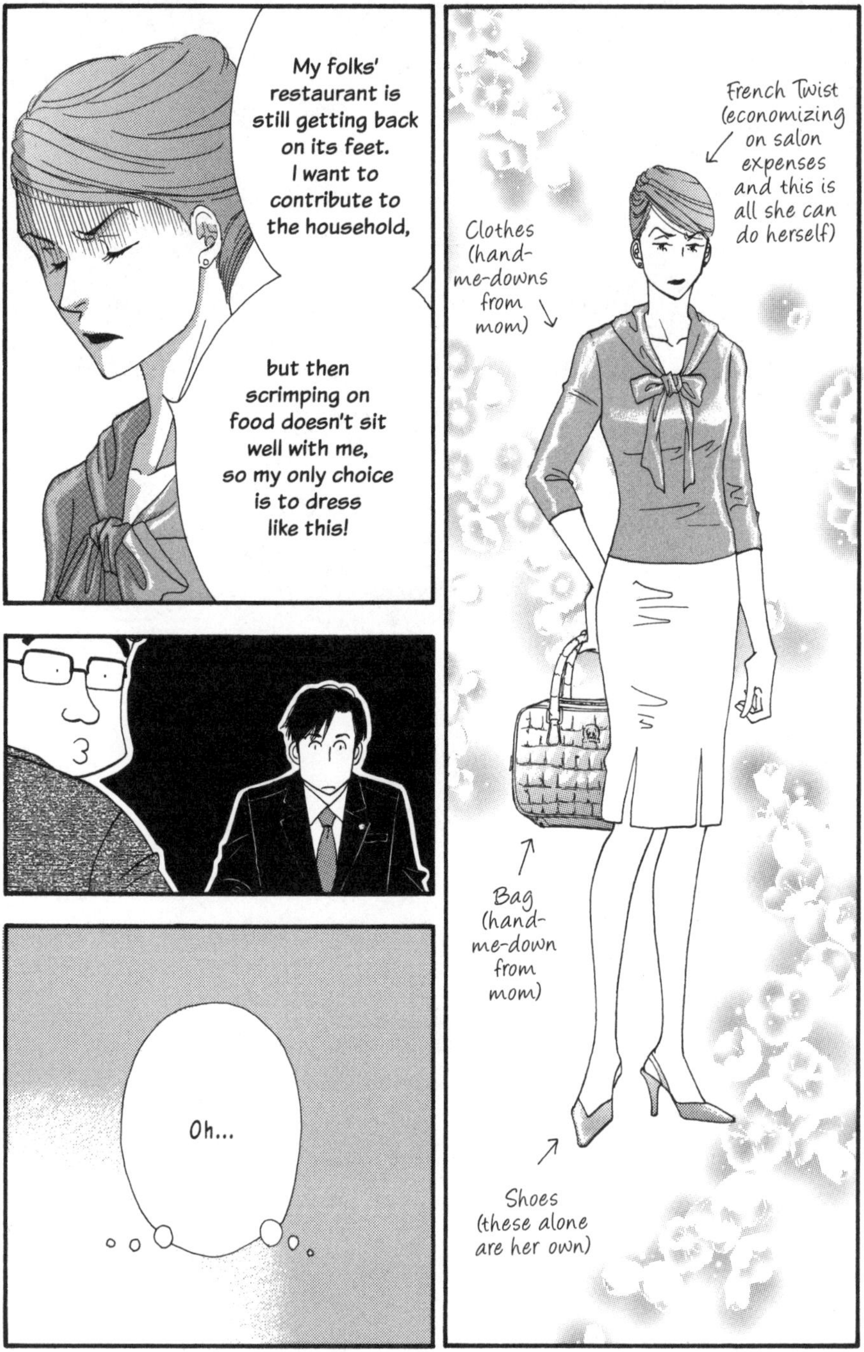
French Twist (economizing on salon expenses and this is all she can do herself)
Clothes (hand-me-downs from mom)
Bag (hand-me-down from mom)
Shoes (these alone are her own)
My folks' restaurant is still getting back on its feet. I want to contribute to the household,
but then scrimping on food doesn't sit well with me, so my only choice is to dress like this!
Oh...

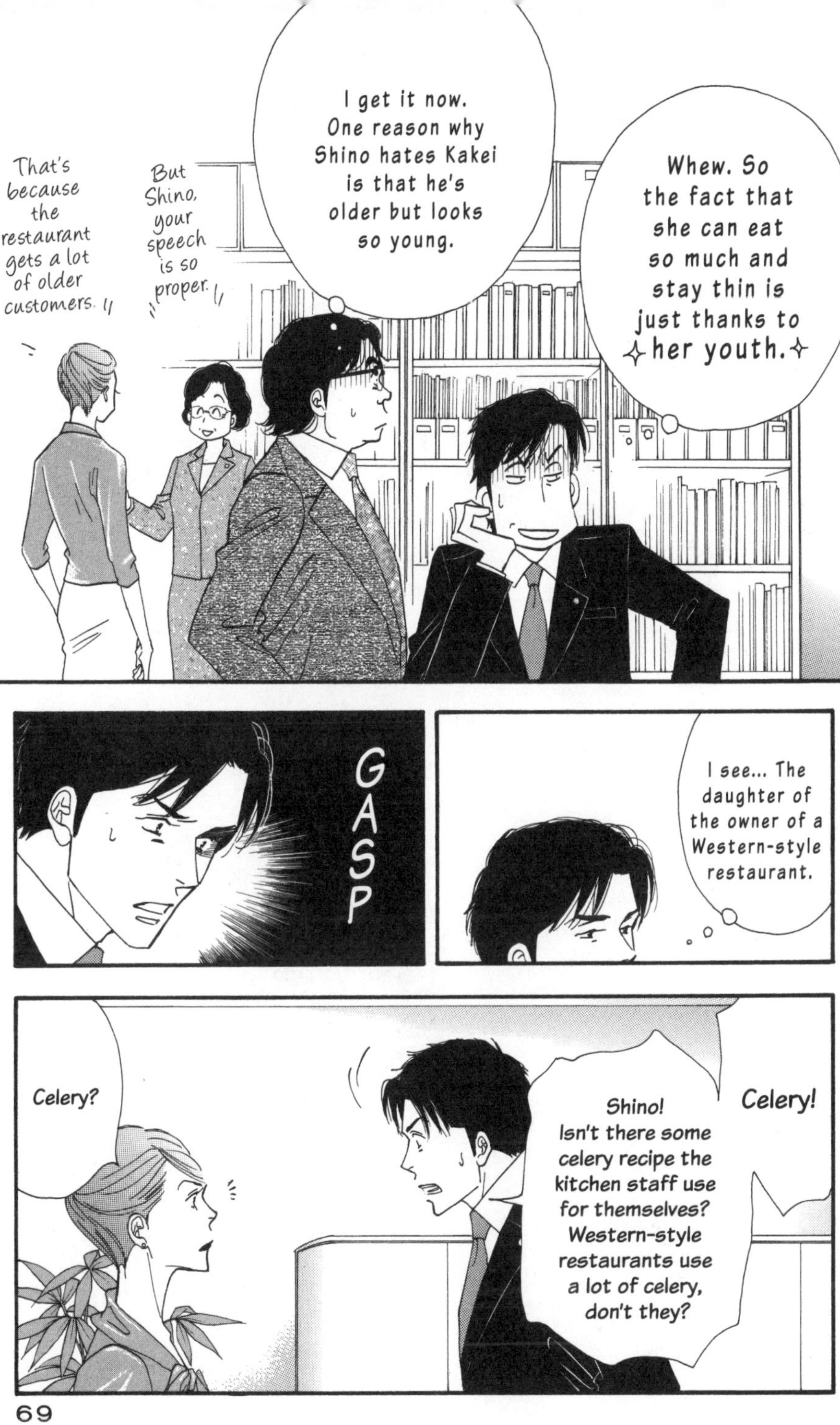

Whew. So the fact that she can eat so much and stay thin is just thanks to ✧her youth.✧
I get it now. One reason why Shino hates Kakei is that he's older but looks so young.
But Shino, your speech is so proper.
That's because the restaurant gets a lot of older customers.
I see... The daughter of the owner of a Western-style restaurant.
GASP
Celery!
Shino! Isn't there some celery recipe the kitchen staff use for themselves? Western-style restaurants use a lot of celery, don't they?
Celery?

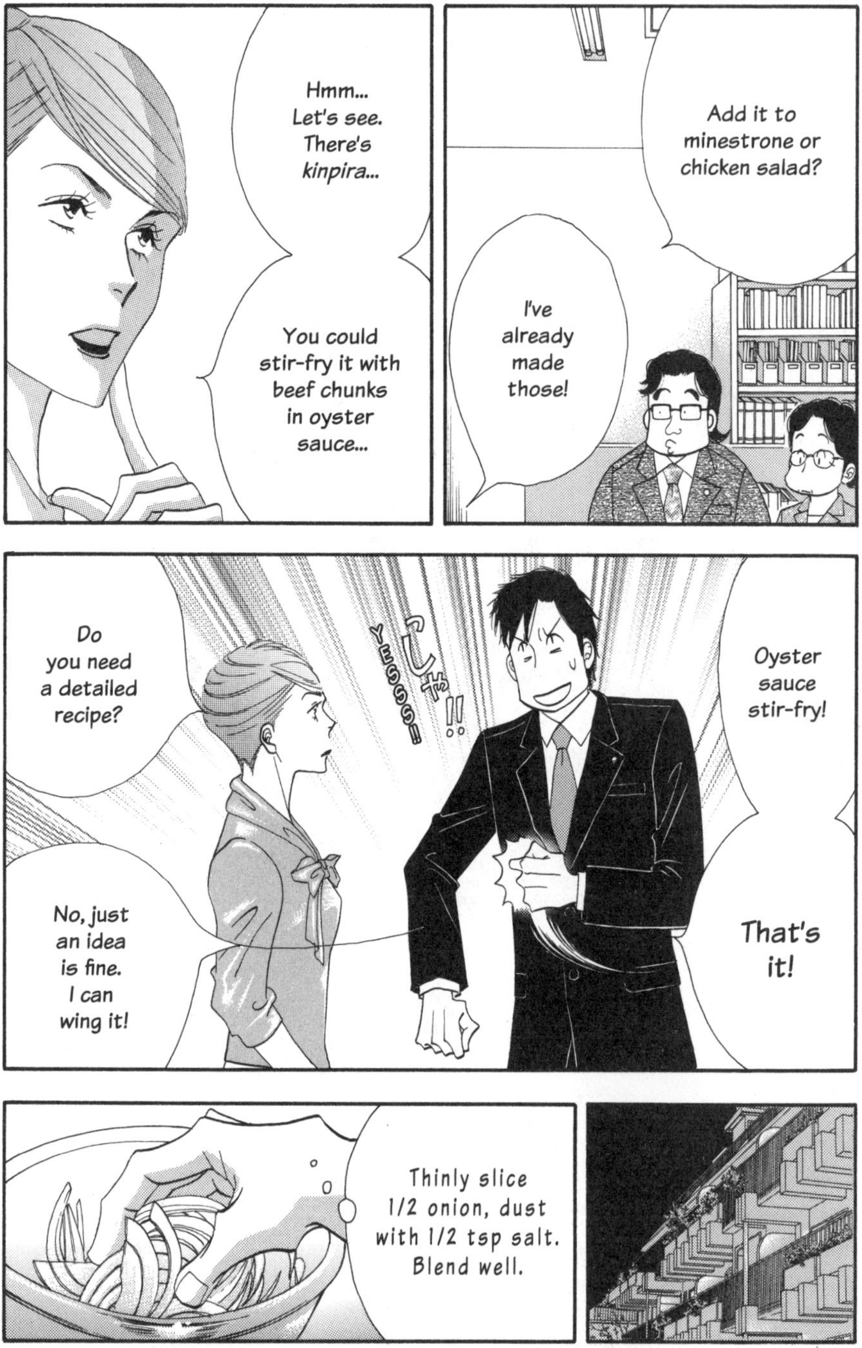

Add it to minestrone or chicken salad?
I've already made those!
Hmm... Let's see. There's *kinpira*...
You could stir-fry it with beef chunks in oyster sauce...
Oyster sauce stir-fry!
YESSS!!
That's it!
Do you need a detailed recipe?
No, just an idea is fine. I can wing it!
Thinly slice 1/2 onion, dust with 1/2 tsp salt. Blend well.

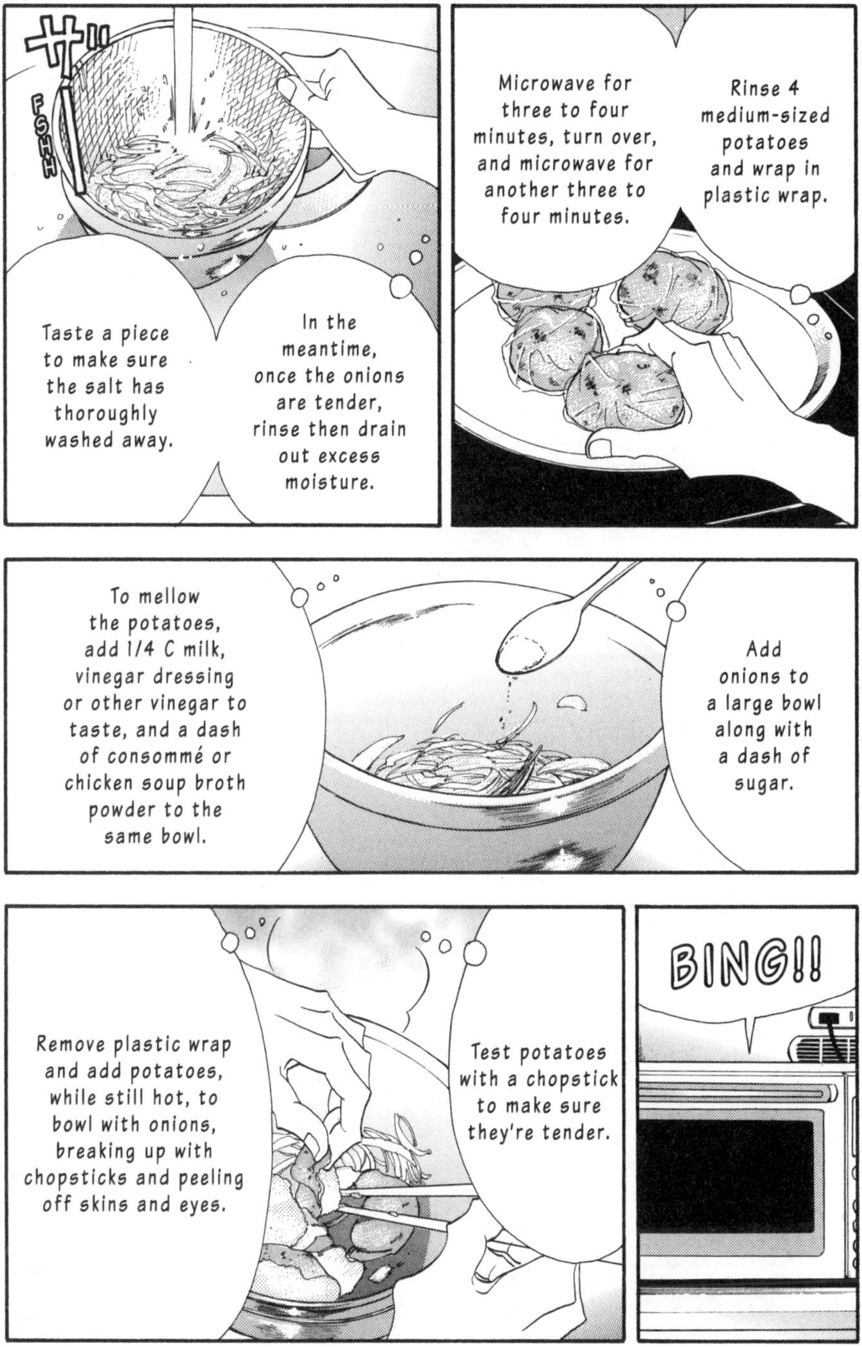
Rinse 4 medium-sized potatoes and wrap in plastic wrap.
Microwave for three to four minutes, turn over, and microwave for another three to four minutes.
FSHH
In the meantime, once the onions are tender, rinse then drain out excess moisture.
Taste a piece to make sure the salt has thoroughly washed away.
Add onions to a large bowl along with a dash of sugar.
To mellow the potatoes, add 1/4 C milk, vinegar dressing or other vinegar to taste, and a dash of consommé or chicken soup broth powder to the same bowl.
BING!!
Test potatoes with a chopstick to make sure they're tender.
Remove plastic wrap and add potatoes, while still hot, to bowl with onions, breaking up with chopsticks and peeling off skins and eyes.

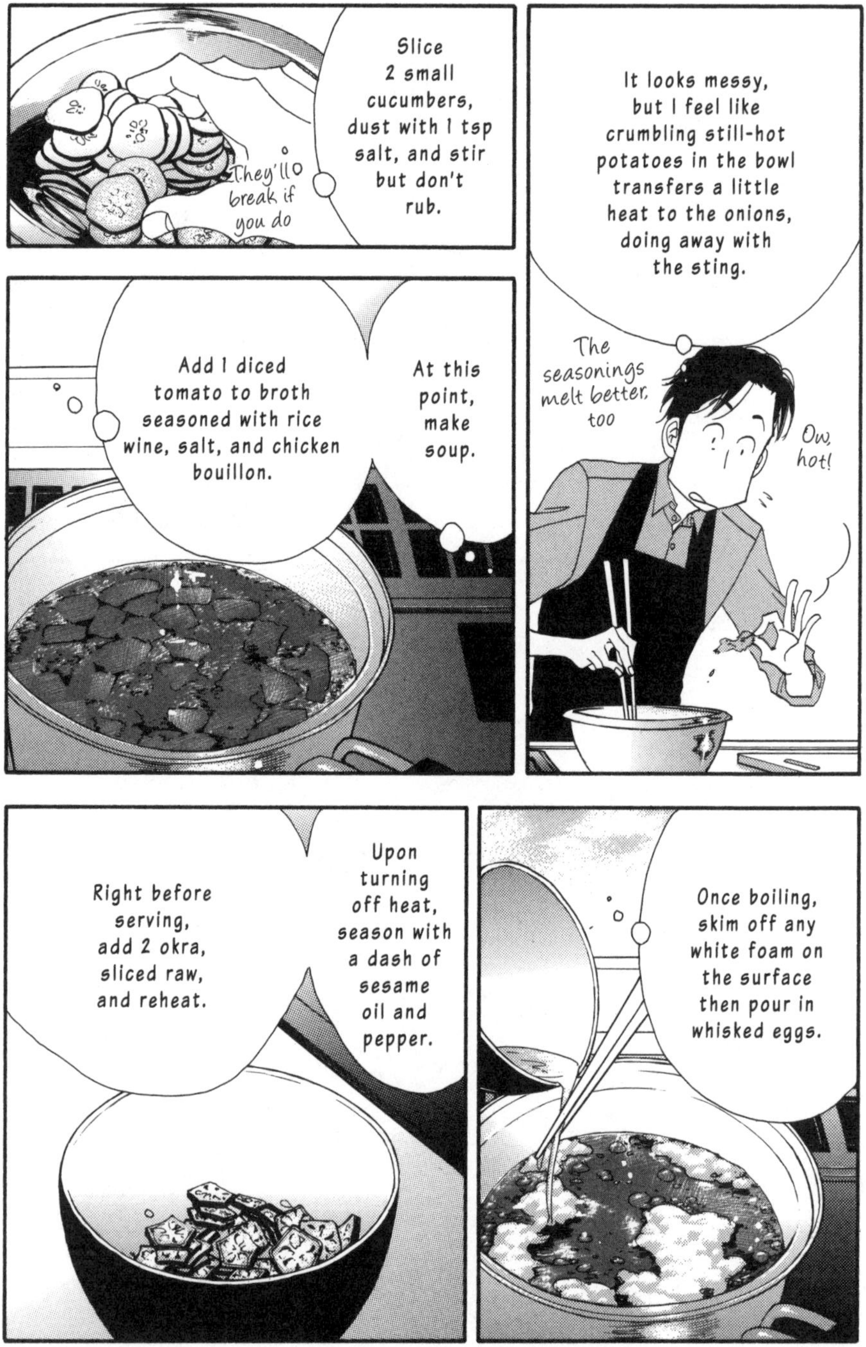
It looks messy, but I feel like crumbling still-hot potatoes in the bowl transfers a little heat to the onions, doing away with the sting.
The seasonings melt better, too
Ow, hot!
Slice 2 small cucumbers, dust with 1 tsp salt, and stir but don't rub.
They'll break if you do
At this point, make soup.
Add 1 diced tomato to broth seasoned with rice wine, salt, and chicken bouillon.
Once boiling, skim off any white foam on the surface then pour in whisked eggs.
Upon turning off heat, season with a dash of sesame oil and pepper.
Right before serving, add 2 okra, sliced raw, and reheat.

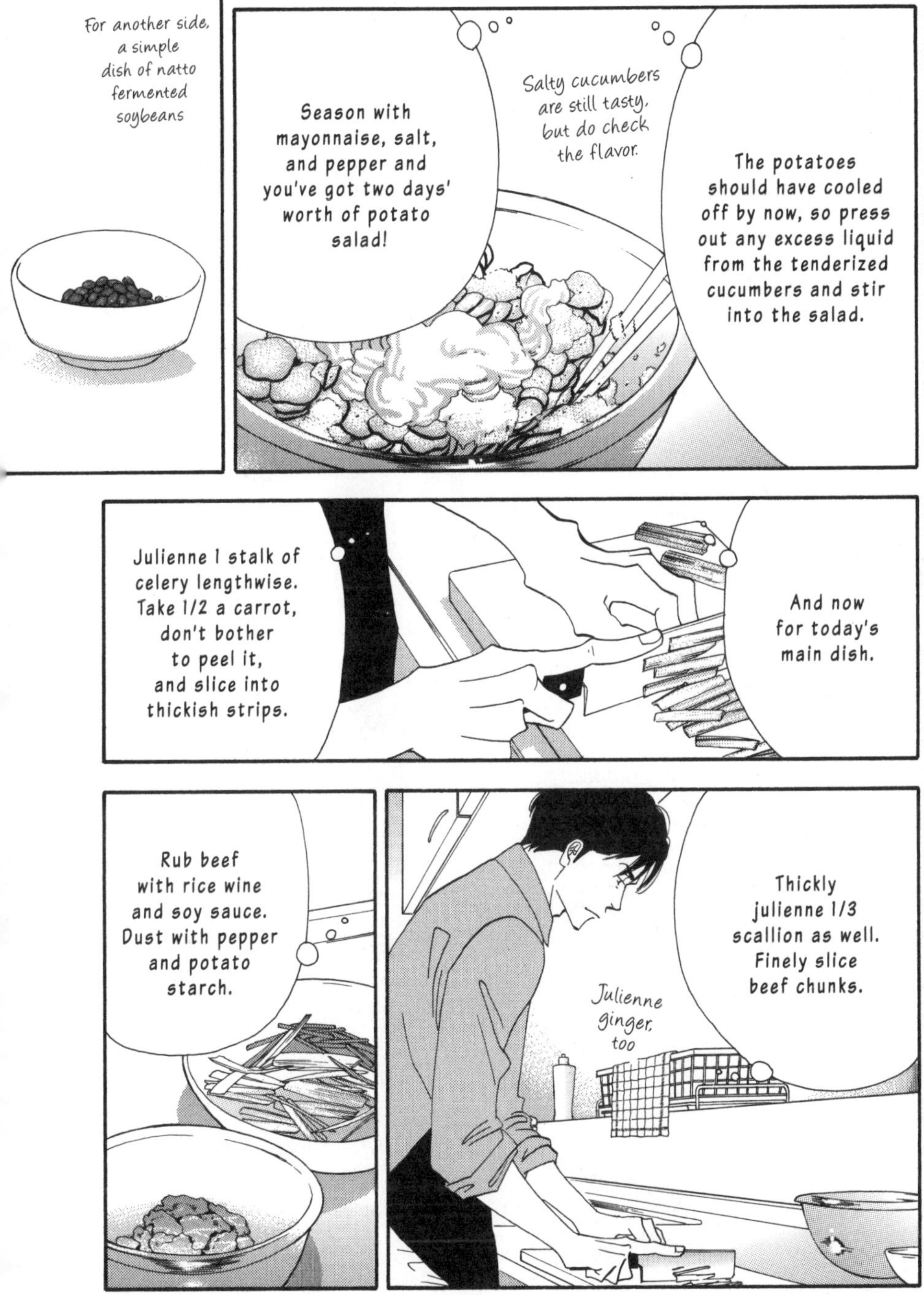
The potatoes should have cooled off by now, so press out any excess liquid from the tenderized cucumbers and stir into the salad.
Salty cucumbers are still tasty, but do check the flavor.
Season with mayonnaise, salt, and pepper and you've got two days' worth of potato salad!
For another side, a simple dish of natto fermented soybeans
And now for today's main dish.
Julienne 1 stalk of celery lengthwise. Take 1/2 a carrot, don't bother to peel it, and slice into thickish strips.
Thickly julienne 1/3 scallion as well. Finely slice beef chunks.
Julienne ginger, too
Rub beef with rice wine and soy sauce. Dust with pepper and potato starch.

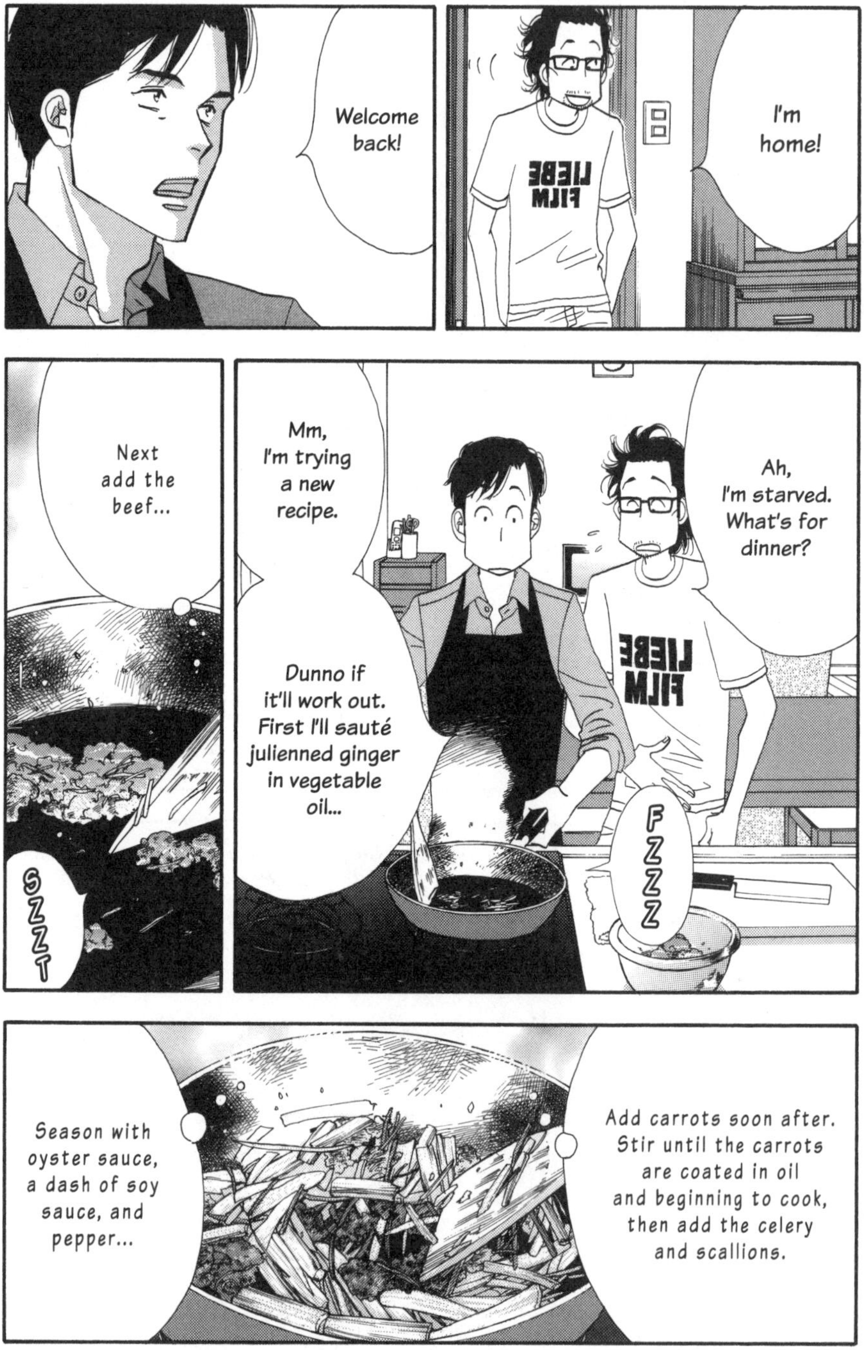
I'm home!
Welcome back!
Ah, I'm starved. What's for dinner?
Mm, I'm trying a new recipe.
Dunno if it'll work out. First I'll sauté julienned ginger in vegetable oil...
FZZZ
Next add the beef...
SZZT
Add carrots soon after. Stir until the carrots are coated in oil and beginning to cook, then add the celery and scallions.
Season with oyster sauce, a dash of soy sauce, and pepper...

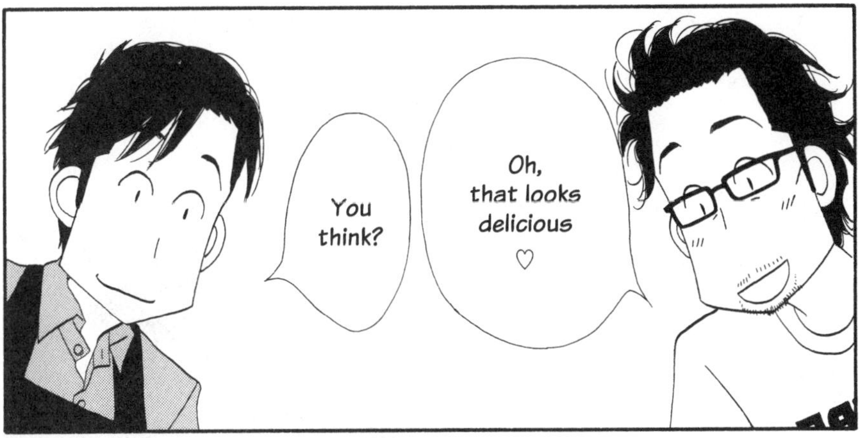
Oh, that looks delicious ♡
You think?

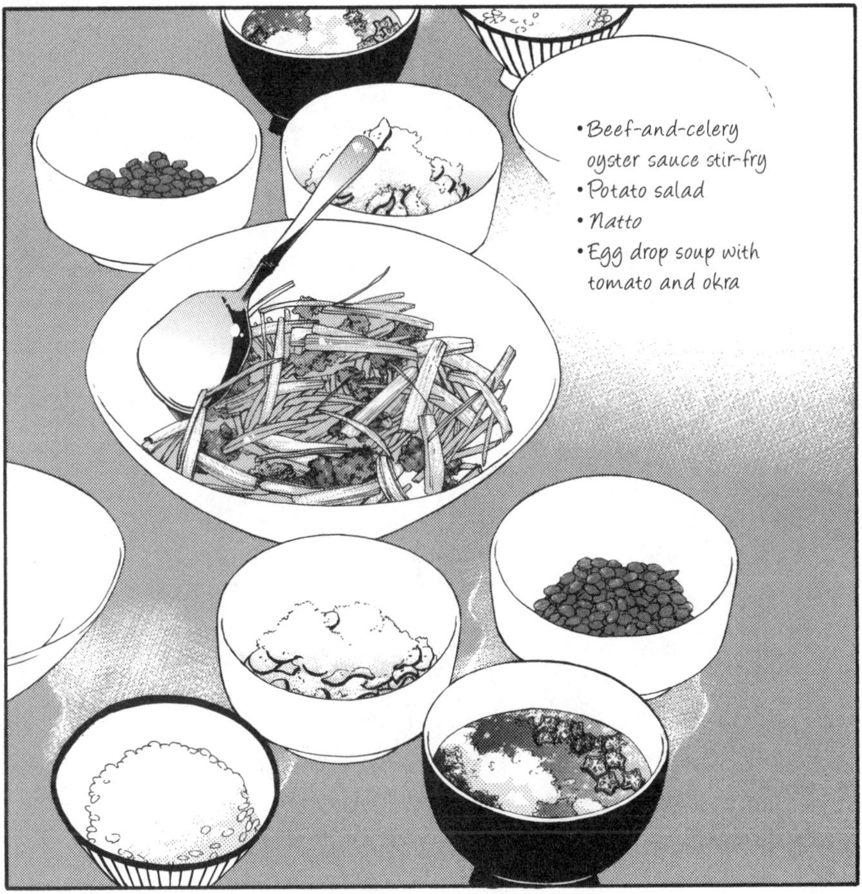
•Beef-and-celery oyster sauce stir-fry
•Potato salad
•Natto
•Egg drop soup with tomato and okra

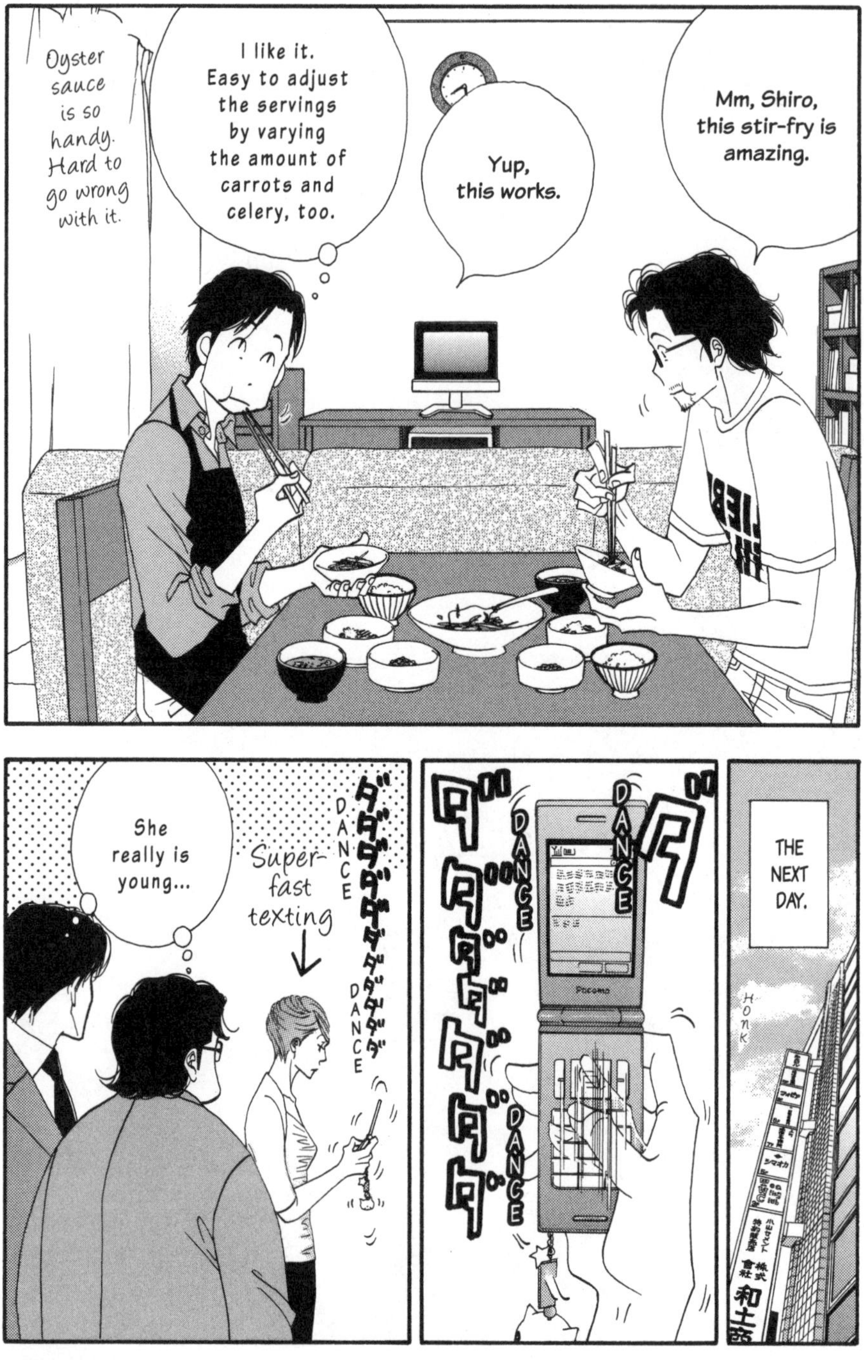
Mm, Shiro, this stir-fry is amazing.
Yup, this works.
I like it. Easy to adjust the servings by varying the amount of carrots and celery, too.
Oyster sauce is so handy. Hard to go wrong with it.
THE NEXT DAY.
HONK
DANCE
DANCE
DANCE
DANCE
She really is young...
Super-fast texting
DANCE
DANCE

#12 END

Beef has a stronger odor than pork,
so it's more suited to stir-frying
with a very fragrant vegetable like celery.
Shiro Kakei doesn't use beef unless
a recipe downright requires it.

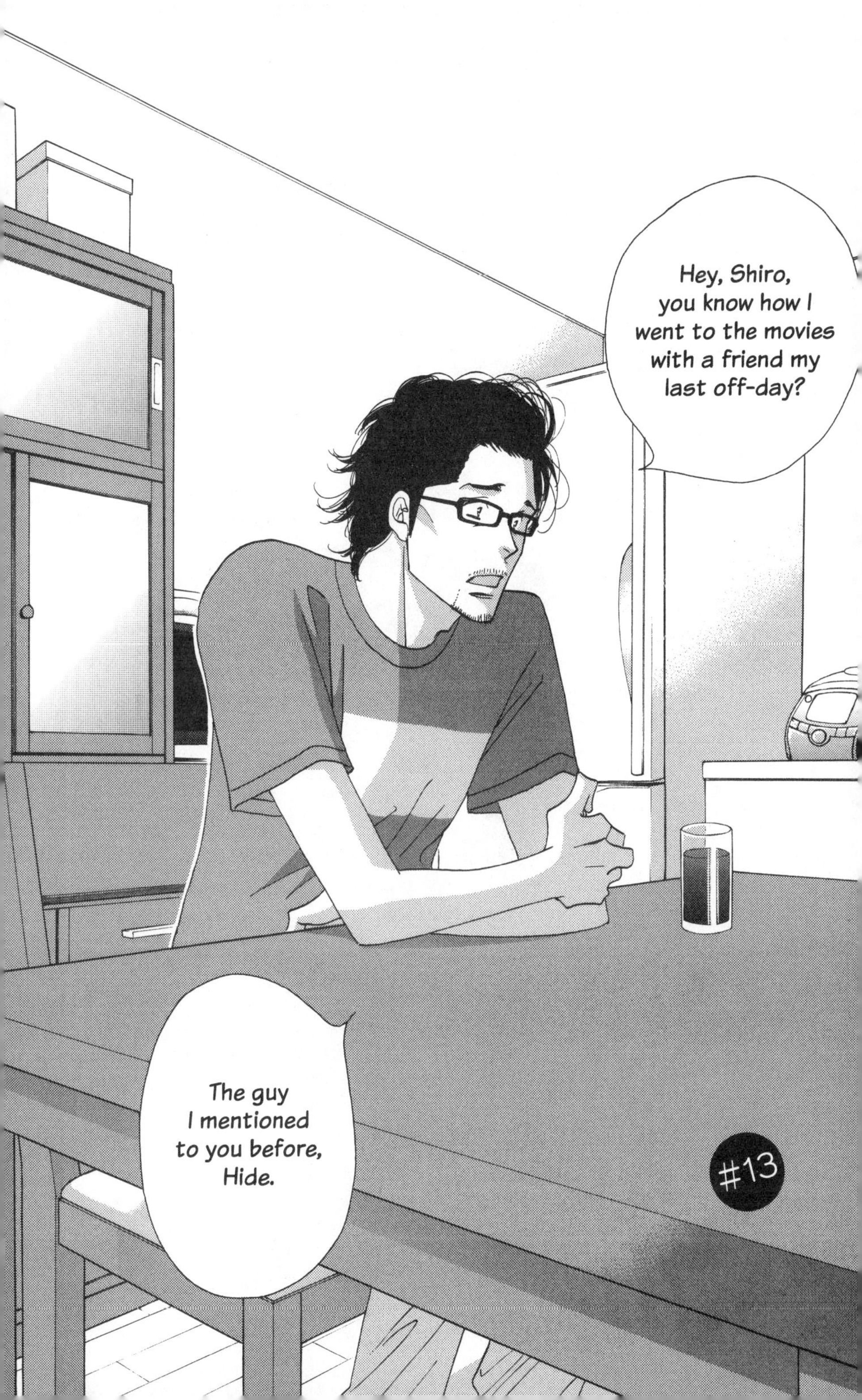
Hey, Shiro, you know how I went to the movies with a friend my last off-day?
The guy I mentioned to you before, Hide.
#13

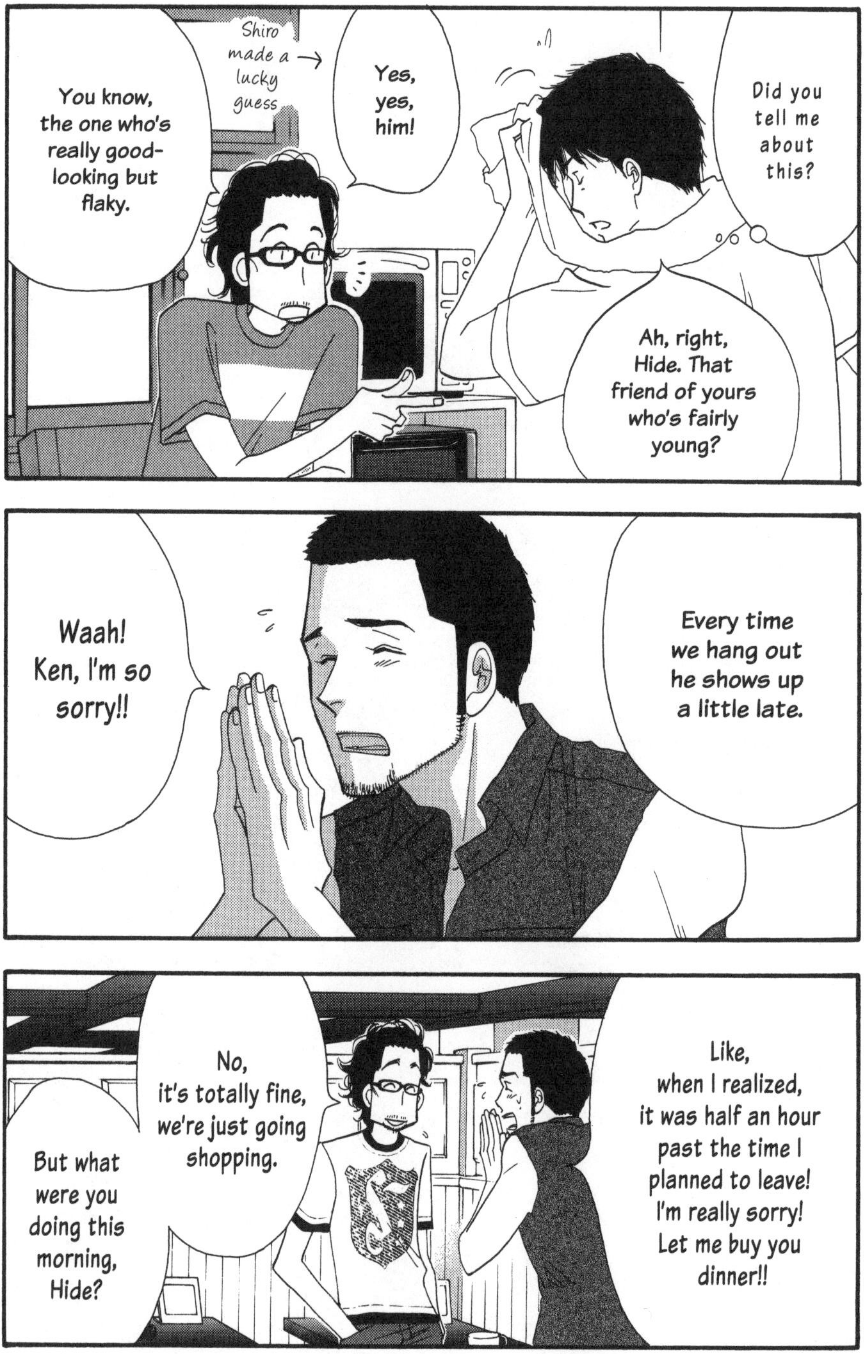
Did you tell me about this?
Ah, right, Hide. That friend of yours who's fairly young?
Yes, yes, him!
Shiro made a lucky guess
You know, the one who's really good-looking but flaky.
Every time we hang out he shows up a little late.
Waah! Ken, I'm so sorry!!
Like, when I realized, it was half an hour past the time I planned to leave! I'm really sorry! Let me buy you dinner!!
No, it's totally fine, we're just going shopping.
But what were you doing this morning, Hide?

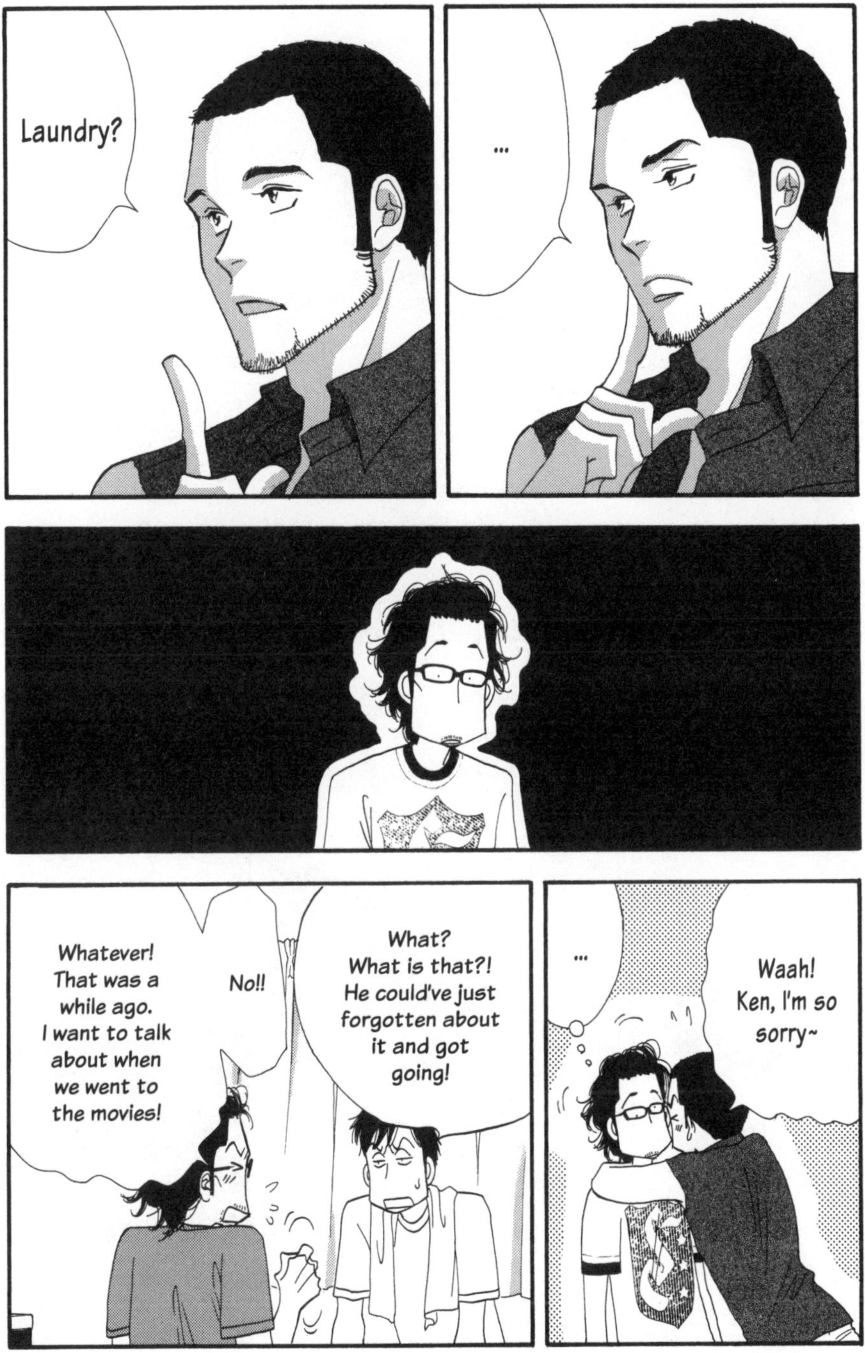

...
Laundry?
...
Waah! Ken, I'm so sorry~
What? What is that?! He could've just forgotten about it and got going!
No!!
Whatever! That was a while ago. I want to talk about when we went to the movies!

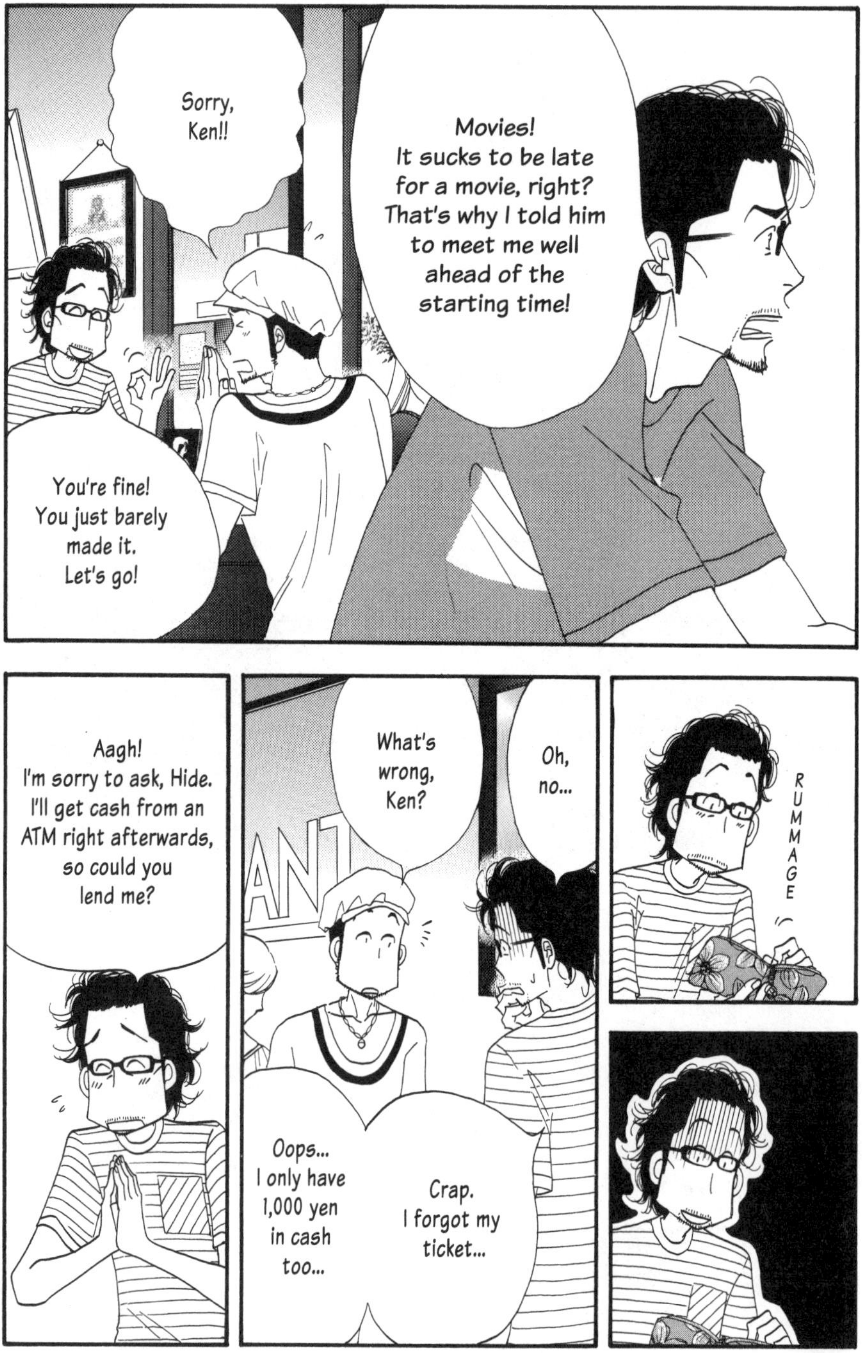
Movies! It sucks to be late for a movie, right? That's why I told him to meet me well ahead of the starting time!
Sorry, Ken!!
You're fine! You just barely made it. Let's go!
RUMMAGE
Oh, no...
What's wrong, Ken?
Crap. I forgot my ticket...
Oops... I only have 1,000 yen in cash too...
Aagh! I'm sorry to ask, Hide. I'll get cash from an ATM right afterwards, so could you lend me?

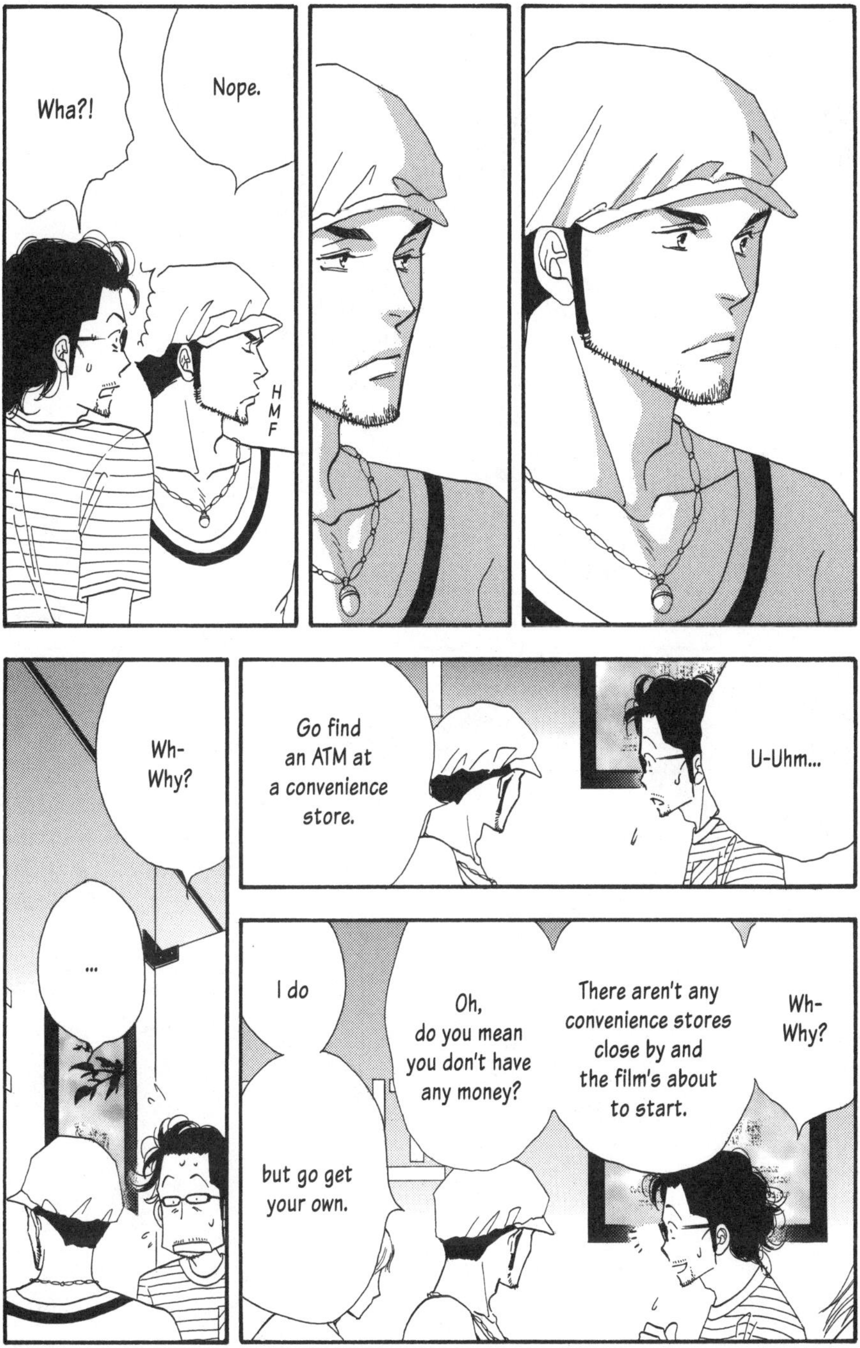
Nope.
Wha?!
HMF
U-Uhm...
Go find an ATM at a convenience store.
Wh- Why?
There aren't any convenience stores close by and the film's about to start.
Oh, do you mean you don't have any money?
I do
but go get your own.
Wh- Why?
...

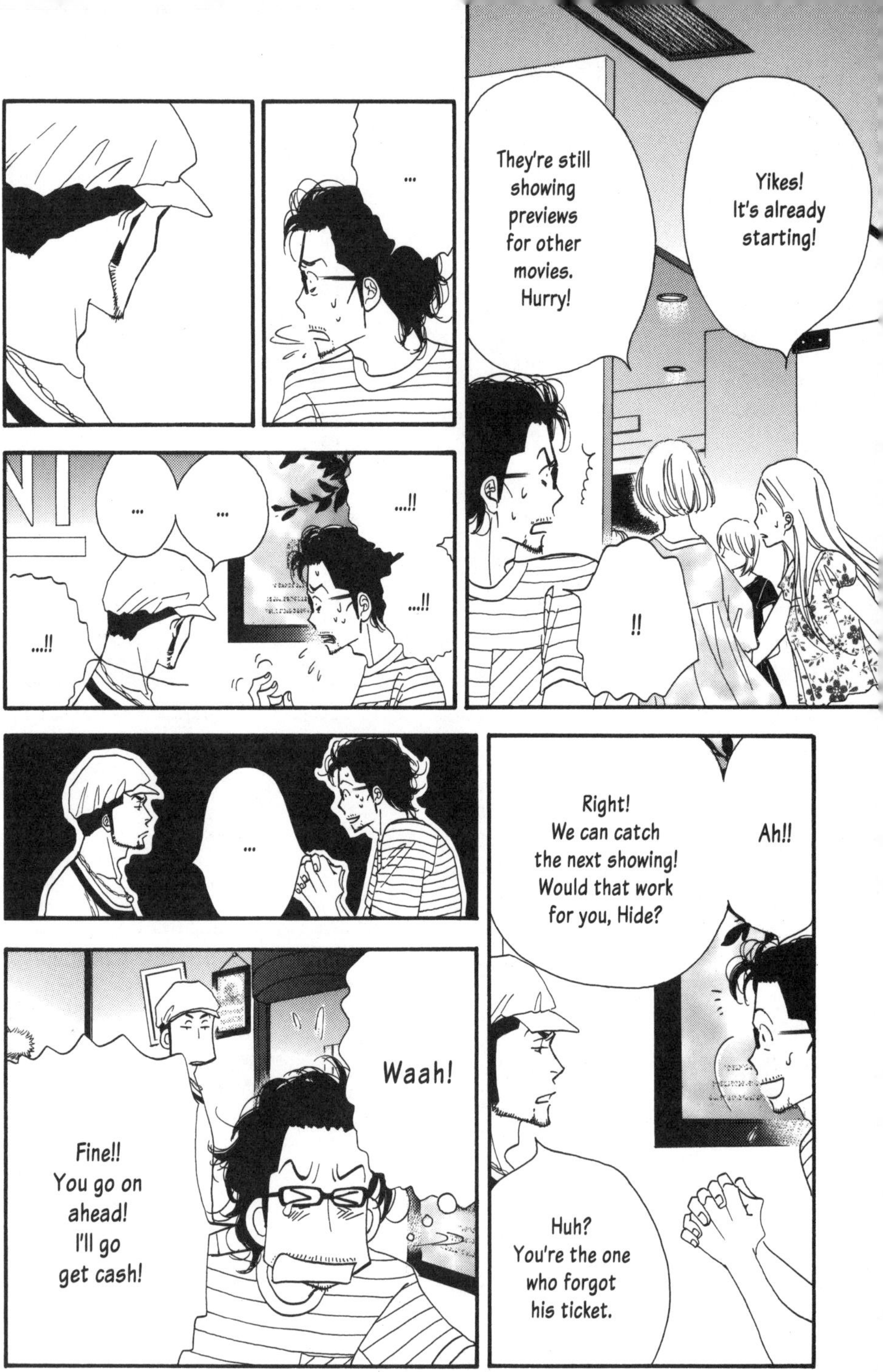
Yikes! It's already starting!
They're still showing previews for other movies. Hurry!
!!
...
...!!
...
...
...!!
...!!
Ah!!
Right! We can catch the next showing! Would that work for you, Hide?
Huh? You're the one who forgot his ticket.
...
Waah!
Fine!! You go on ahead! I'll go get cash!

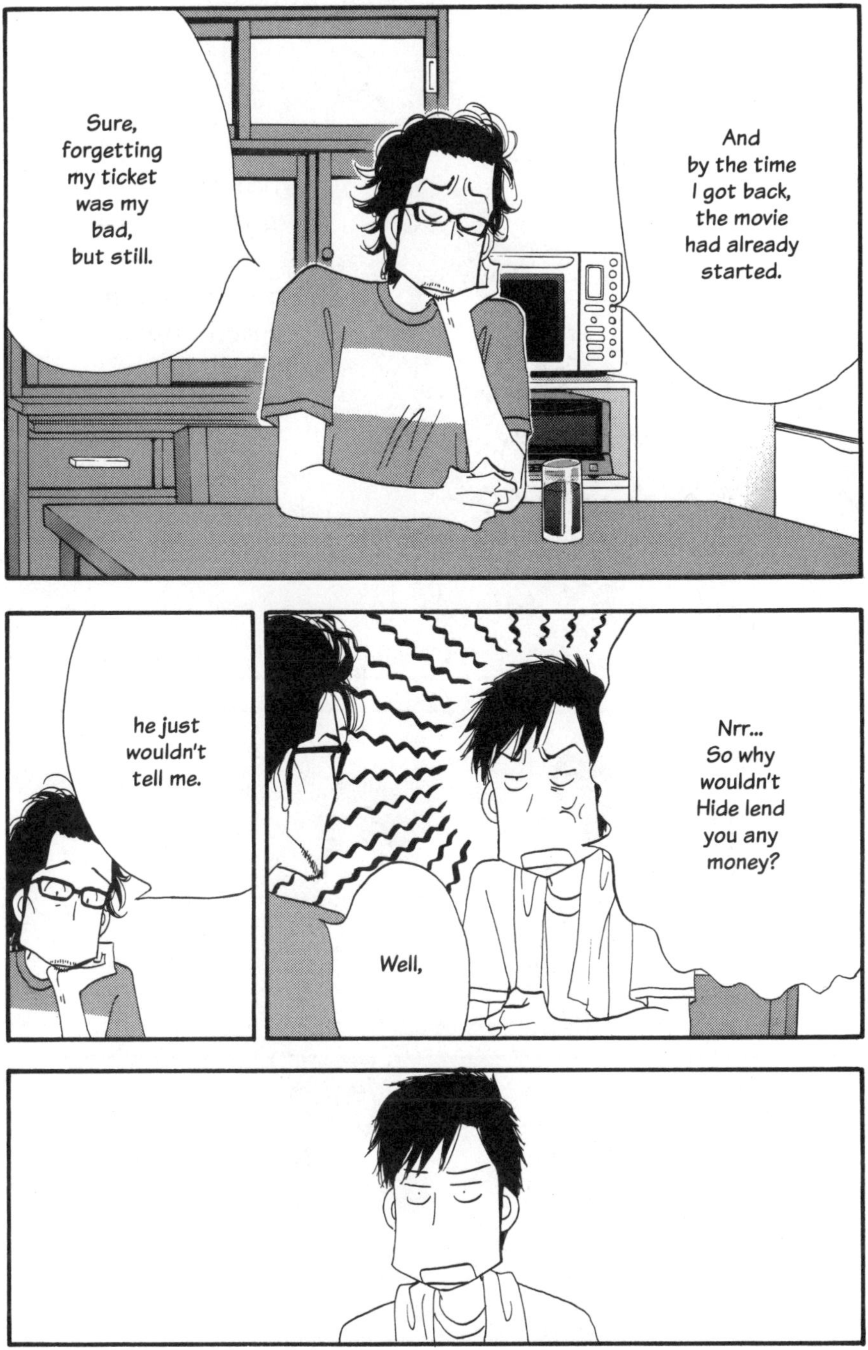
And by the time I got back, the movie had already started.
Sure, forgetting my ticket was my bad, but still.
Nrr... So why wouldn't Hide lend you any money?
Well,
he just wouldn't tell me.

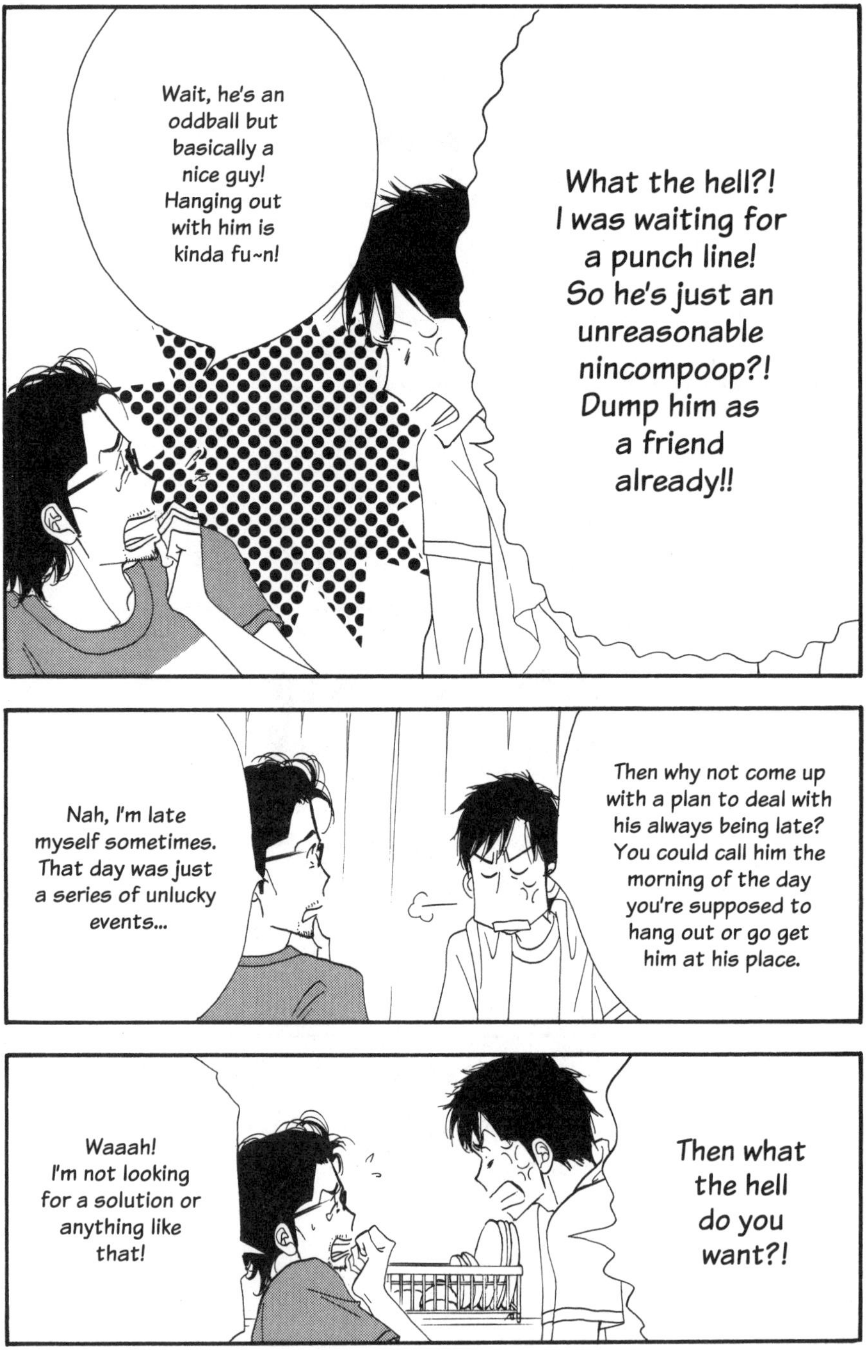
Wait, he's an oddball but basically a nice guy! Hanging out with him is kinda fu~n!
What the hell?! I was waiting for a punch line! So he's just an unreasonable nincompoop?! Dump him as a friend already!!
Nah, I'm late myself sometimes. That day was just a series of unlucky events...
Then why not come up with a plan to deal with his always being late? You could call him the morning of the day you're supposed to hang out or go get him at his place.
Waaah! I'm not looking for a solution or anything like that!
Then what the hell do you want?!

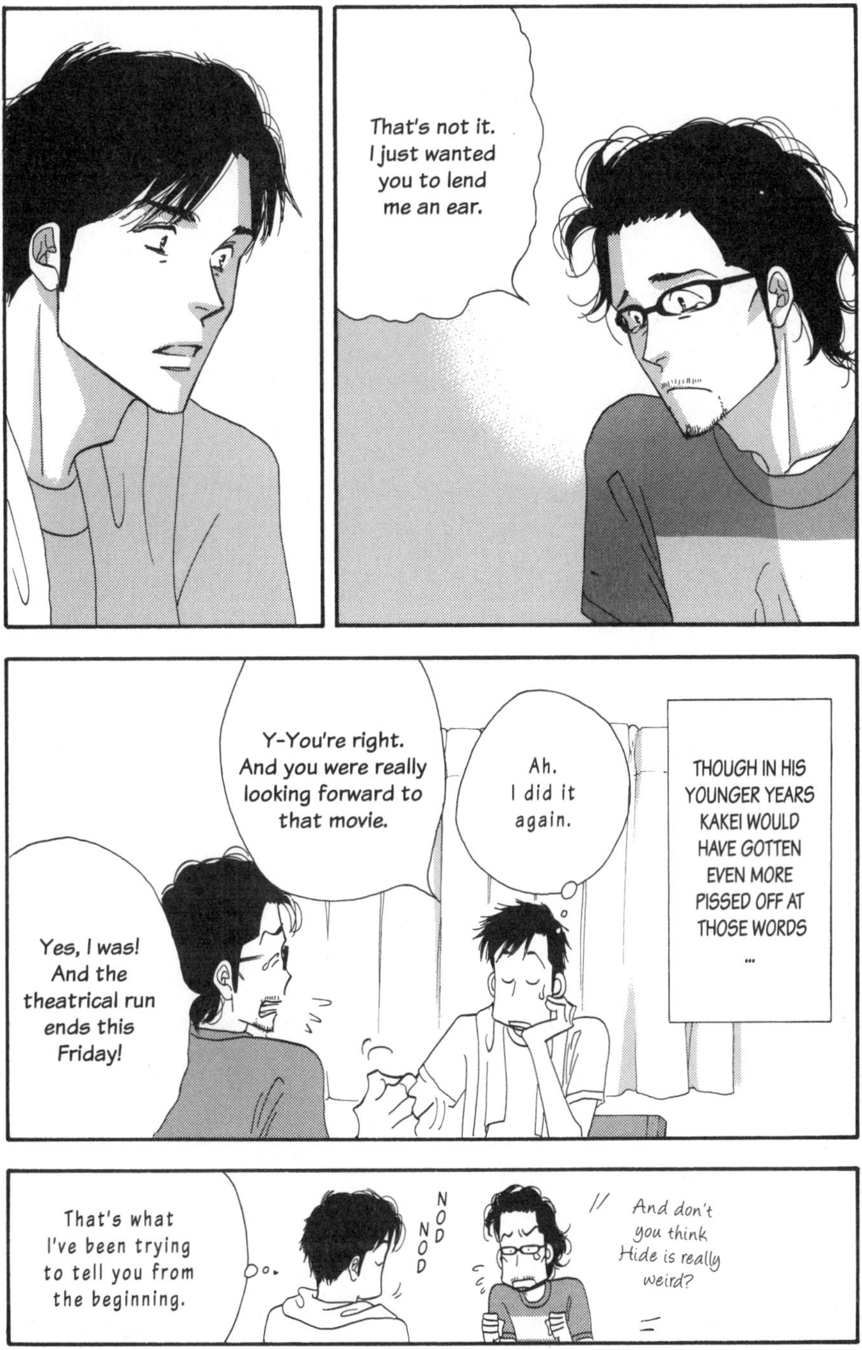
That's not it. I just wanted you to lend me an ear.
THOUGH IN HIS YOUNGER YEARS KAKEI WOULD HAVE GOTTEN EVEN MORE PISSED OFF AT THOSE WORDS ...
Ah. I did it again.
Y-You're right. And you were really looking forward to that movie.
Yes, I was! And the theatrical run ends this Friday!
And don't you think Hide is really weird?
NOD NOD
That's what I've been trying to tell you from the beginning.

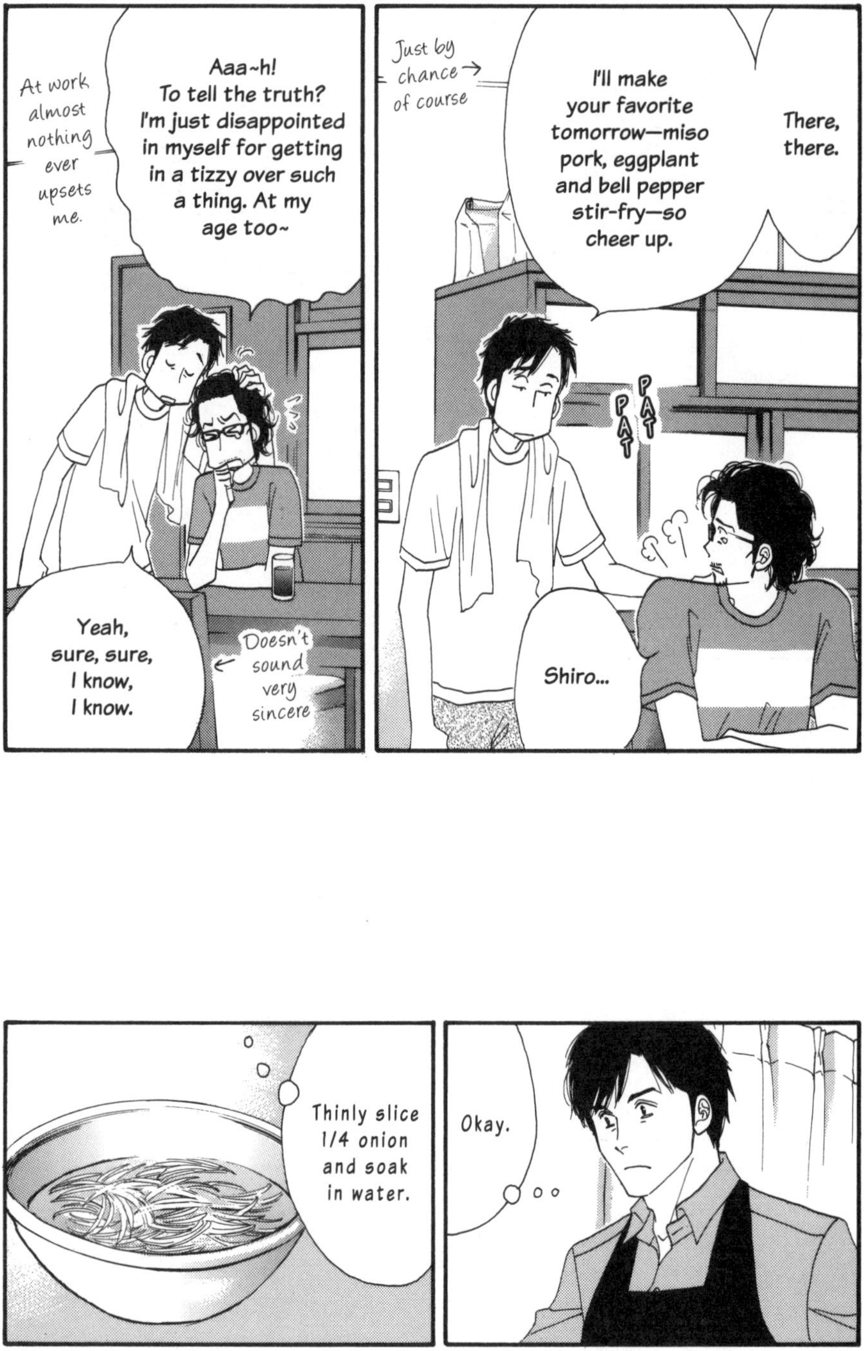
There, there.
I'll make your favorite tomorrow—miso pork, eggplant and bell pepper stir-fry—so cheer up.
Just by chance of course
PAT PAT
Shiro...
Aaa~h! To tell the truth? I'm just disappointed in myself for getting in a tizzy over such a thing. At my age too~
At work almost nothing ever upsets me.
Yeah, sure, sure, I know, I know.
Doesn't sound very sincere
Okay.
Thinly slice 1/4 onion and soak in water.

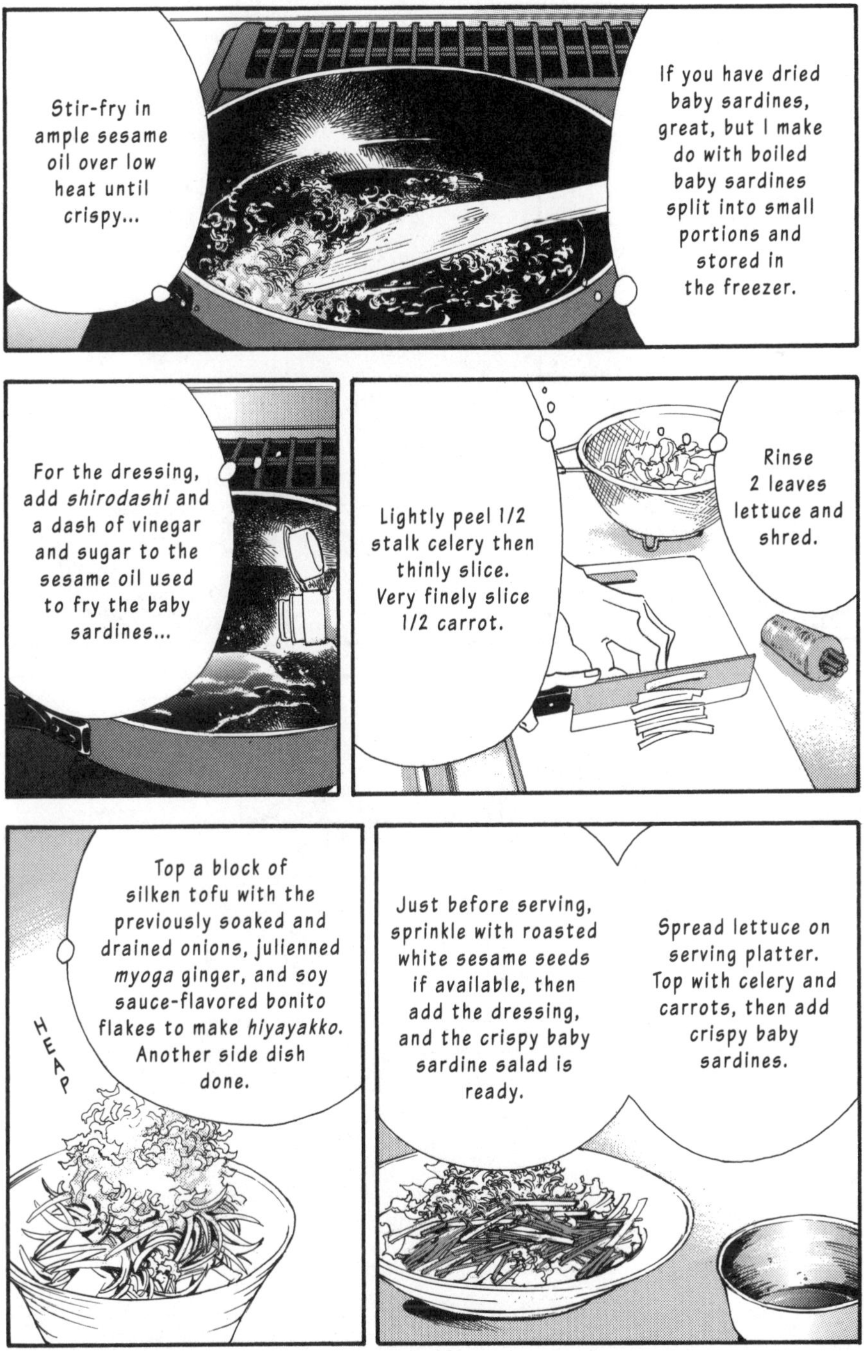

If you have dried baby sardines, great, but I make do with boiled baby sardines split into small portions and stored in the freezer.
Stir-fry in ample sesame oil over low heat until crispy...
Rinse 2 leaves lettuce and shred.
Lightly peel 1/2 stalk celery then thinly slice. Very finely slice 1/2 carrot.
For the dressing, add *shirodashi* and a dash of vinegar and sugar to the sesame oil used to fry the baby sardines...
Spread lettuce on serving platter. Top with celery and carrots, then add crispy baby sardines.
Just before serving, sprinkle with roasted white sesame seeds if available, then add the dressing, and the crispy baby sardine salad is ready.
Top a block of silken tofu with the previously soaked and drained onions, julienned *myoga* ginger, and soy sauce-flavored bonito flakes to make *hiyayakko*. Another side dish done.
HEAP

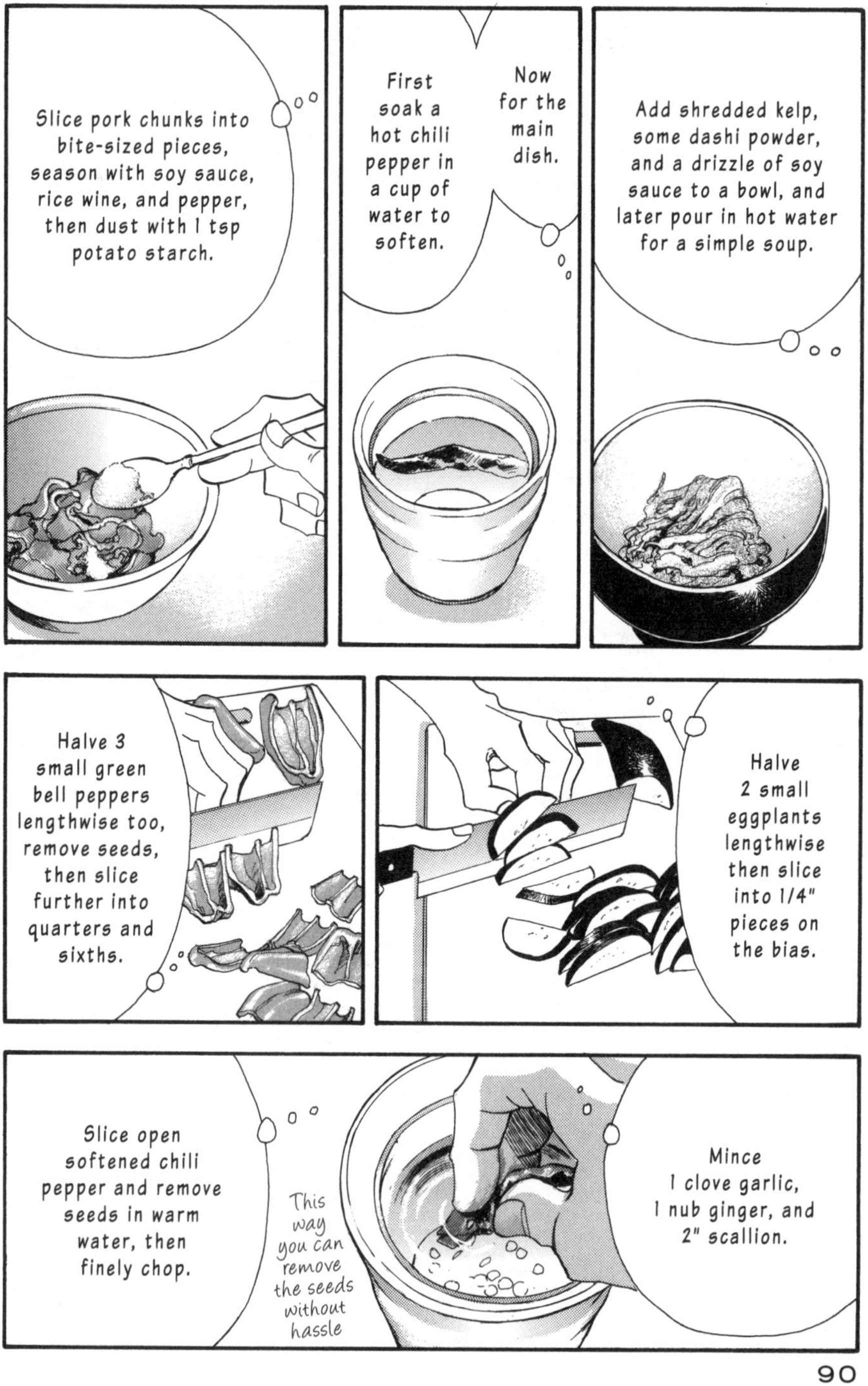
Add shredded kelp, some dashi powder, and a drizzle of soy sauce to a bowl, and later pour in hot water for a simple soup.
Now for the main dish.
First soak a hot chili pepper in a cup of water to soften.
Slice pork chunks into bite-sized pieces, season with soy sauce, rice wine, and pepper, then dust with 1 tsp potato starch.
Halve 2 small eggplants lengthwise then slice into 1/4" pieces on the bias.
Halve 3 small green bell peppers lengthwise too, remove seeds, then slice further into quarters and sixths.
Mince 1 clove garlic, 1 nub ginger, and 2" scallion.
Slice open softened chili pepper and remove seeds in warm water, then finely chop.
This way you can remove the seeds without hassle

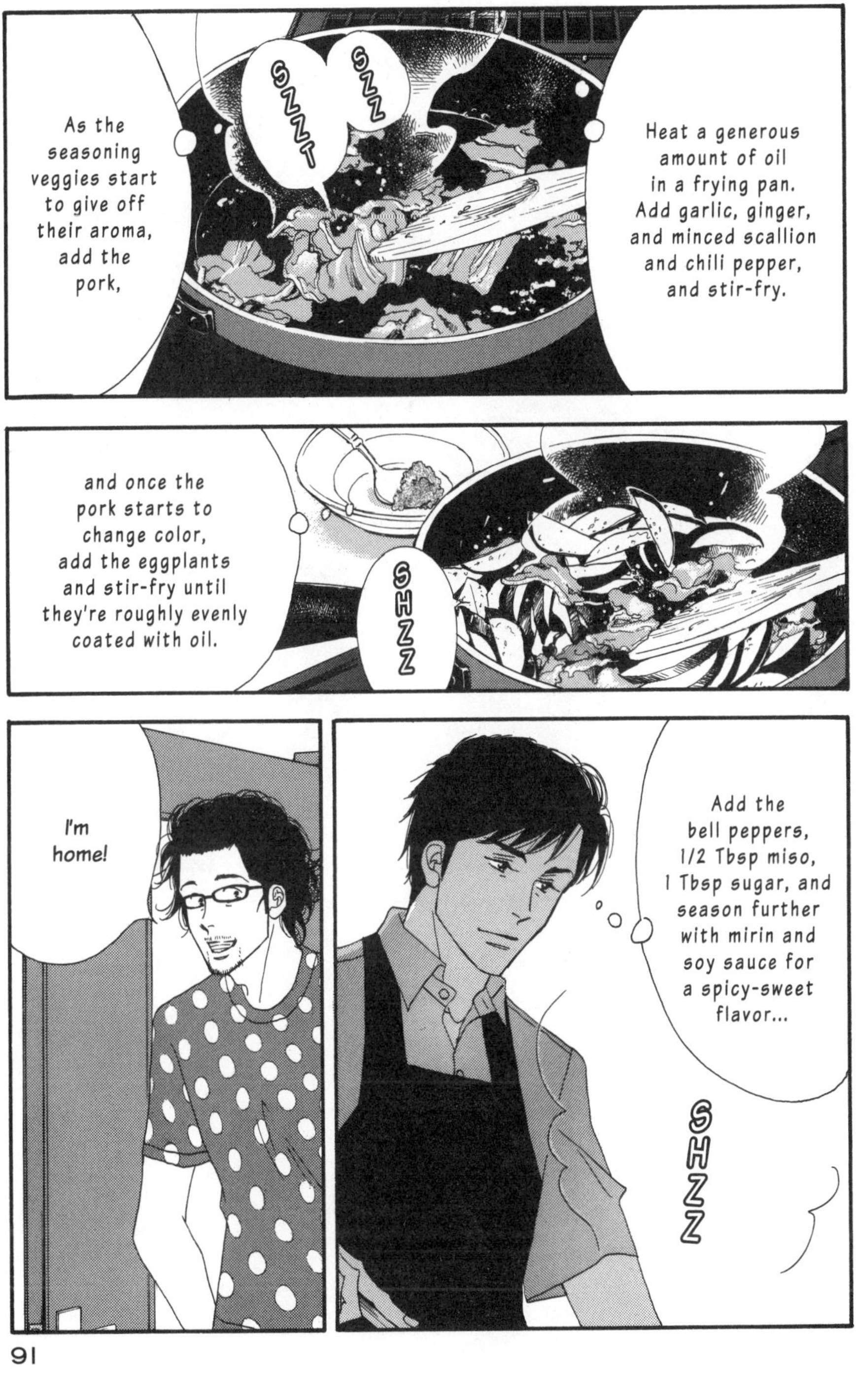
Heat a generous amount of oil in a frying pan. Add garlic, ginger, and minced scallion and chili pepper, and stir-fry.
SZZ
SZZZT
As the seasoning veggies start to give off their aroma, add the pork,
and once the pork starts to change color, add the eggplants and stir-fry until they're roughly evenly coated with oil.
SHZZ
Add the bell peppers, 1/2 Tbsp miso, 1 Tbsp sugar, and season further with mirin and soy sauce for a spicy-sweet flavor...
SHZZ
I'm home!

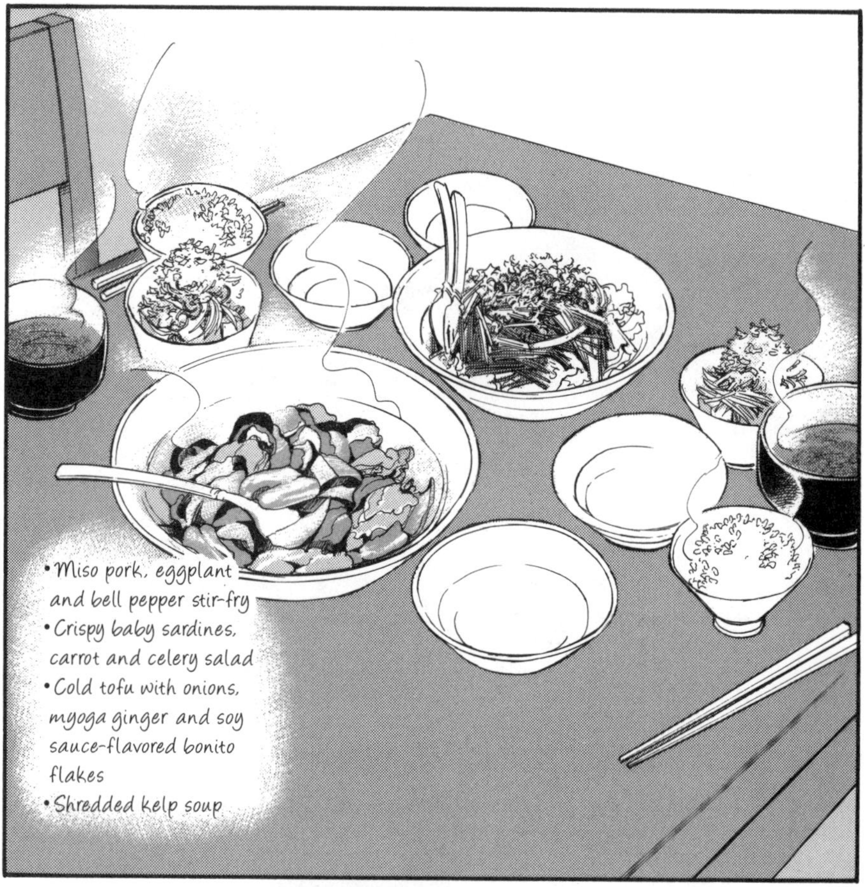
•Miso pork, eggplant and bell pepper stir-fry
•Crispy baby sardines, carrot and celery salad
•Cold tofu with onions, myoga ginger and soy sauce-flavored bonito flakes
•Shredded kelp soup

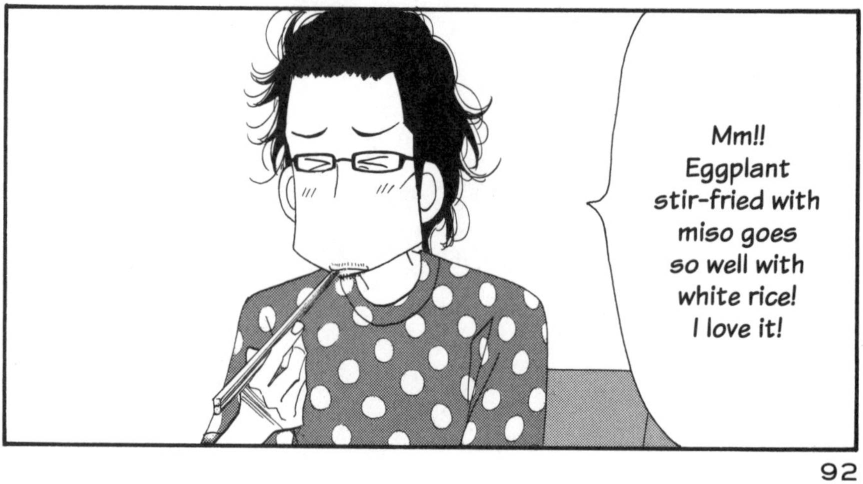
Mm!! Eggplant stir-fried with miso goes so well with white rice! I love it!

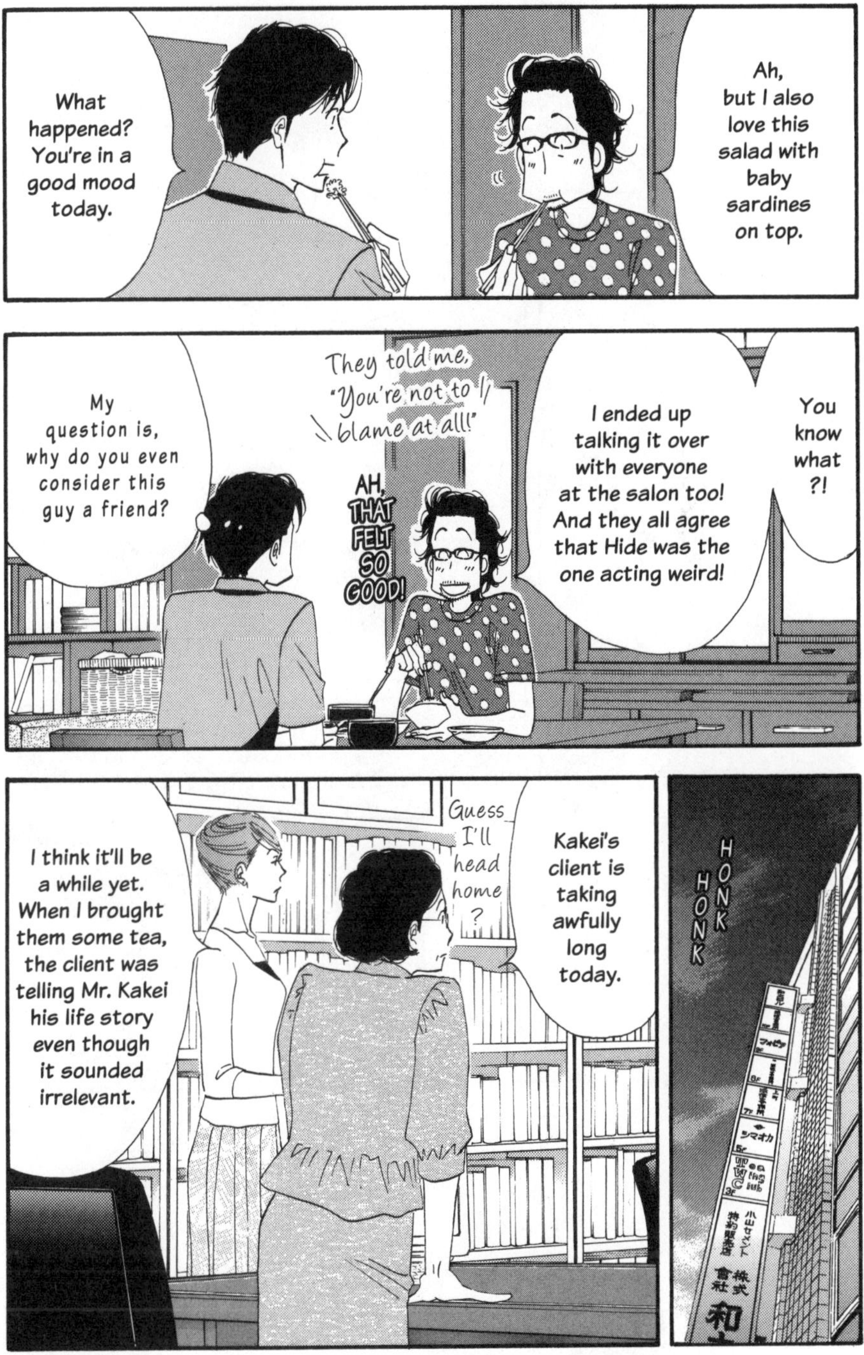
Ah, but I also love this salad with baby sardines on top.
What happened? You're in a good mood today.
You know what?!
I ended up talking it over with everyone at the salon too! And they all agree that Hide was the one acting weird!
They told me, "You're not to blame at all!"
AH, THAT FELT SO GOOD!
My question is, why do you even consider this guy a friend?
HONK HONK
Kakei's client is taking awfully long today.
Guess I'll head home?
I think it'll be a while yet. When I brought them some tea, the client was telling Mr. Kakei his life story even though it sounded irrelevant.

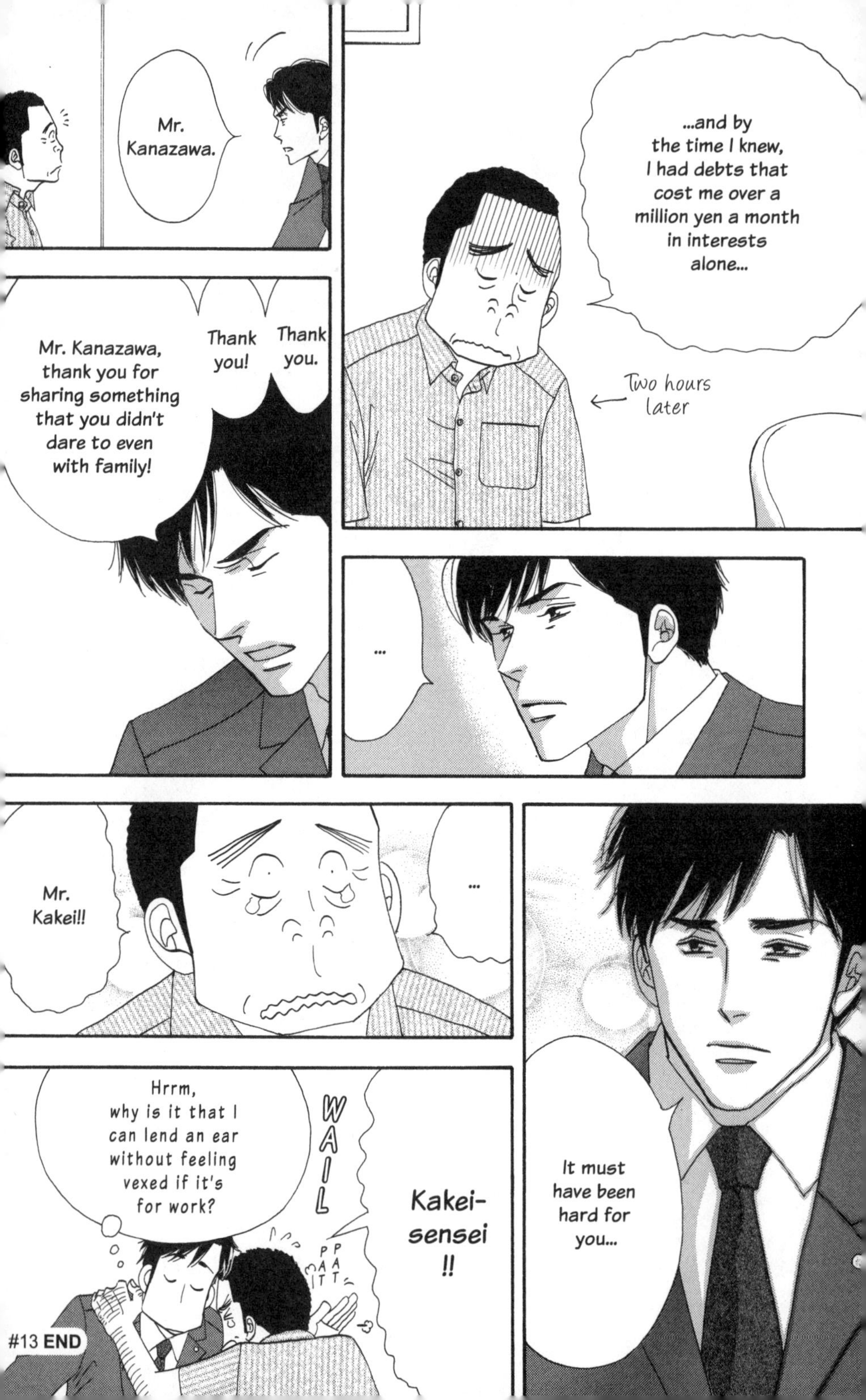
...and by the time I knew, I had debts that cost me over a million yen a month in interests alone...
Two hours later
Mr. Kanazawa.
Thank you.
Thank you!
Mr. Kanazawa, thank you for sharing something that you didn't dare to even with family!
...
It must have been hard for you...
...
Mr. Kakei!!
Kakei-sensei !!
WAIL
PAT PAT
Hrrm, why is it that I can lend an ear without feeling vexed if it's for work?
#13 END

For the carrots in **the crispy baby sardine, carrot and celery salad,** slice as thinly as possible for maximum deliciousness.
Also, don't let the chili pepper sit for too long in lukewarm water as all the spiciness will seep out.

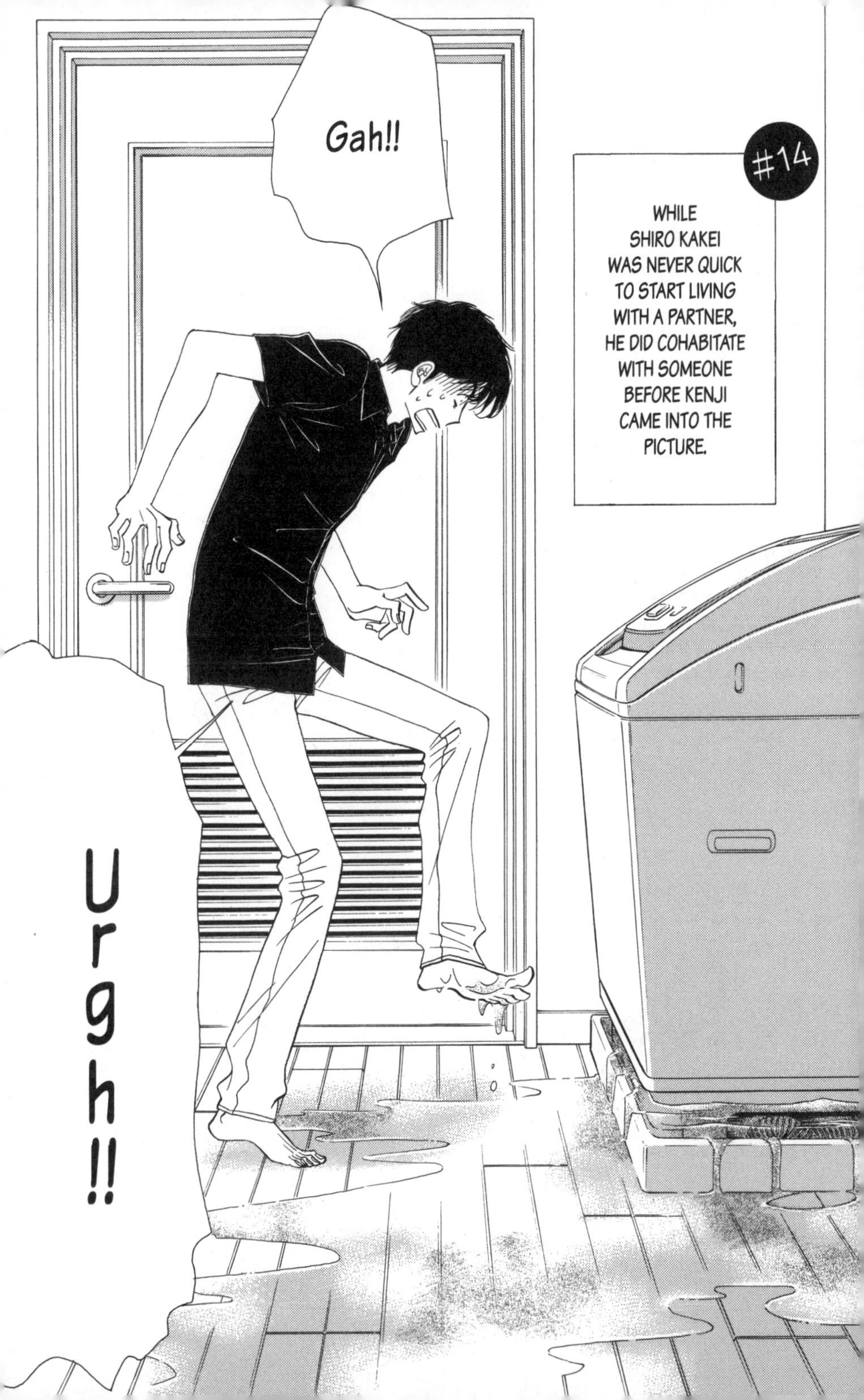
#14
WHILE SHIRO KAKEI WAS NEVER QUICK TO START LIVING WITH A PARTNER, HE DID COHABITATE WITH SOMEONE BEFORE KENJI CAME INTO THE PICTURE.
Gah!!
Urgh!!

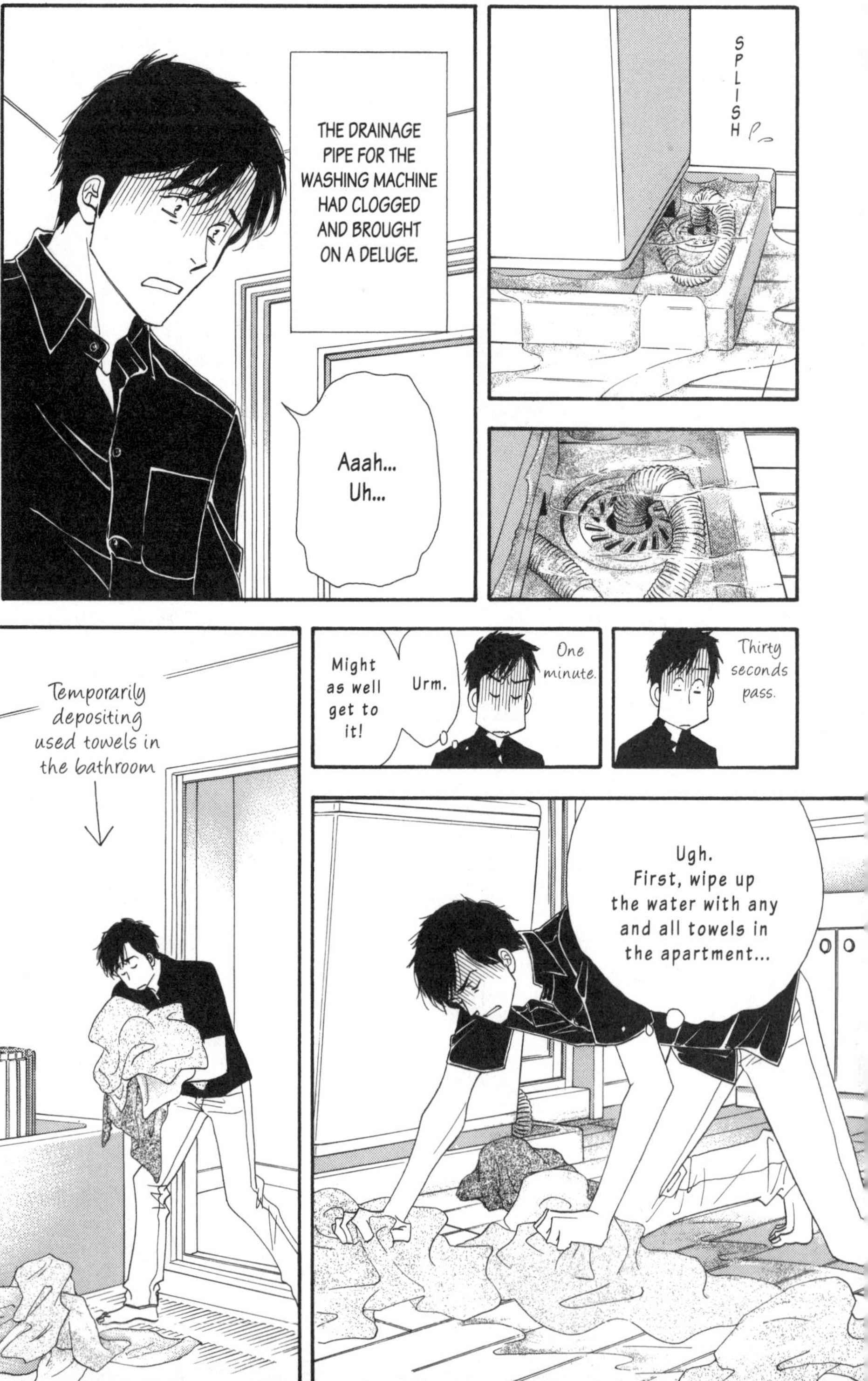
SPLISH
THE DRAINAGE PIPE FOR THE WASHING MACHINE HAD CLOGGED AND BROUGHT ON A DELUGE.
Aaah... Uh...
Thirty seconds pass.
One minute.
Urm.
Might as well get to it!
Ugh. First, wipe up the water with any and all towels in the apartment...
Temporarily depositing used towels in the bathroom

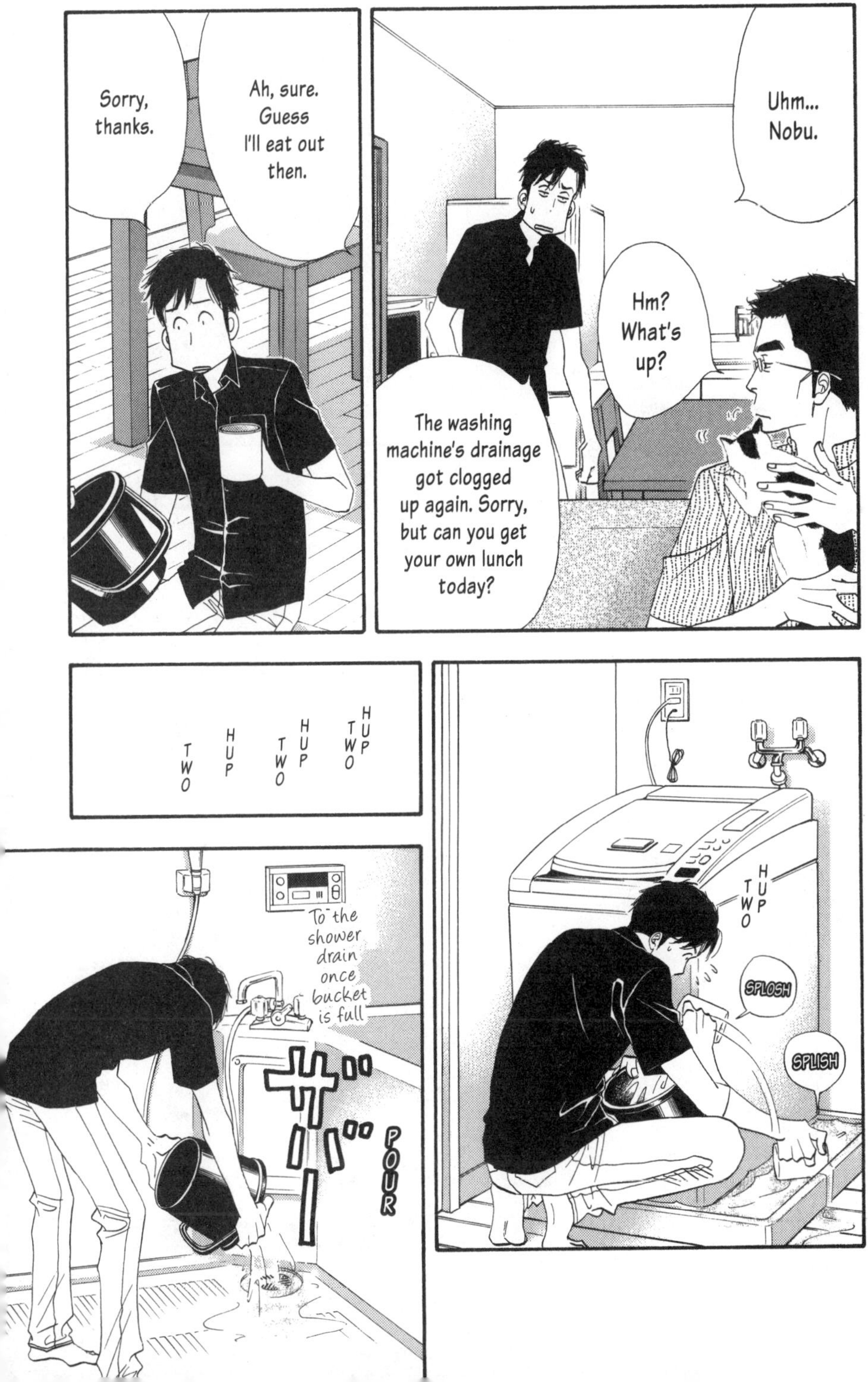
Uhm... Nobu.
Hm? What's up?
The washing machine's drainage got clogged up again. Sorry, but can you get your own lunch today?
Ah, sure. Guess I'll eat out then.
Sorry, thanks.
HUP TWO
SPLOSH
SPLISH
HUP TWO
HUP TWO
HUP TWO
To the shower drain once bucket is full
POUR

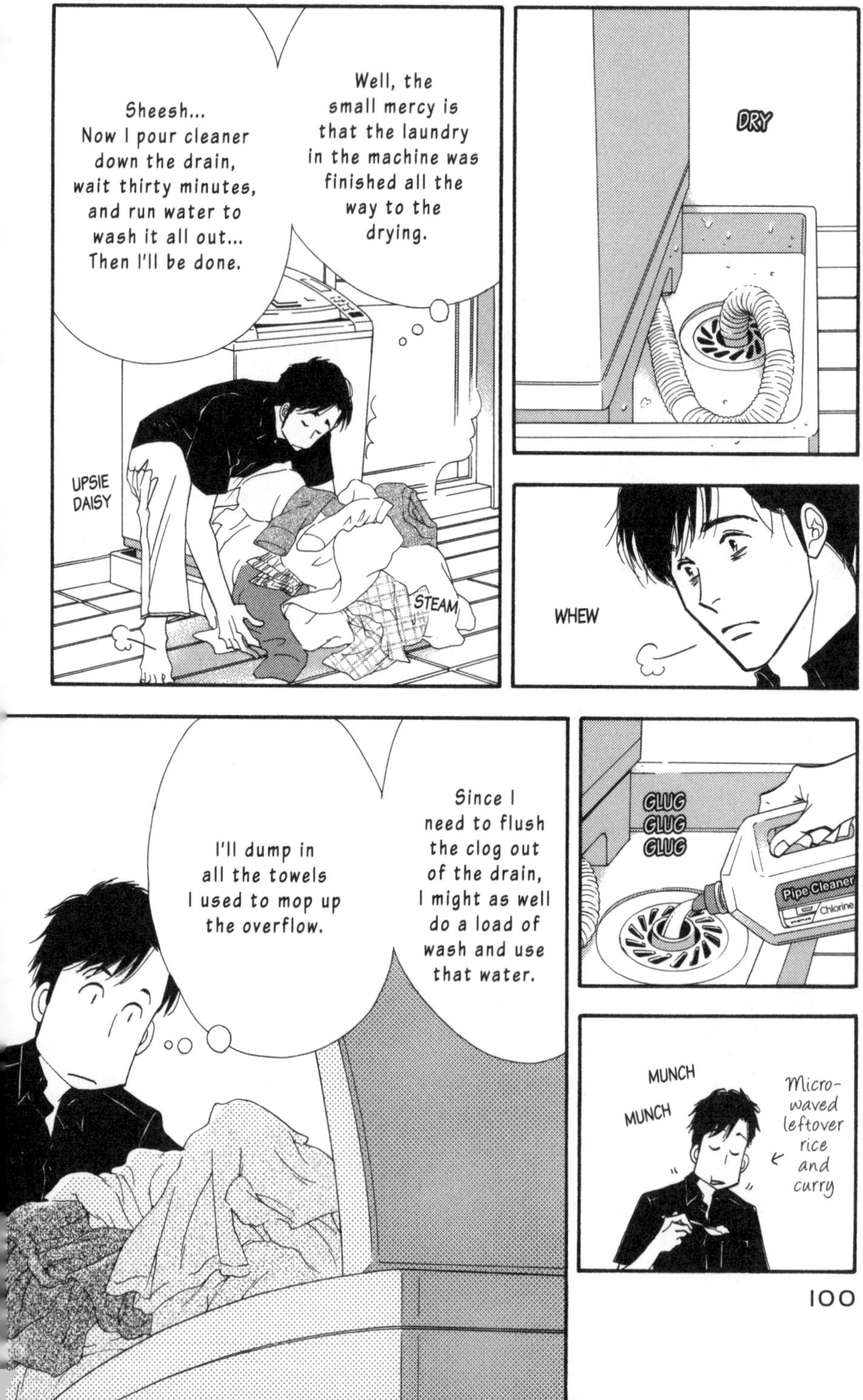
DRY
WHEW
Well, the small mercy is that the laundry in the machine was finished all the way to the drying.
Sheesh... Now I pour cleaner down the drain, wait thirty minutes, and run water to wash it all out... Then I'll be done.
STEAM
UPSIE DAISY
GLUG GLUG GLUG
Pipe Cleaner
Chlorine
MUNCH
MUNCH
Micro-waved leftover rice and curry
Since I need to flush the clog out of the drain, I might as well do a load of wash and use that water.
I'll dump in all the towels I used to mop up the overflow.

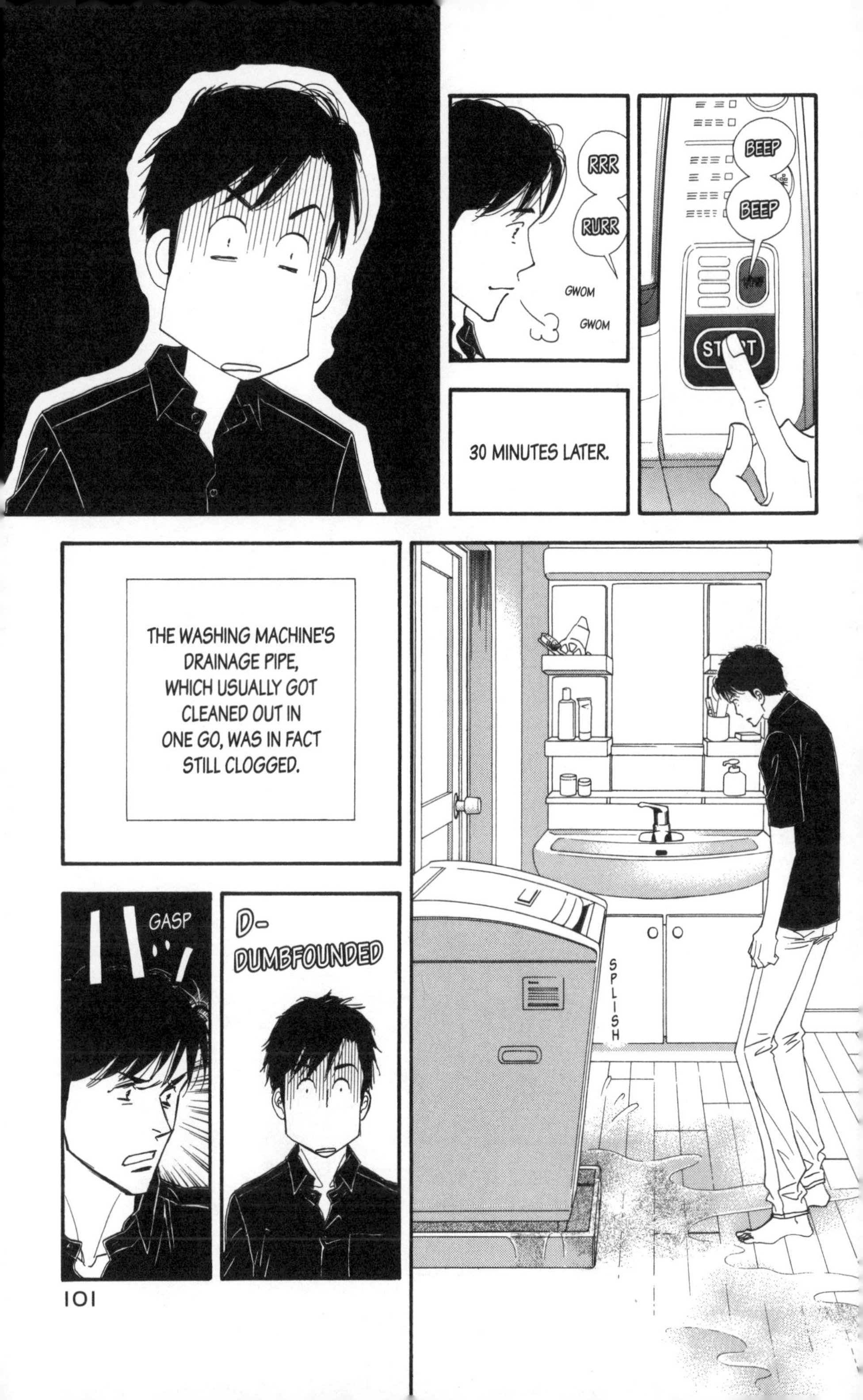
BEEP
BEEP
START
RRR
RURR
GWOM
GWOM
30 MINUTES LATER.
SPLISH
THE WASHING MACHINE'S DRAINAGE PIPE, WHICH USUALLY GOT CLEANED OUT IN ONE GO, WAS IN FACT STILL CLOGGED.
D-DUMBFOUNDED
GASP

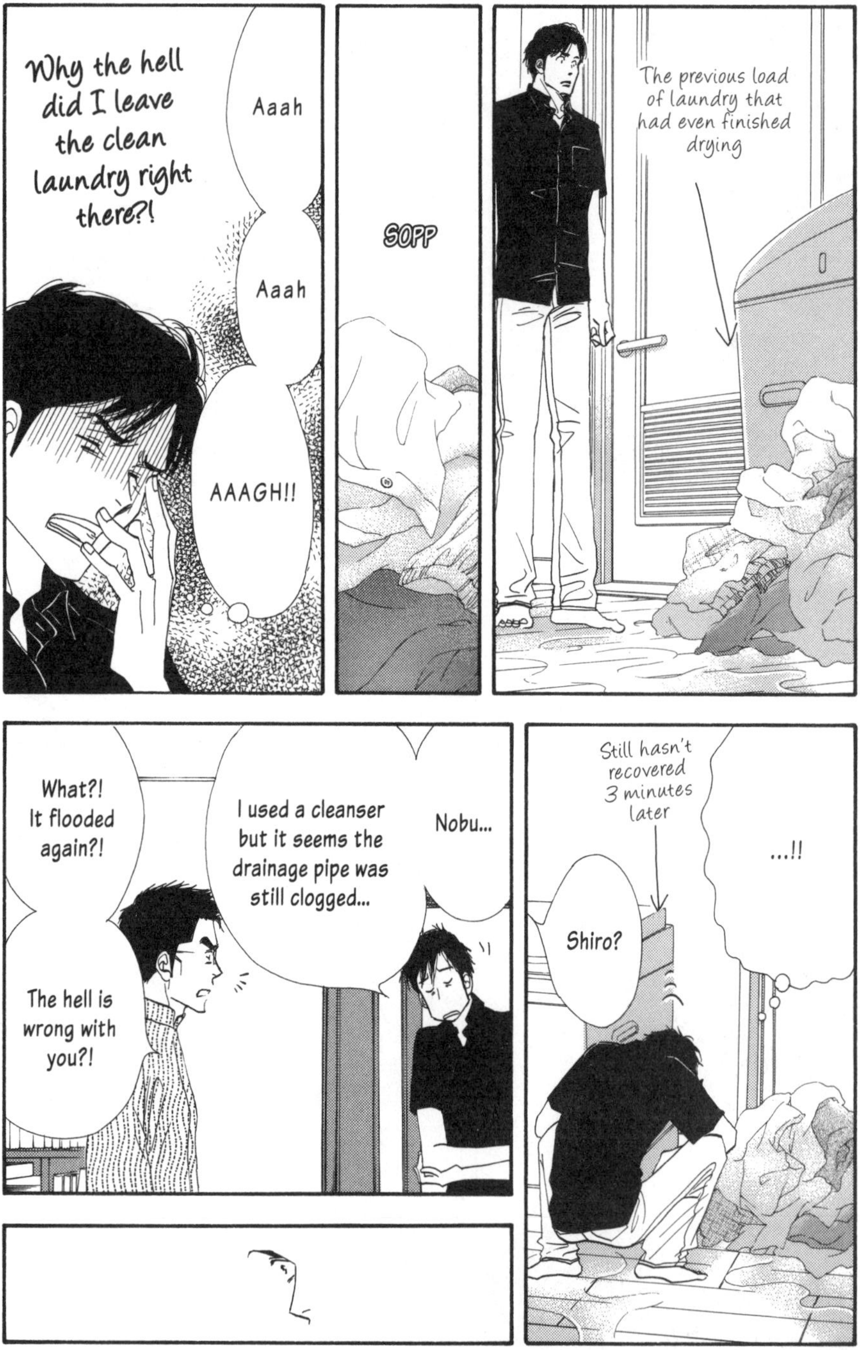
The previous load of laundry that had even finished drying
SOPP
Aaah
Aaah
AAAGH!!
Why the hell did I leave the clean laundry right there?!
...!!
Still hasn't recovered 3 minutes later
Shiro?
Nobu...
I used a cleanser but it seems the drainage pipe was still clogged...
What?! It flooded again?!
The hell is wrong with you?!

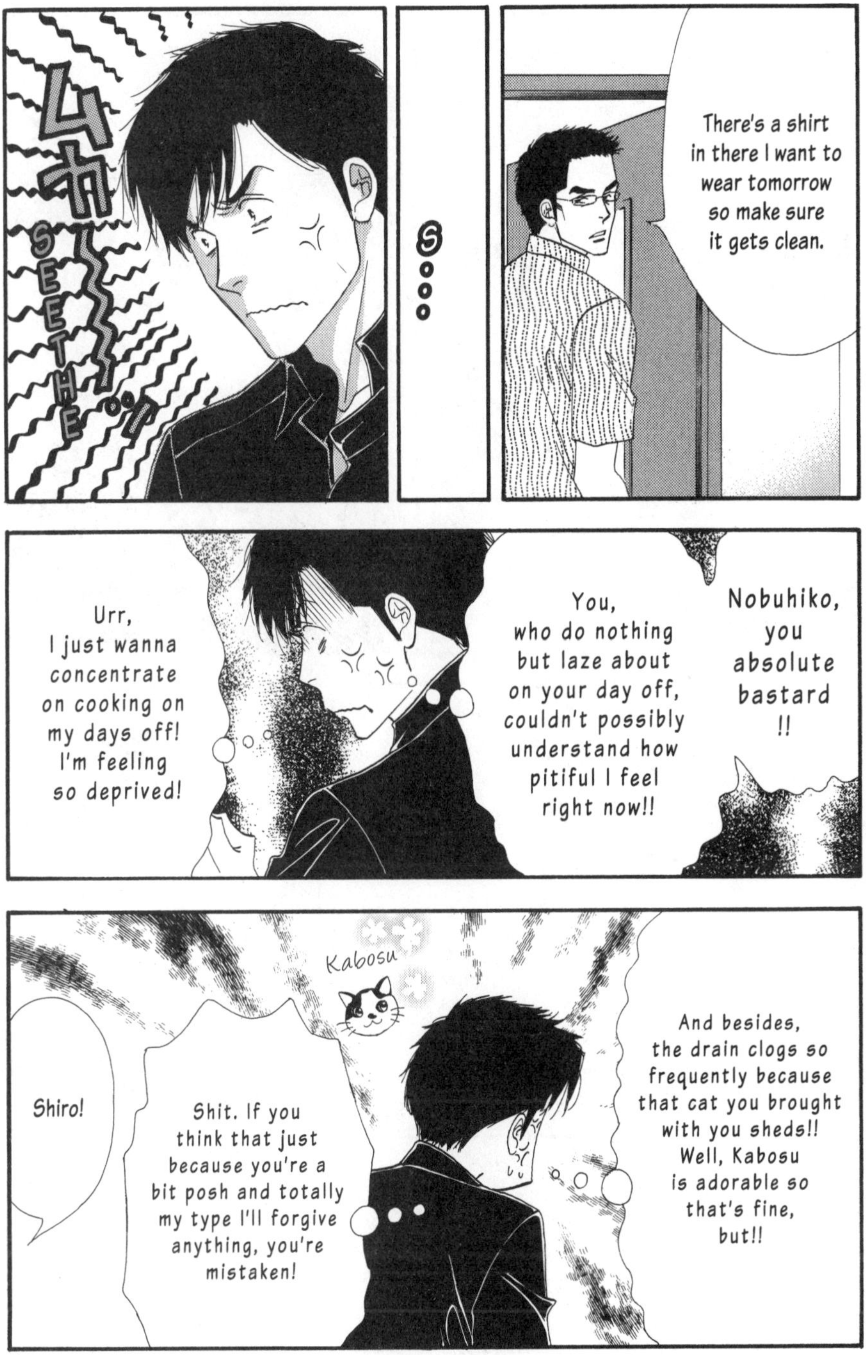
There's a shirt in there I want to wear tomorrow so make sure it gets clean.
Sooo
ムカ
SEETHE...!
Nobuhiko, you absolute bastard!!
You, who do nothing but laze about on your day off, couldn't possibly understand how pitiful I feel right now!!
Urr, I just wanna concentrate on cooking on my days off! I'm feeling so deprived!
And besides, the drain clogs so frequently because that cat you brought with you sheds!! Well, Kabosu is adorable so that's fine, but!!
Kabosu
Shit. If you think that just because you're a bit posh and totally my type I'll forgive anything, you're mistaken!
Shiro!

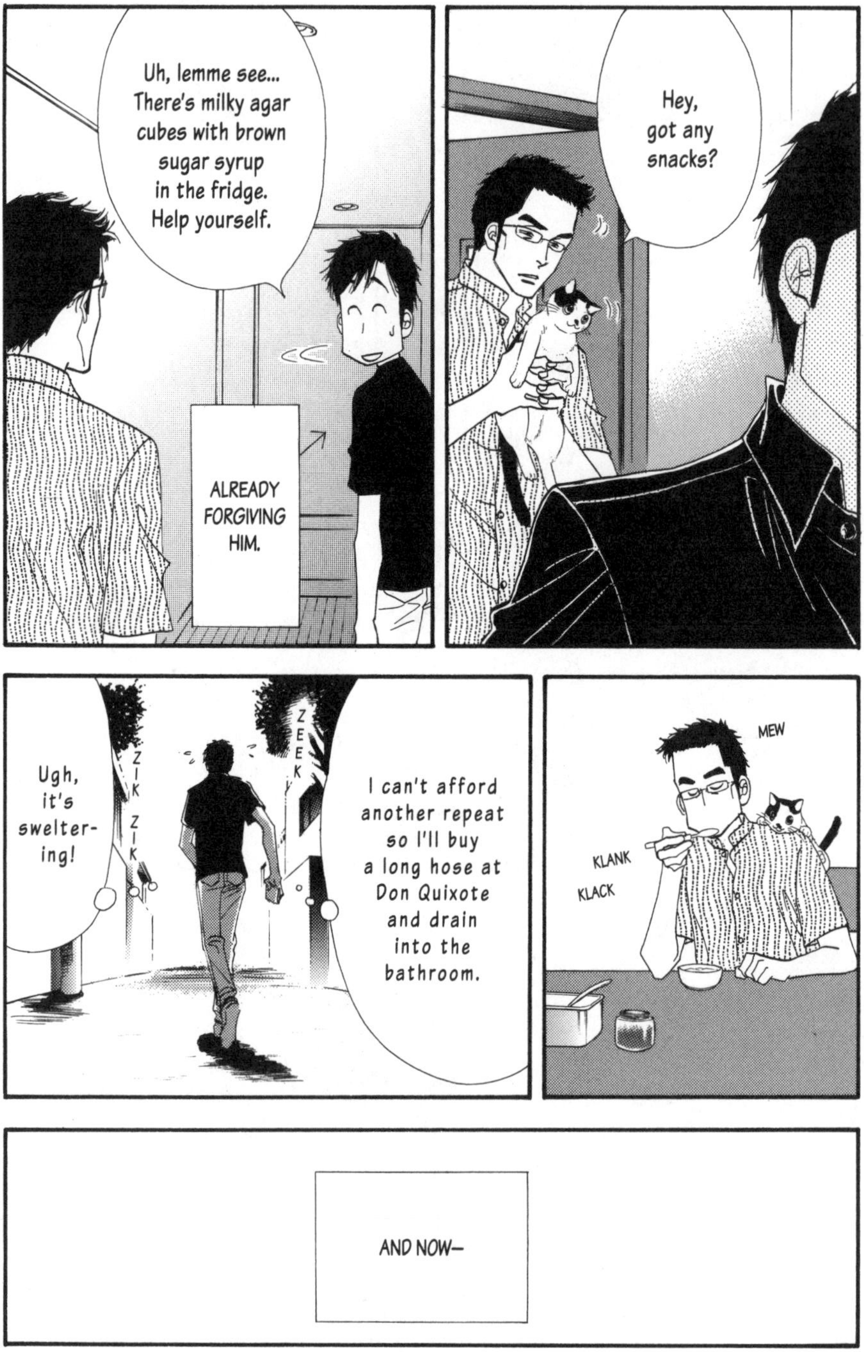
Hey, got any snacks?
Uh, lemme see... There's milky agar cubes with brown sugar syrup in the fridge. Help yourself.
ALREADY FORGIVING HIM.
MEW
KLANK
KLACK
I can't afford another repeat so I'll buy a long hose at Don Quixote and drain into the bathroom.
ZEEK
ZIK ZIK
Ugh, it's swelter-ing!
AND NOW—

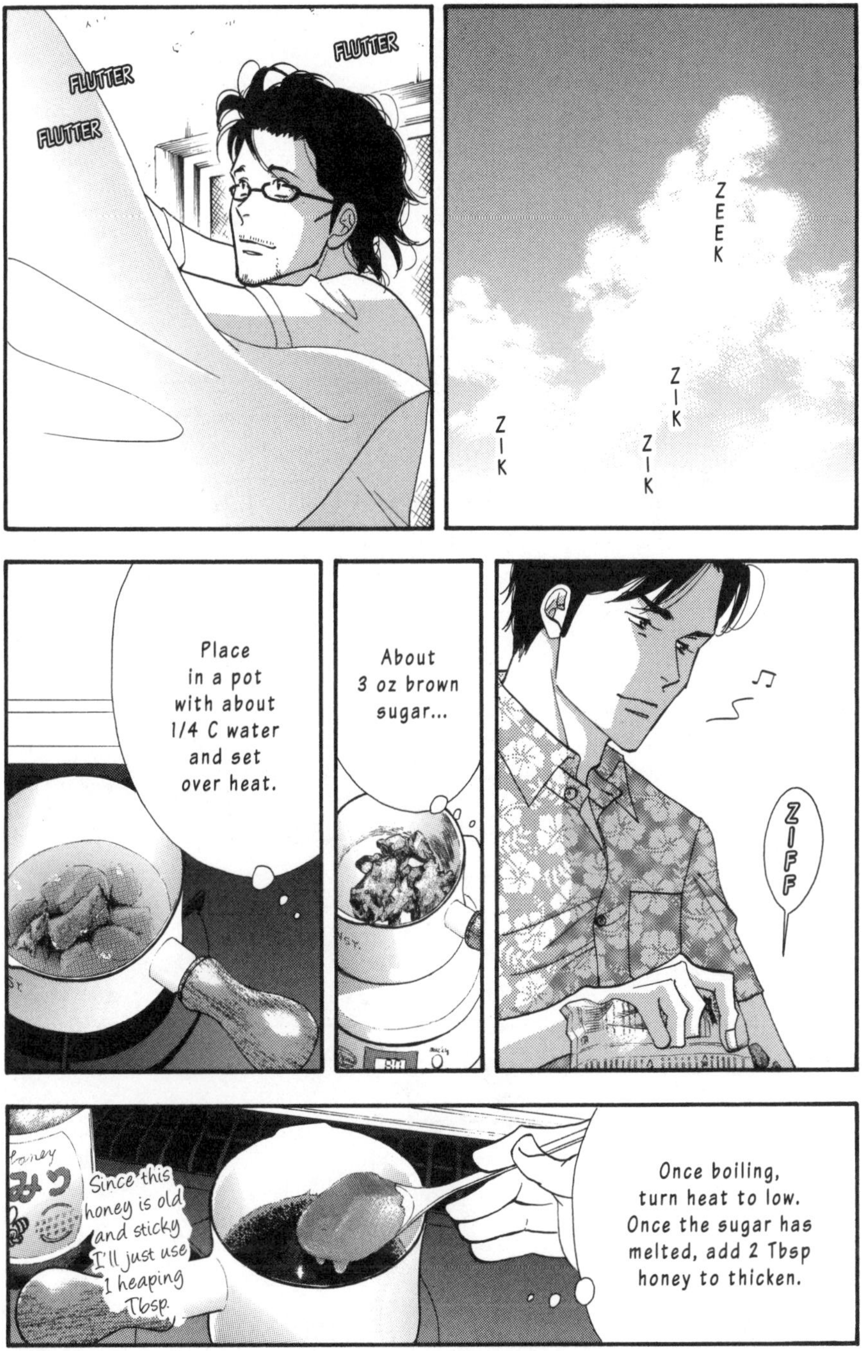
ZEEK
ZIK
ZIK
ZIK
FLUTTER
FLUTTER
FLUTTER
ZIFF
About 3 oz brown sugar...
Place in a pot with about 1/4 C water and set over heat.
Once boiling, turn heat to low. Once the sugar has melted, add 2 Tbsp honey to thicken.
Since this honey is old and sticky I'll just use 1 heaping Tbsp.

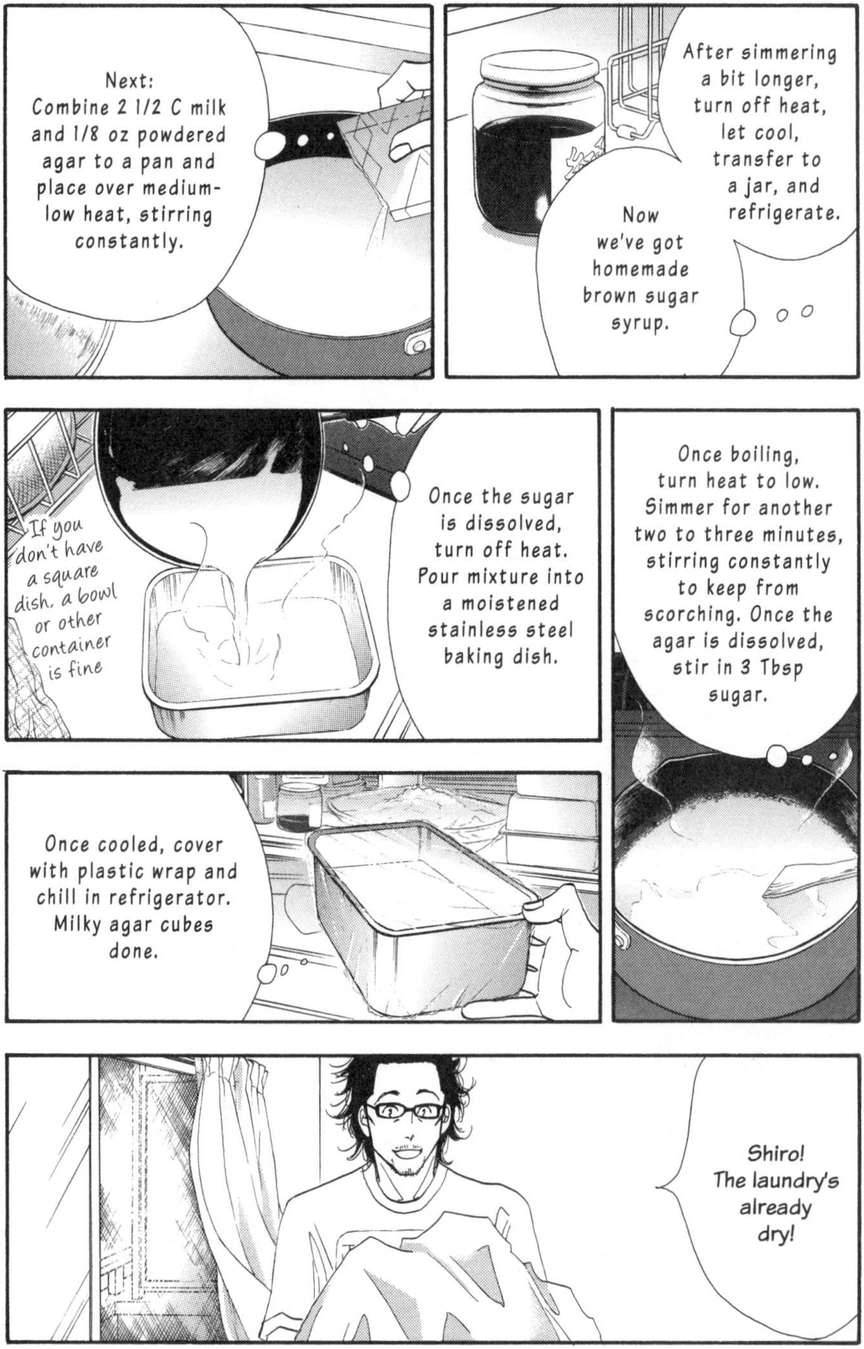
After simmering a bit longer, turn off heat, let cool, transfer to a jar, and refrigerate.
Now we've got homemade brown sugar syrup.
Next: Combine 2 1/2 C milk and 1/8 oz powdered agar to a pan and place over medium-low heat, stirring constantly.
Once boiling, turn heat to low. Simmer for another two to three minutes, stirring constantly to keep from scorching. Once the agar is dissolved, stir in 3 Tbsp sugar.
Once the sugar is dissolved, turn off heat. Pour mixture into a moistened stainless steel baking dish.
If you don't have a square dish, a bowl or other container is fine
Once cooled, cover with plastic wrap and chill in refrigerator. Milky agar cubes done.
Shiro! The laundry's already dry!

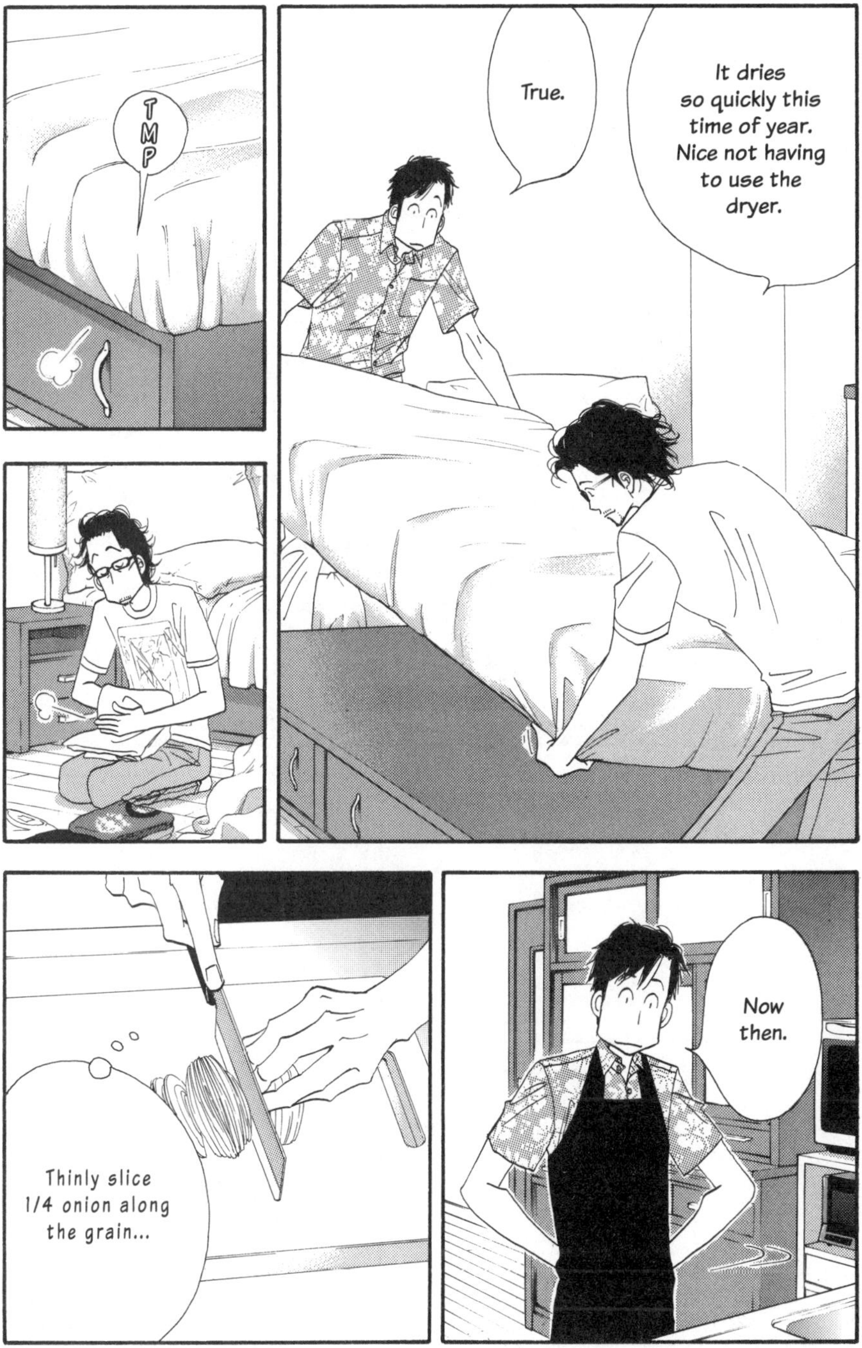
It dries so quickly this time of year. Nice not having to use the dryer.
True.
TMP
Now then.
Thinly slice 1/4 onion along the grain...

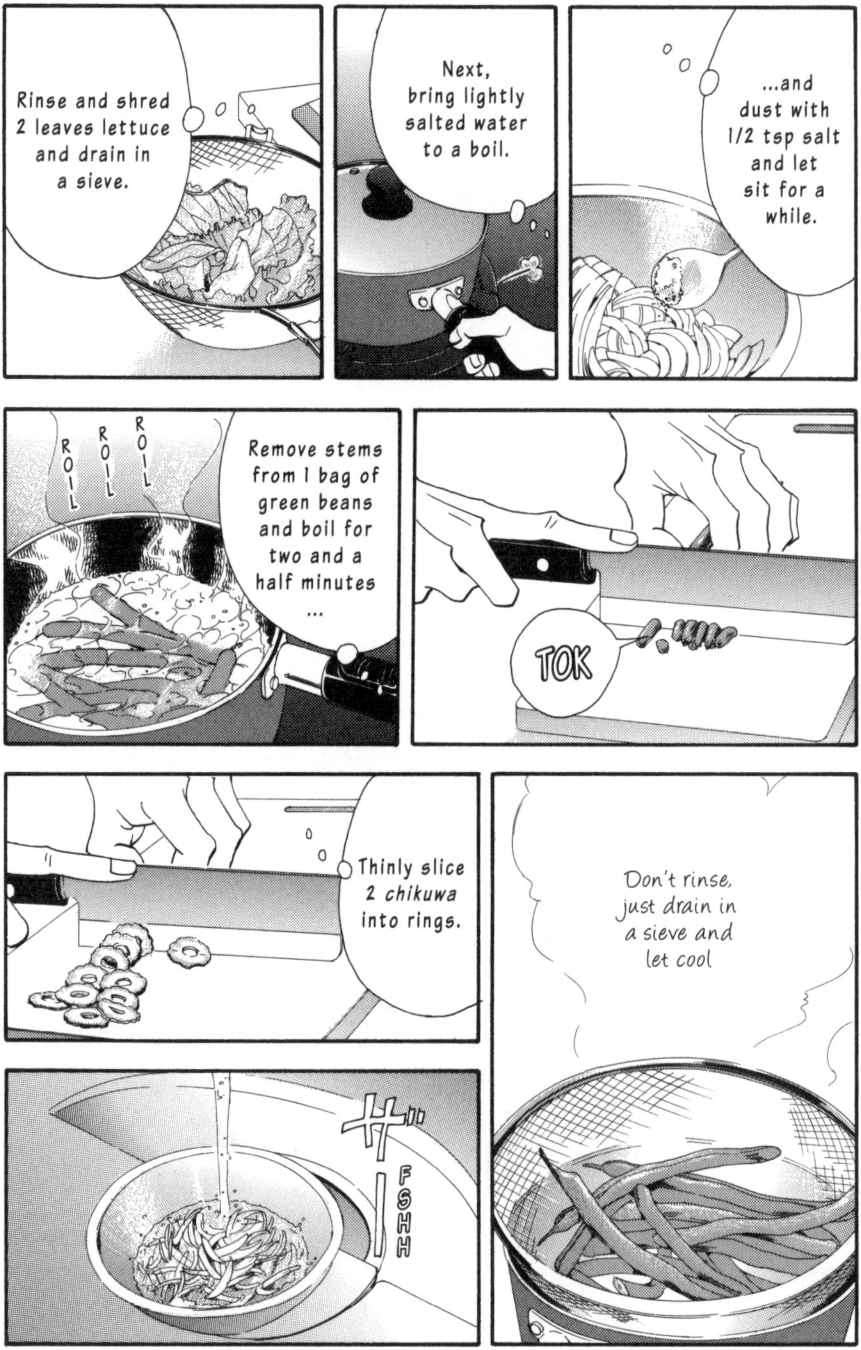
...and dust with 1/2 tsp salt and let sit for a while.
Next, bring lightly salted water to a boil.
Rinse and shred 2 leaves lettuce and drain in a sieve.
TOK
Remove stems from 1 bag of green beans and boil for two and a half minutes ...
ROLL ROLL ROLL
Don't rinse, just drain in a sieve and let cool
Thinly slice 2 chikuwa into rings.
FSHH

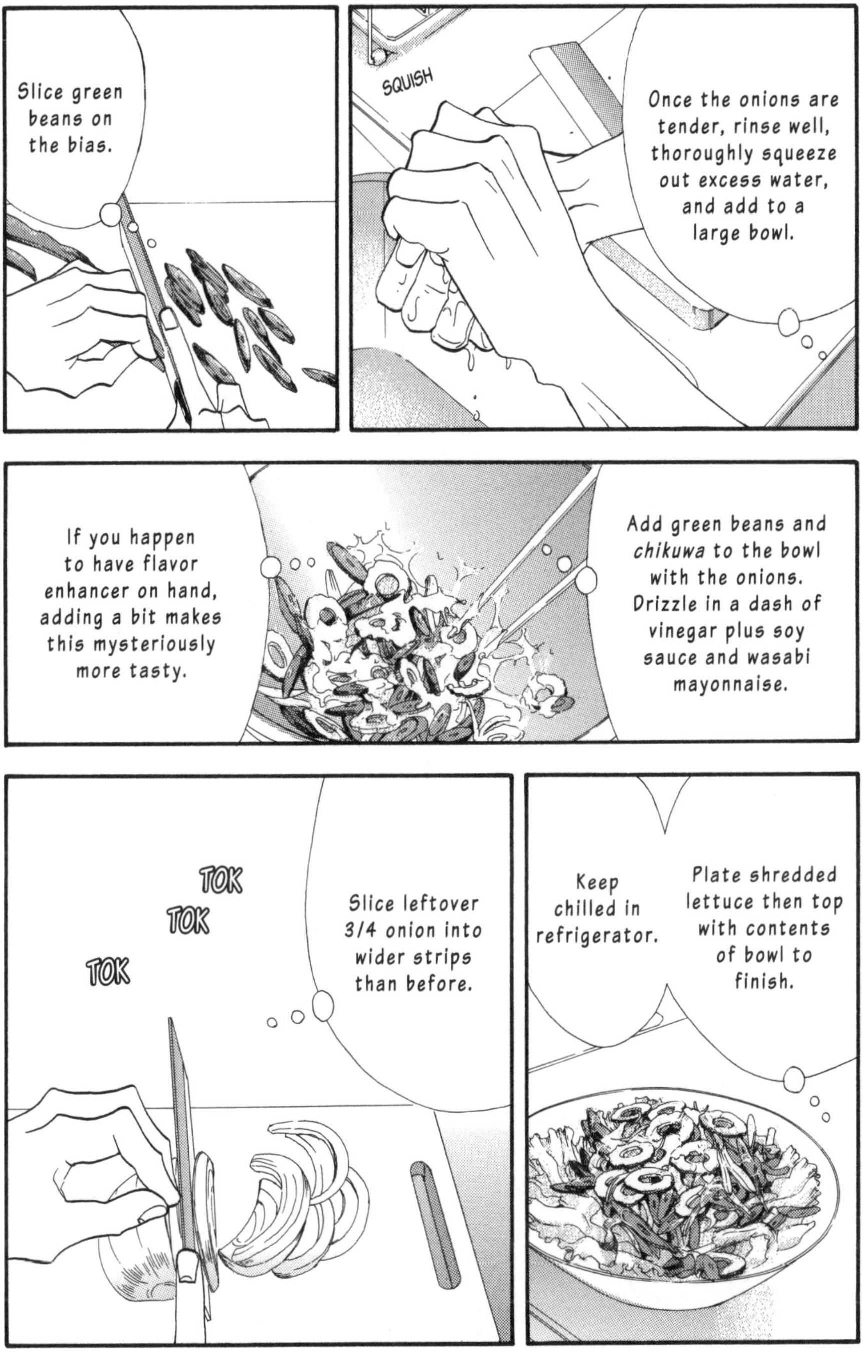
Once the onions are tender, rinse well, thoroughly squeeze out excess water, and add to a large bowl.
SQUISH
Slice green beans on the bias.
Add green beans and *chikuwa* to the bowl with the onions. Drizzle in a dash of vinegar plus soy sauce and wasabi mayonnaise.
If you happen to have flavor enhancer on hand, adding a bit makes this mysteriously more tasty.
Plate shredded lettuce then top with contents of bowl to finish.
Keep chilled in refrigerator.
Slice leftover 3/4 onion into wider strips than before.
TOK
TOK
TOK

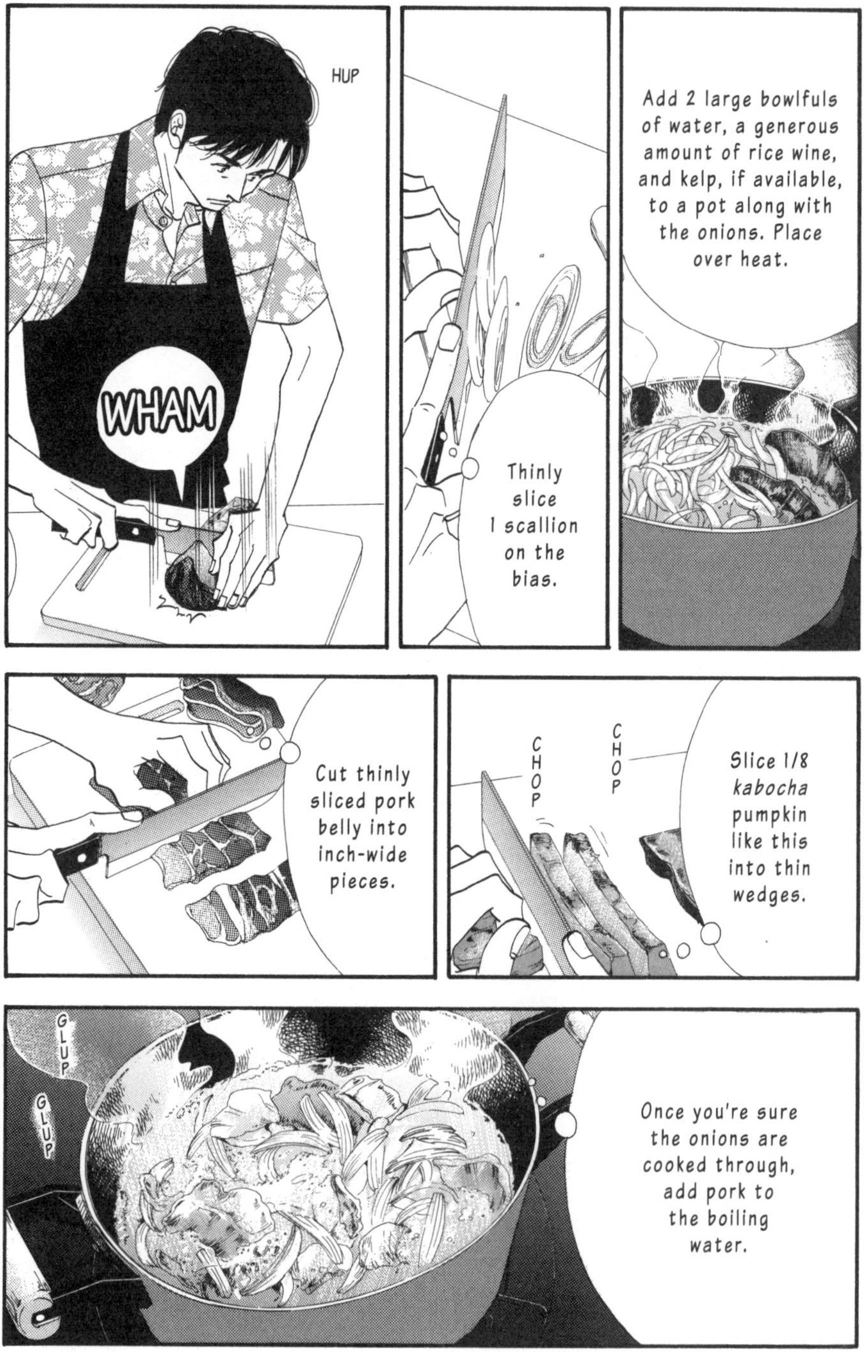
Add 2 large bowlfuls of water, a generous amount of rice wine, and kelp, if available, to a pot along with the onions. Place over heat.
Thinly slice 1 scallion on the bias.
HUP
WHAM
CHOP
CHOP
Slice 1/8 *kabocha* pumpkin like this into thin wedges.
Cut thinly sliced pork belly into inch-wide pieces.
Once you're sure the onions are cooked through, add pork to the boiling water.
GLUP
GLUP

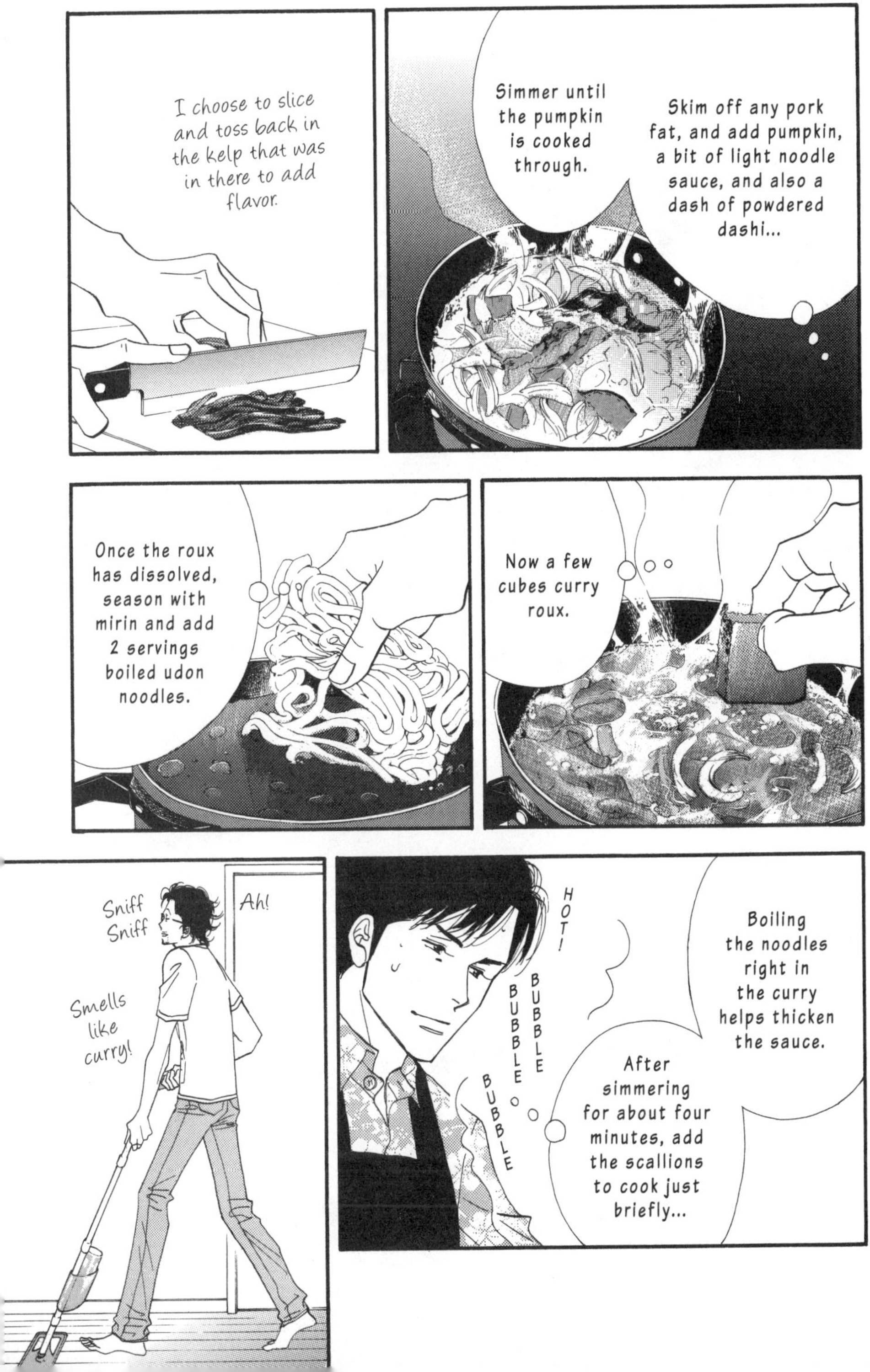
Skim off any pork fat, and add pumpkin, a bit of light noodle sauce, and also a dash of powdered dashi...
Simmer until the pumpkin is cooked through.
I choose to slice and toss back in the kelp that was in there to add flavor.
Now a few cubes curry roux.
Once the roux has dissolved, season with mirin and add 2 servings boiled udon noodles.
HOT!
Boiling the noodles right in the curry helps thicken the sauce.
BUBBLE BUBBLE
After simmering for about four minutes, add the scallions to cook just briefly...
BUBBLE
Ah!
Sniff Sniff
Smells like curry!

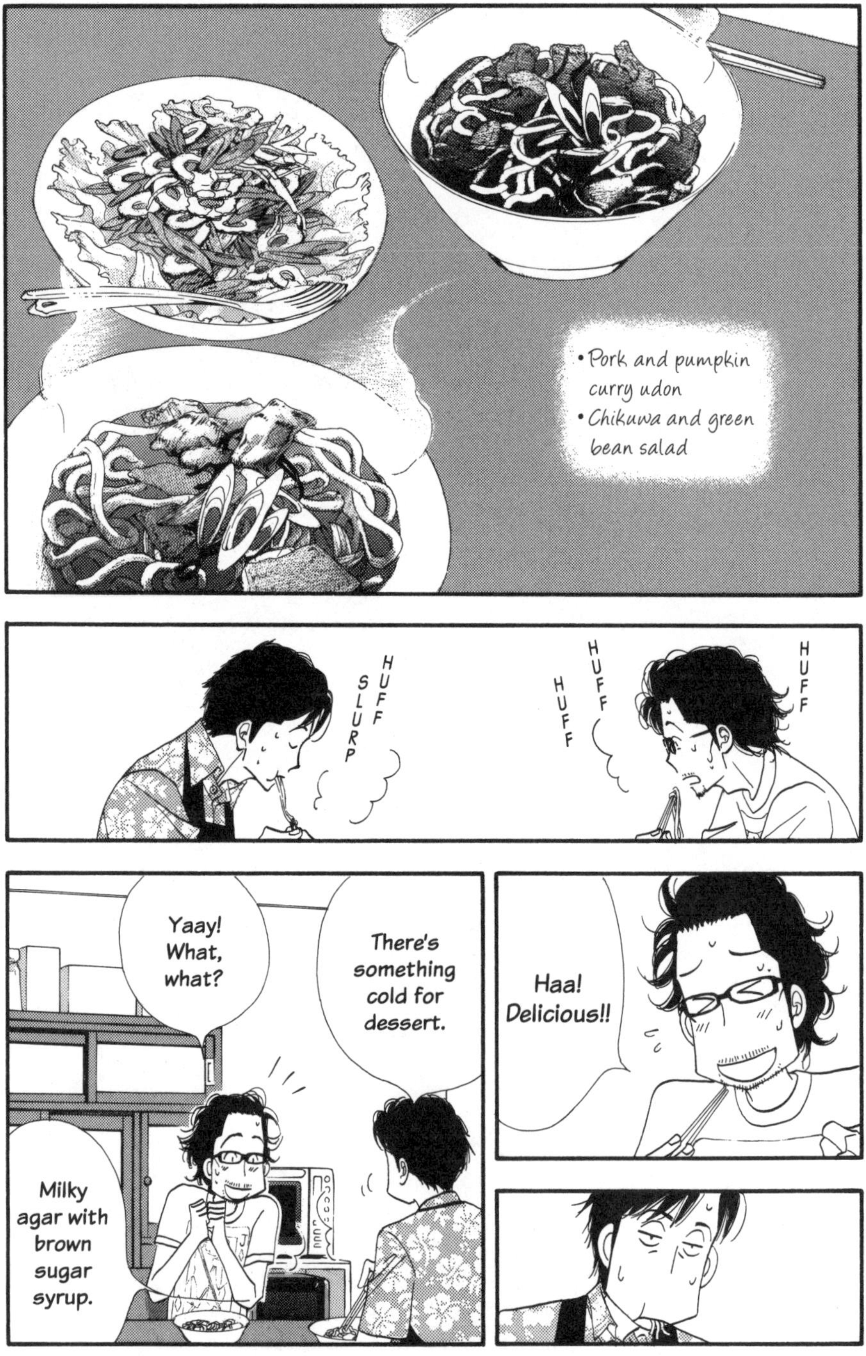

•Pork and pumpkin curry udon
•Chikuwa and green bean salad
HUFF
HUFF
HUFF
HUFF
SLURP
Haa! Delicious!!
There's something cold for dessert.
Yaay! What, what?
Milky agar with brown sugar syrup.

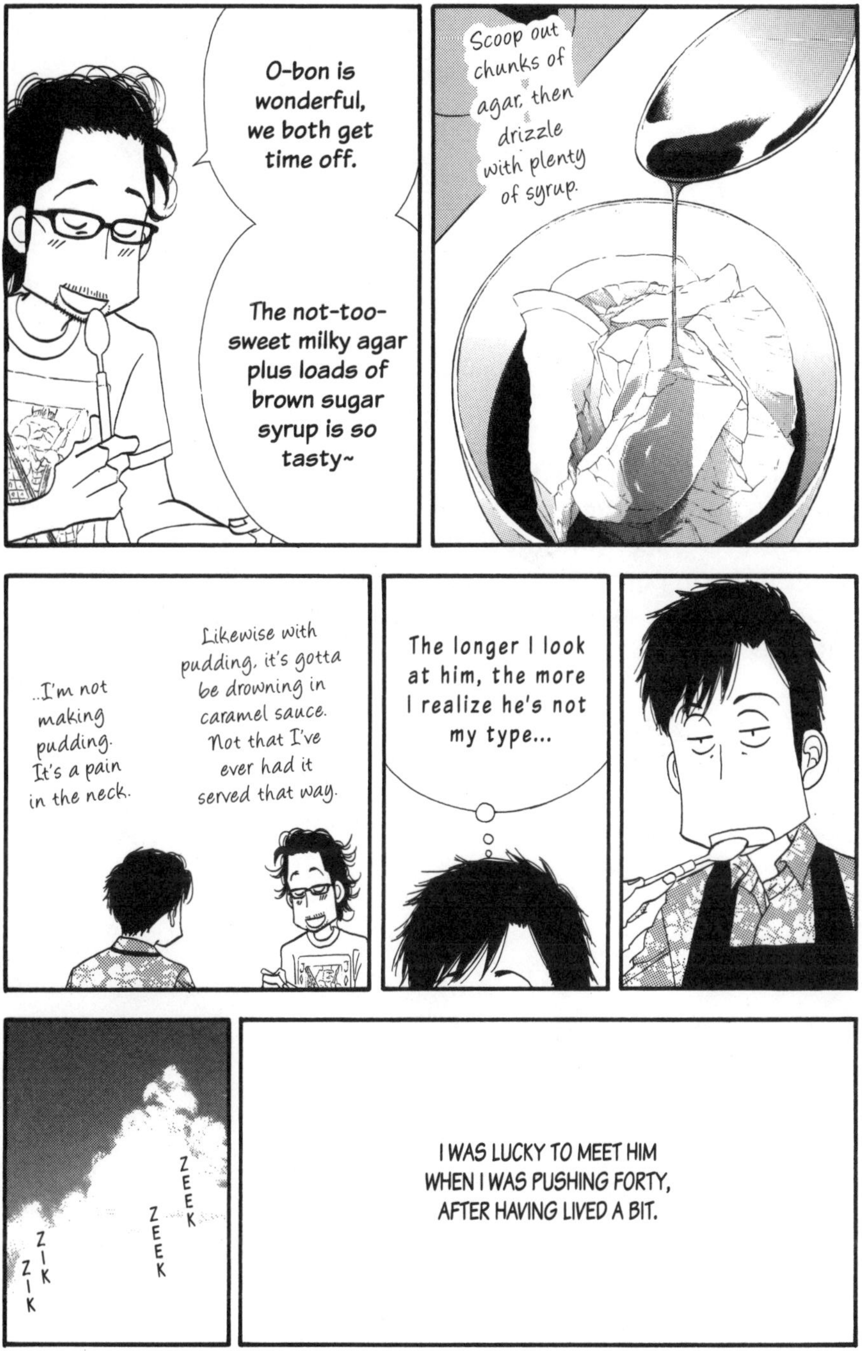
Scoop out chunks of agar, then drizzle with plenty of syrup.
O-bon is wonderful, we both get time off.
The not-too-sweet milky agar plus loads of brown sugar syrup is so tasty~
The longer I look at him, the more I realize he's not my type...
Likewise with pudding, it's gotta be drowning in caramel sauce. Not that I've ever had it served that way.
...I'm not making pudding. It's a pain in the neck.
I WAS LUCKY TO MEET HIM WHEN I WAS PUSHING FORTY, AFTER HAVING LIVED A BIT.
ZEEK
ZEEK
ZIK
ZIK

#14 END

Use slightly more milk than indicated
on the package directions for **gelling agar (*kanten*)**
for a more evanescent mouthfeel.
For the pumpkin curry, also try stir-frying the onions
and pork in a small amount of vegetable oil before
adding the water.

#15

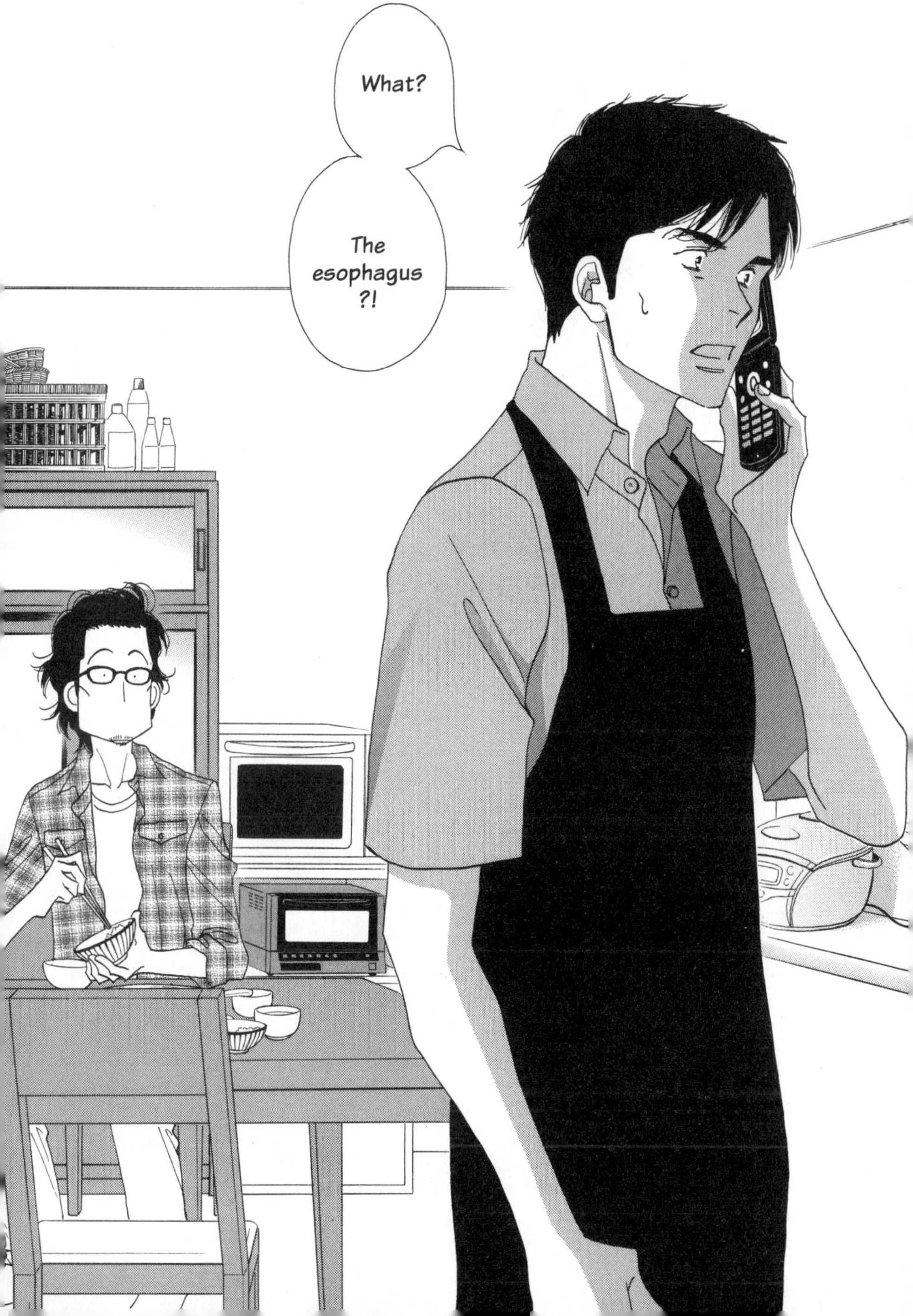
What?
The esophagus ?!

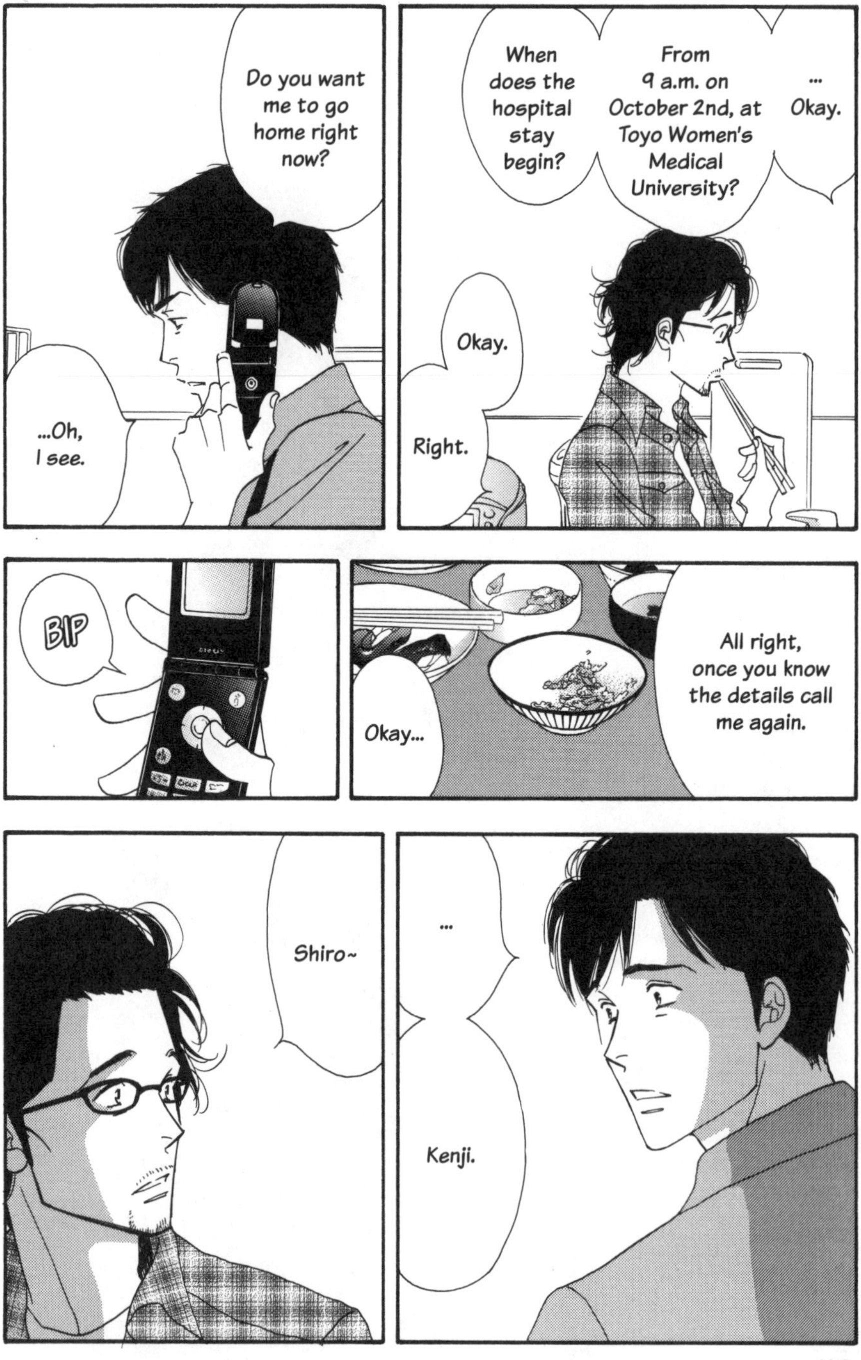

... Okay.
From 9 a.m. on October 2nd, at Toyo Women's Medical University?
When does the hospital stay begin?
Okay.
Right.
Do you want me to go home right now?
...Oh, I see.
All right, once you know the details call me again.
Okay...
BIP
...
Kenji.
Shiro~

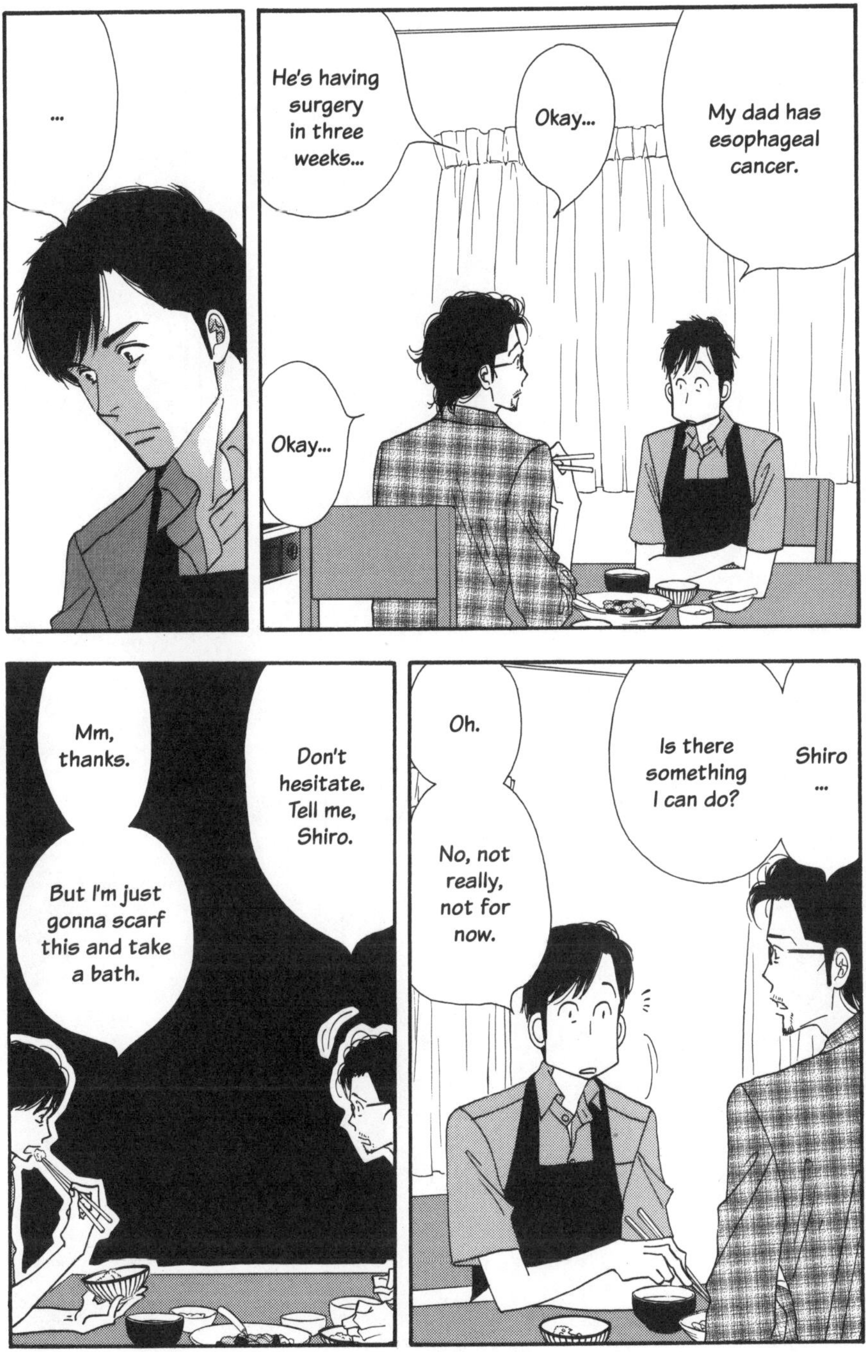
My dad has esophageal cancer.
Okay...
He's having surgery in three weeks...
Okay...
...
Shiro ...
Is there something I can do?
Oh.
No, not really, not for now.
Don't hesitate. Tell me, Shiro.
Mm, thanks.
But I'm just gonna scarf this and take a bath.

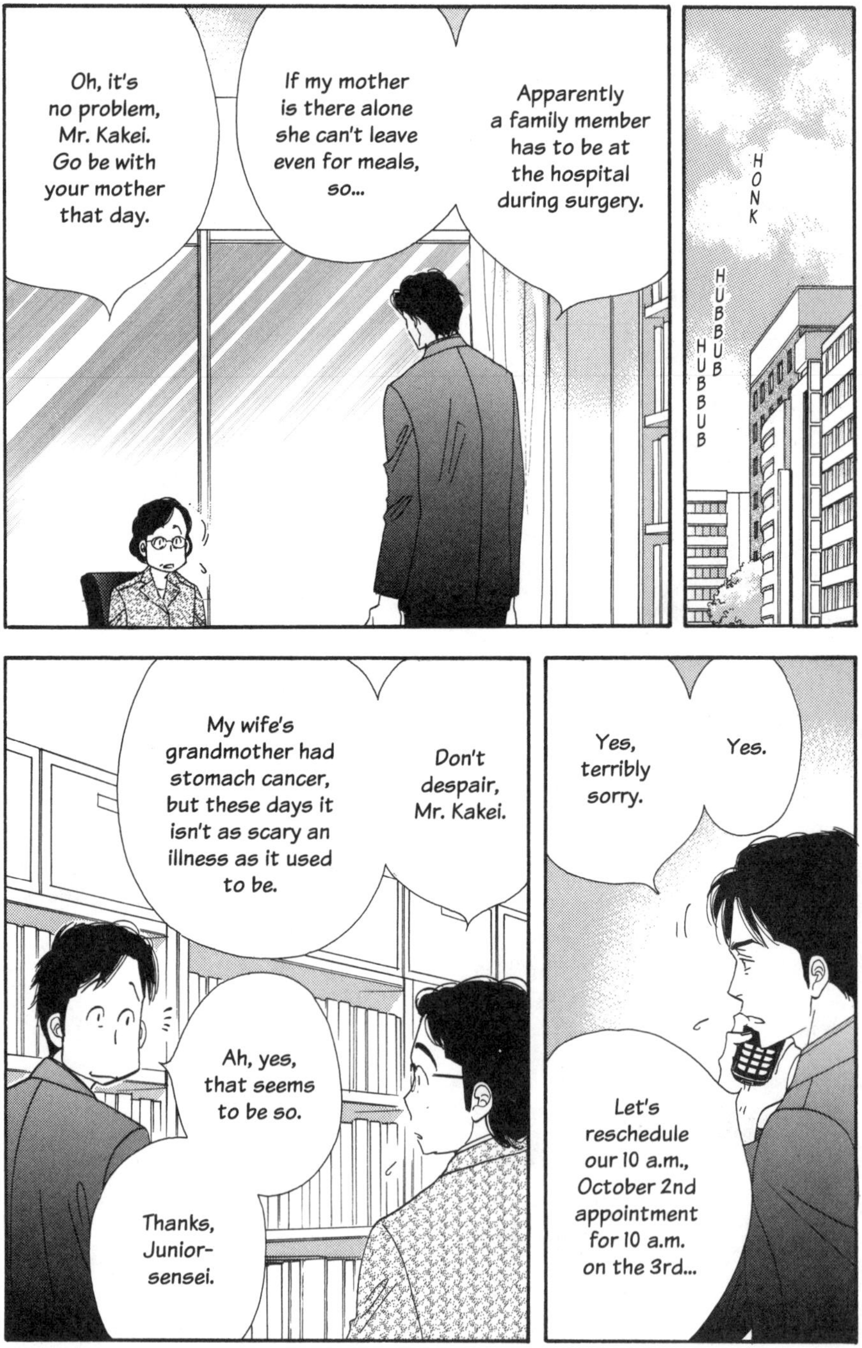
HONK
HUBBUB
HUBBUB
Apparently a family member has to be at the hospital during surgery.
If my mother is there alone she can't leave even for meals, so...
Oh, it's no problem, Mr. Kakei. Go be with your mother that day.
Yes.
Yes, terribly sorry.
Let's reschedule our 10 a.m., October 2nd appointment for 10 a.m. on the 3rd...
Don't despair, Mr. Kakei.
My wife's grandmother had stomach cancer, but these days it isn't as scary an illness as it used to be.
Ah, yes, that seems to be so.
Thanks, Junior-sensei.

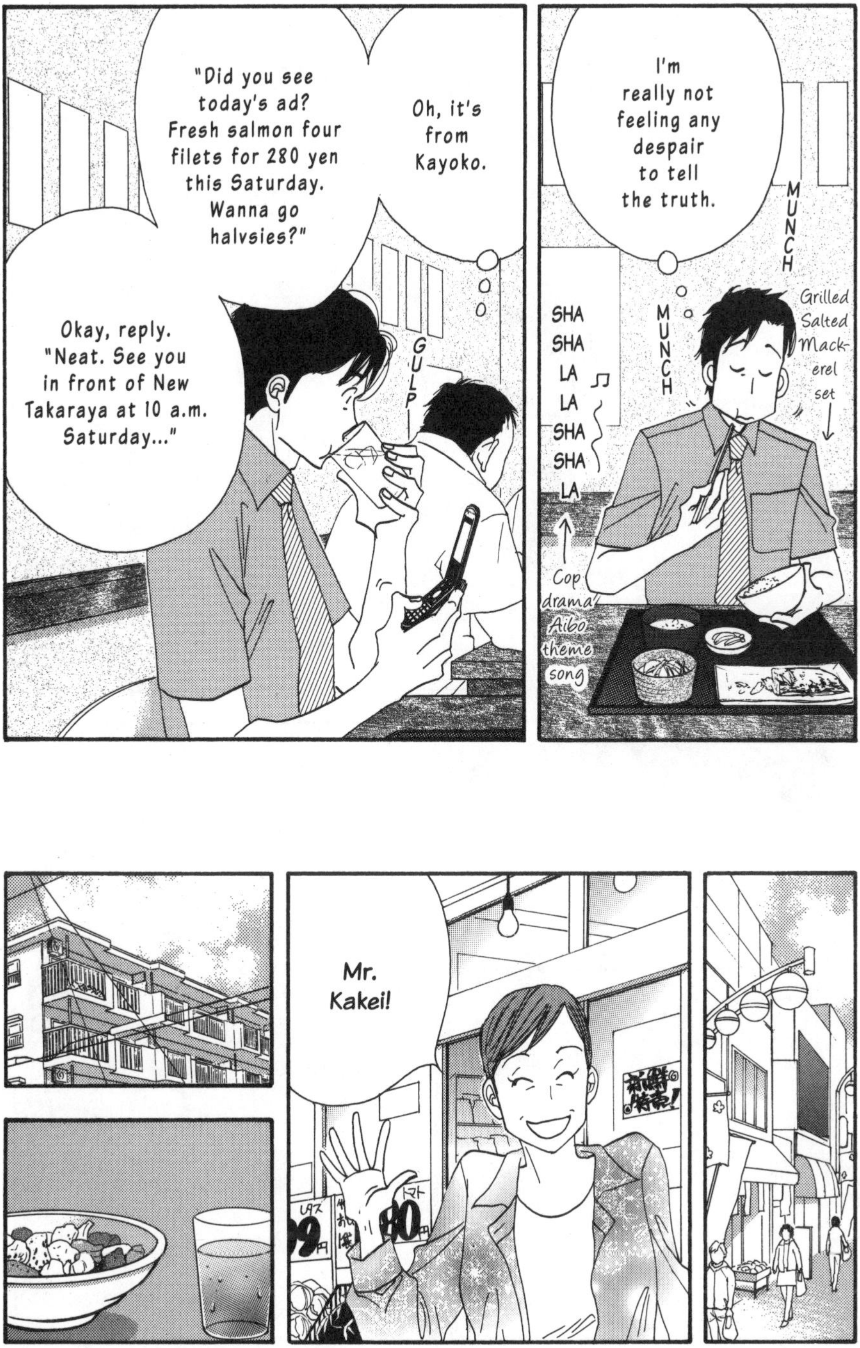
I'm really not feeling any despair to tell the truth.
MUNCH
MUNCH
Grilled Salted Mackerel set
SHA SHA LA LA SHA SHA LA
Cop drama Aibo theme song
Oh, it's from Kayoko.
"Did you see today's ad? Fresh salmon four filets for 280 yen this Saturday. Wanna go halvsies?"
GULP
Okay, reply. "Neat. See you in front of New Takaraya at 10 a.m. Saturday..."
Mr. Kakei!

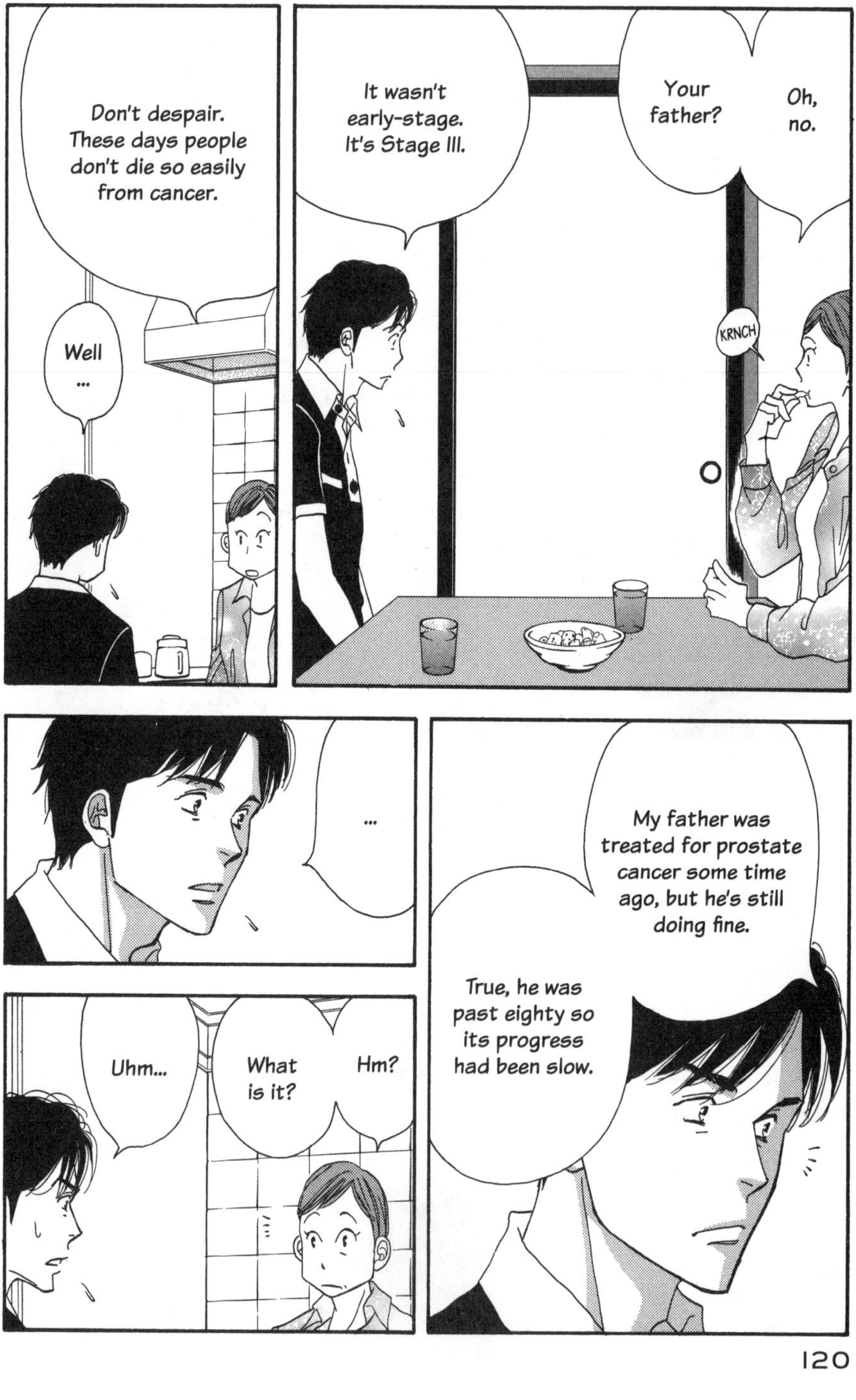
Oh, no.
Your father?
It wasn't early-stage. It's Stage III.
KRNCH
Don't despair. These days people don't die so easily from cancer.
Well ...
My father was treated for prostate cancer some time ago, but he's still doing fine.
True, he was past eighty so its progress had been slow.
...
Hm?
What is it?
Uhm...

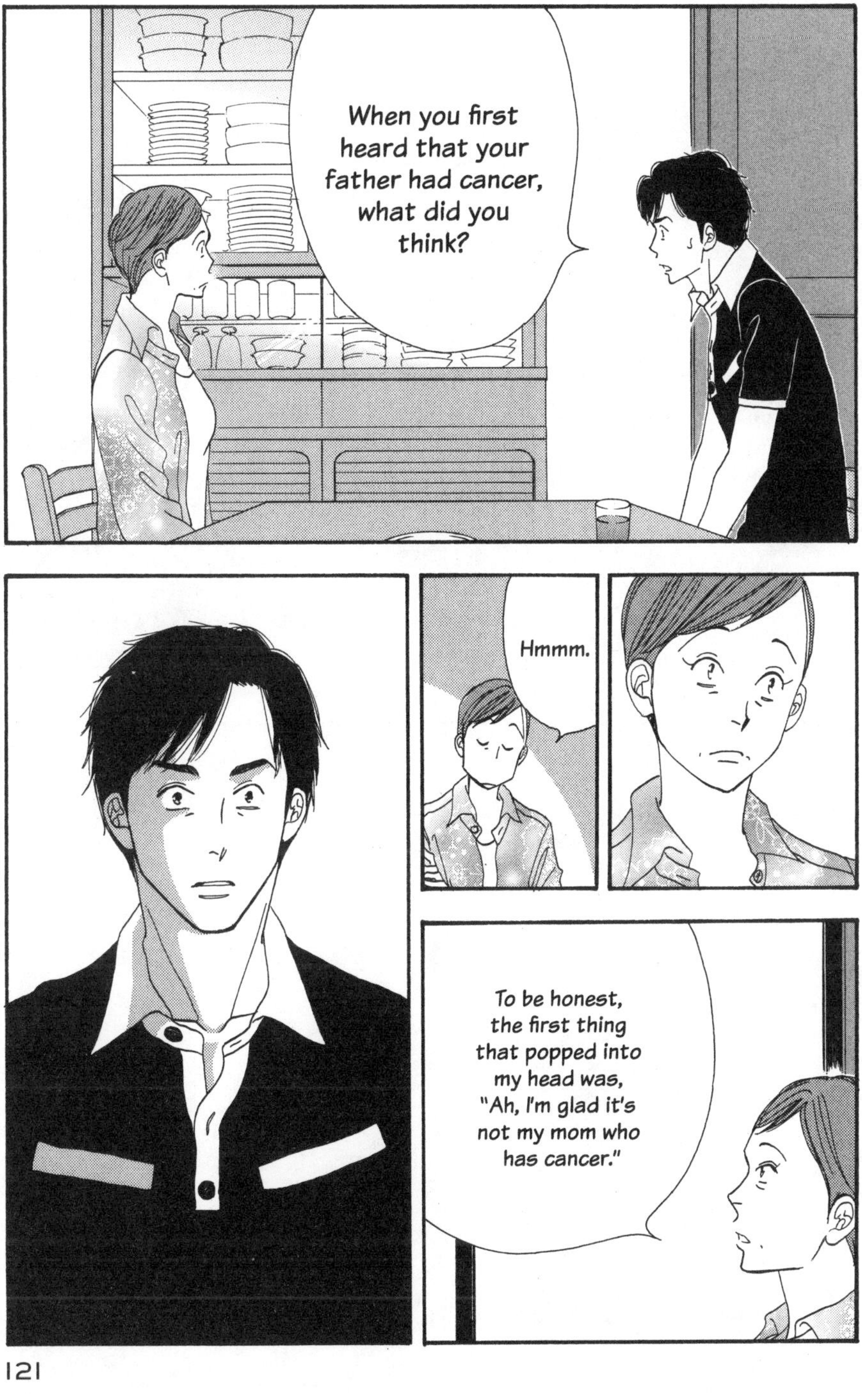
When you first heard that your father had cancer, what did you think?
Hmmm.
To be honest, the first thing that popped into my head was, "Ah, I'm glad it's not my mom who has cancer."

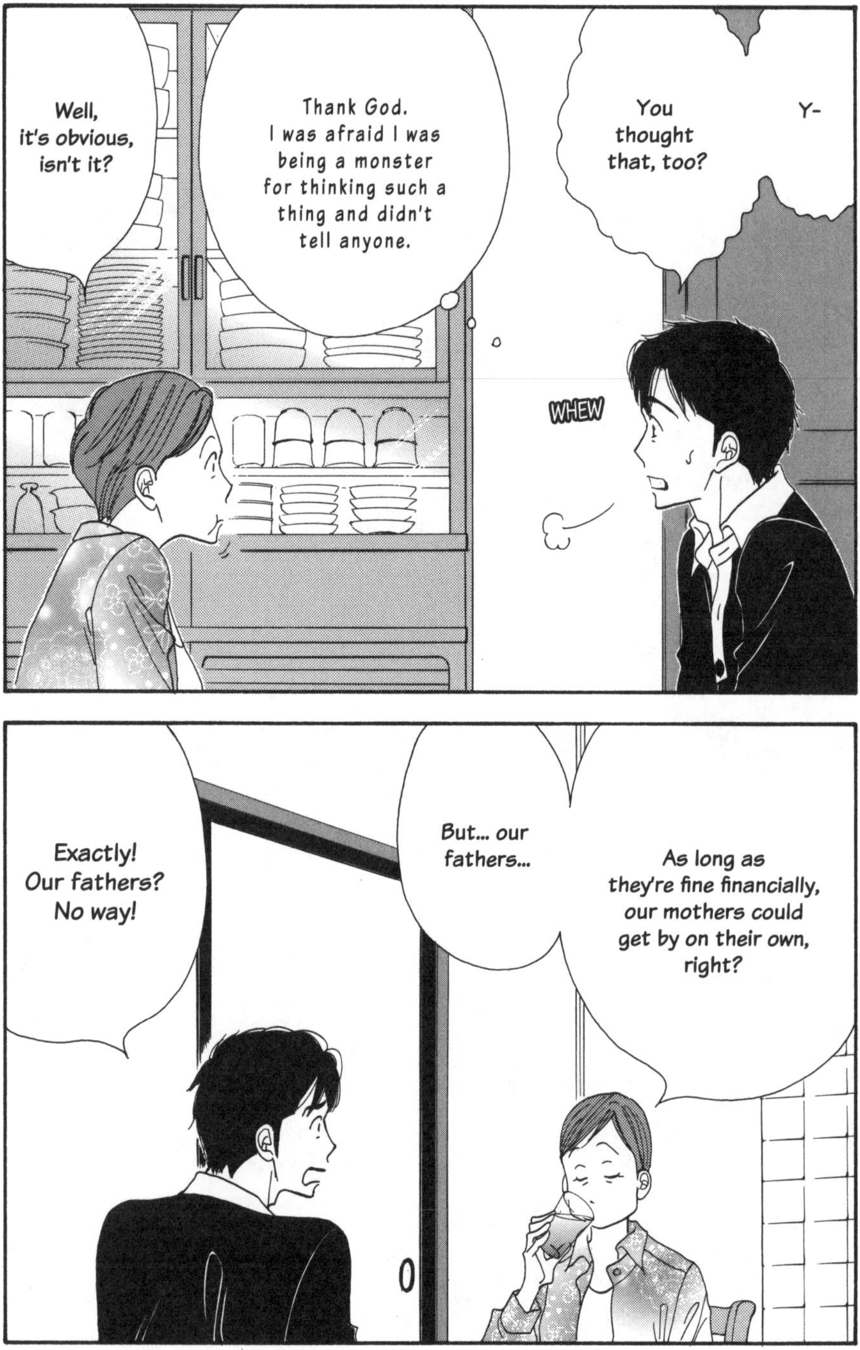
Y-
You thought that, too?
WHEW
Thank God. I was afraid I was being a monster for thinking such a thing and didn't tell anyone.
Well, it's obvious, isn't it?
As long as they're fine financially, our mothers could get by on their own, right?
But... our fathers...
Exactly! Our fathers? No way!

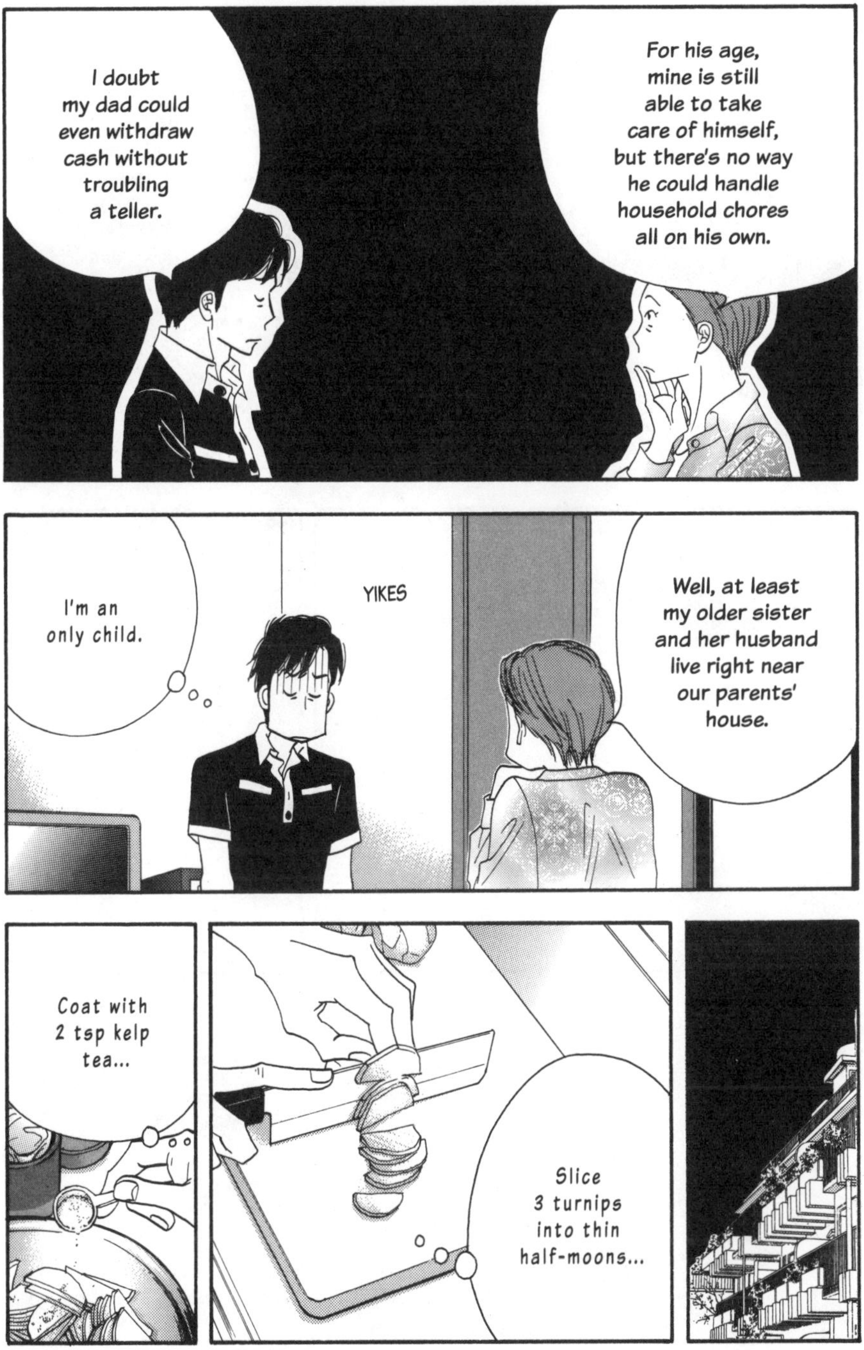
For his age, mine is still able to take care of himself, but there's no way he could handle household chores all on his own.
I doubt my dad could even withdraw cash without troubling a teller.
Well, at least my older sister and her husband live right near our parents' house.
YIKES
I'm an only child.
Slice 3 turnips into thin half-moons...
Coat with 2 tsp kelp tea...

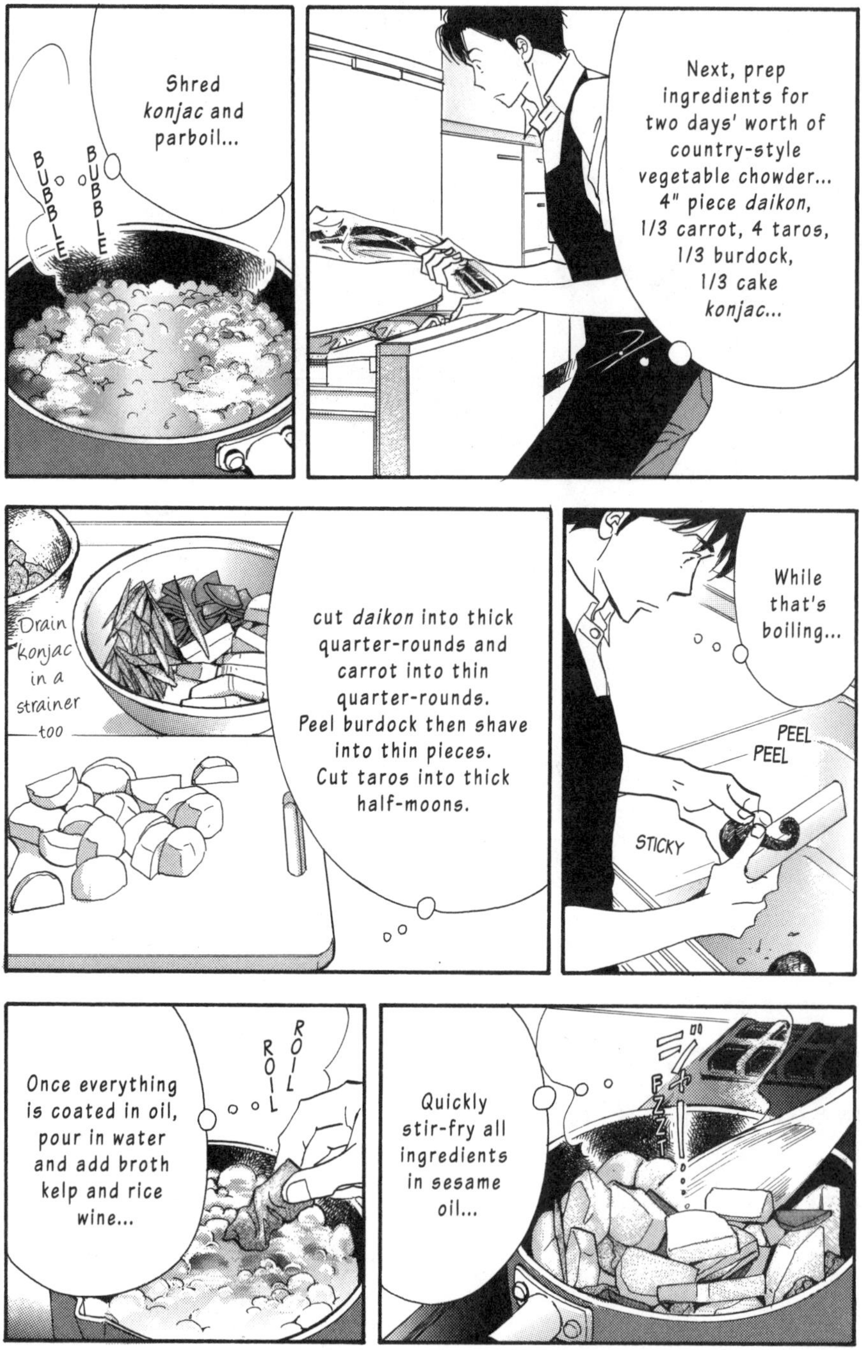
Next, prep ingredients for two days' worth of country-style vegetable chowder... 4" piece *daikon*, 1/3 carrot, 4 taros, 1/3 burdock, 1/3 cake *konjac*...
Shred *konjac* and parboil...
BUBBLE
BUBBLE
While that's boiling...
PEEL
PEEL
STICKY
cut *daikon* into thick quarter-rounds and carrot into thin quarter-rounds. Peel burdock then shave into thin pieces. Cut taros into thick half-moons.
Drain konjac in a strainer too
Quickly stir-fry all ingredients in sesame oil...
FZZT
Once everything is coated in oil, pour in water and add broth kelp and rice wine...
ROIL
ROIL

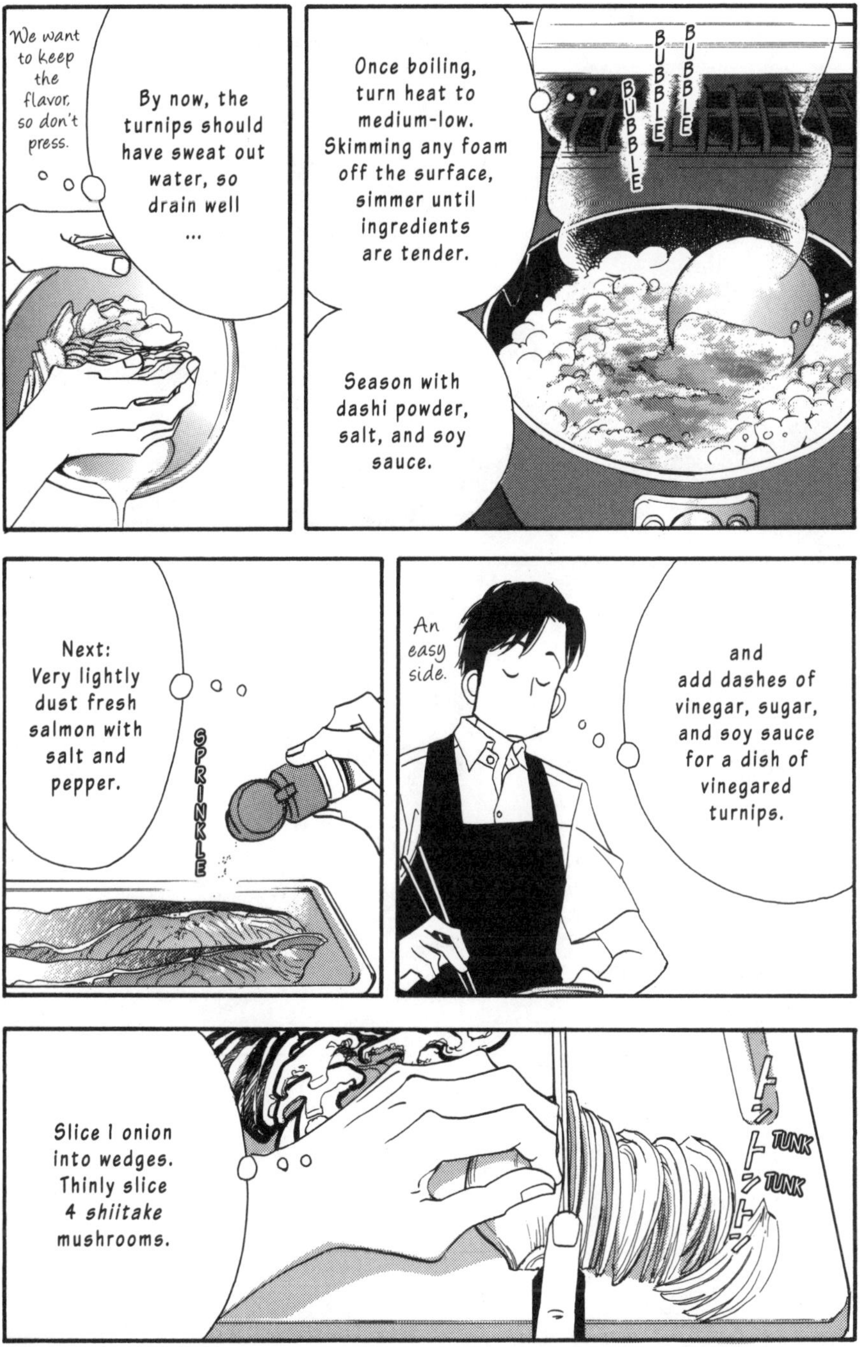
BUBBLE
BUBBLE
BUBBLE
Once boiling, turn heat to medium-low. Skimming any foam off the surface, simmer until ingredients are tender.
Season with dashi powder, salt, and soy sauce.
By now, the turnips should have sweat out water, so drain well ...
We want to keep the flavor, so don't press.
and add dashes of vinegar, sugar, and soy sauce for a dish of vinegared turnips.
An easy side.
Next: Very lightly dust fresh salmon with salt and pepper.
SPRINKLE
TUNK
TUNK
Slice 1 onion into wedges. Thinly slice 4 *shiitake* mushrooms.

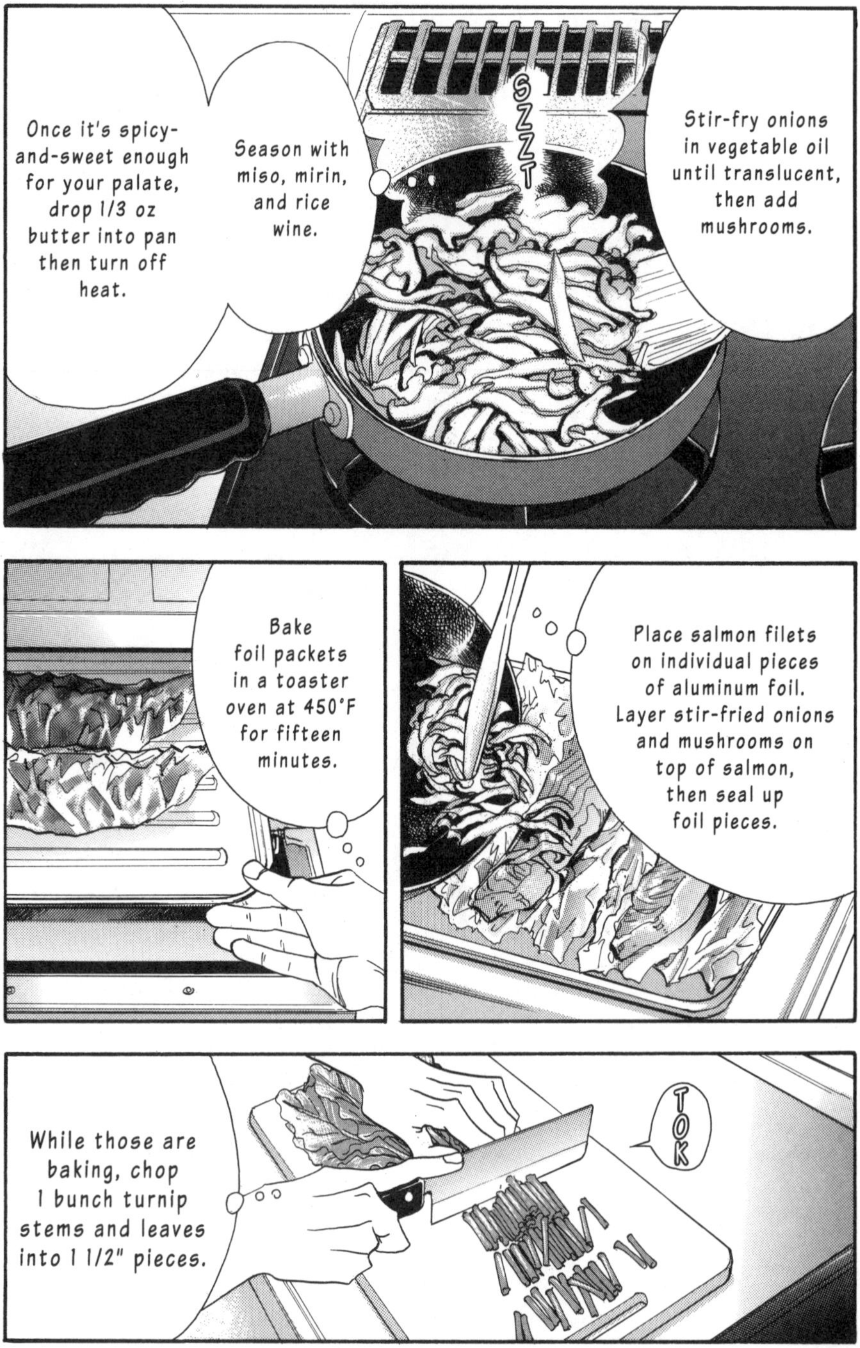
Stir-fry onions in vegetable oil until translucent, then add mushrooms.
SZZT
Season with miso, mirin, and rice wine.
Once it's spicy-and-sweet enough for your palate, drop 1/3 oz butter into pan then turn off heat.
Place salmon filets on individual pieces of aluminum foil. Layer stir-fried onions and mushrooms on top of salmon, then seal up foil pieces.
Bake foil packets in a toaster oven at 450°F for fifteen minutes.
TOK
While those are baking, chop 1 bunch turnip stems and leaves into 1 1/2" pieces.

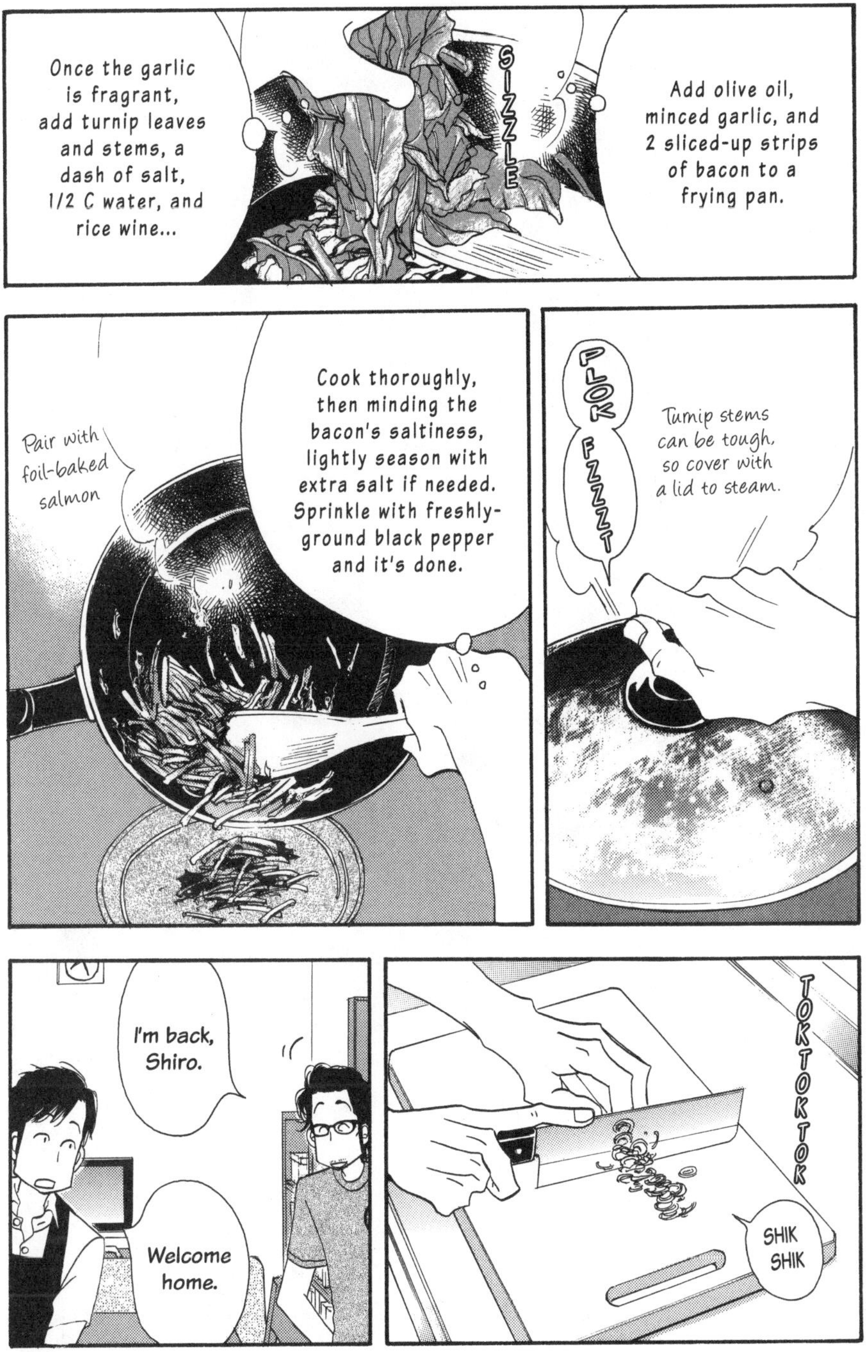
Add olive oil, minced garlic, and 2 sliced-up strips of bacon to a frying pan.
SIZZLE
Once the garlic is fragrant, add turnip leaves and stems, a dash of salt, 1/2 C water, and rice wine...
Turnip stems can be tough, so cover with a lid to steam.
PLOK
FZZZT
Cook thoroughly, then minding the bacon's saltiness, lightly season with extra salt if needed. Sprinkle with freshly-ground black pepper and it's done.
Pair with foil-baked salmon
TOKTOKTOK
SHIK SHIK
I'm back, Shiro.
Welcome home.

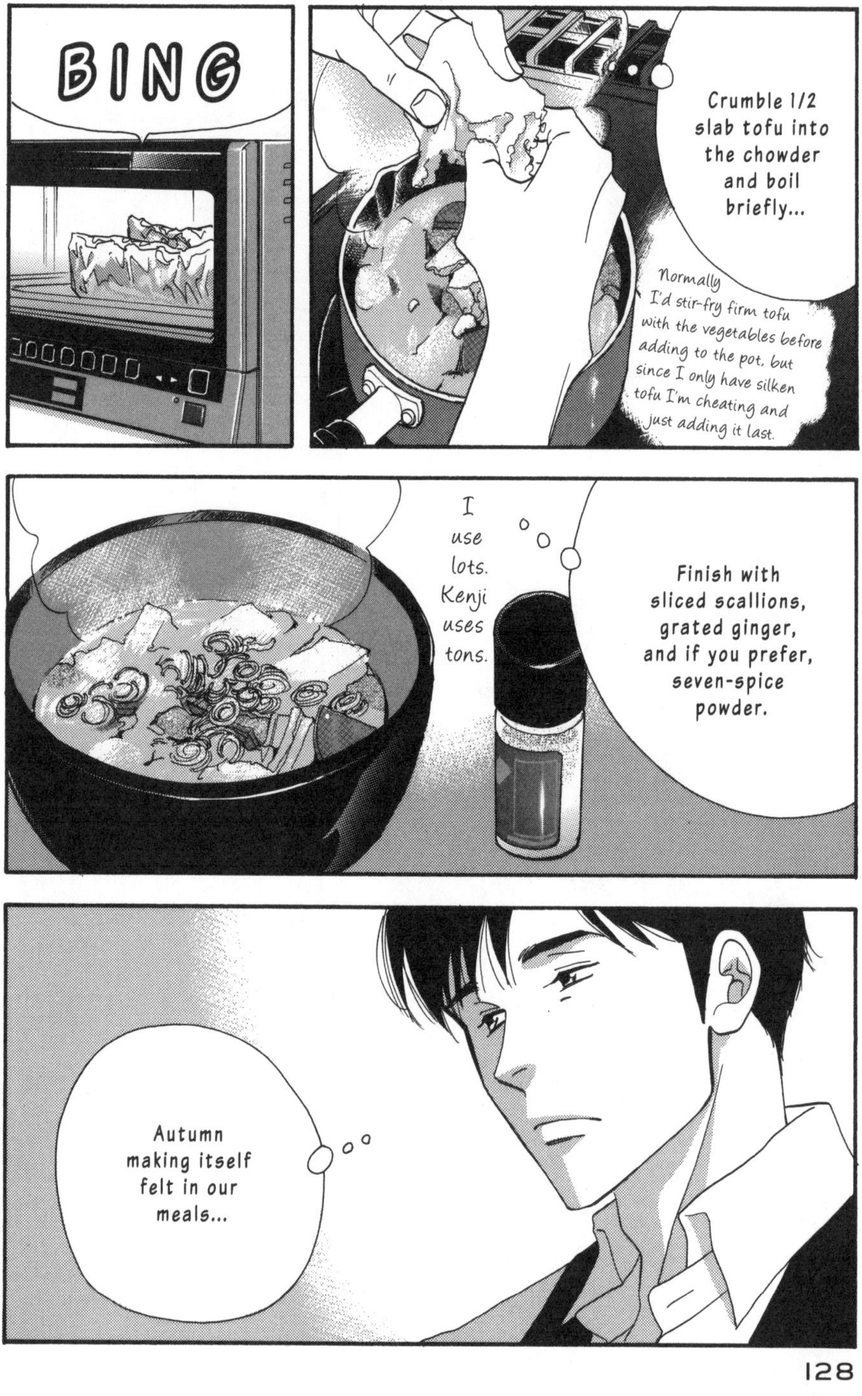
Crumble 1/2 slab tofu into the chowder and boil briefly...
Normally I'd stir-fry firm tofu with the vegetables before adding to the pot, but since I only have silken tofu I'm cheating and just adding it last.
BING
Finish with sliced scallions, grated ginger, and if you prefer, seven-spice powder.
I use lots. Kenji uses tons.
Autumn making itself felt in our meals...

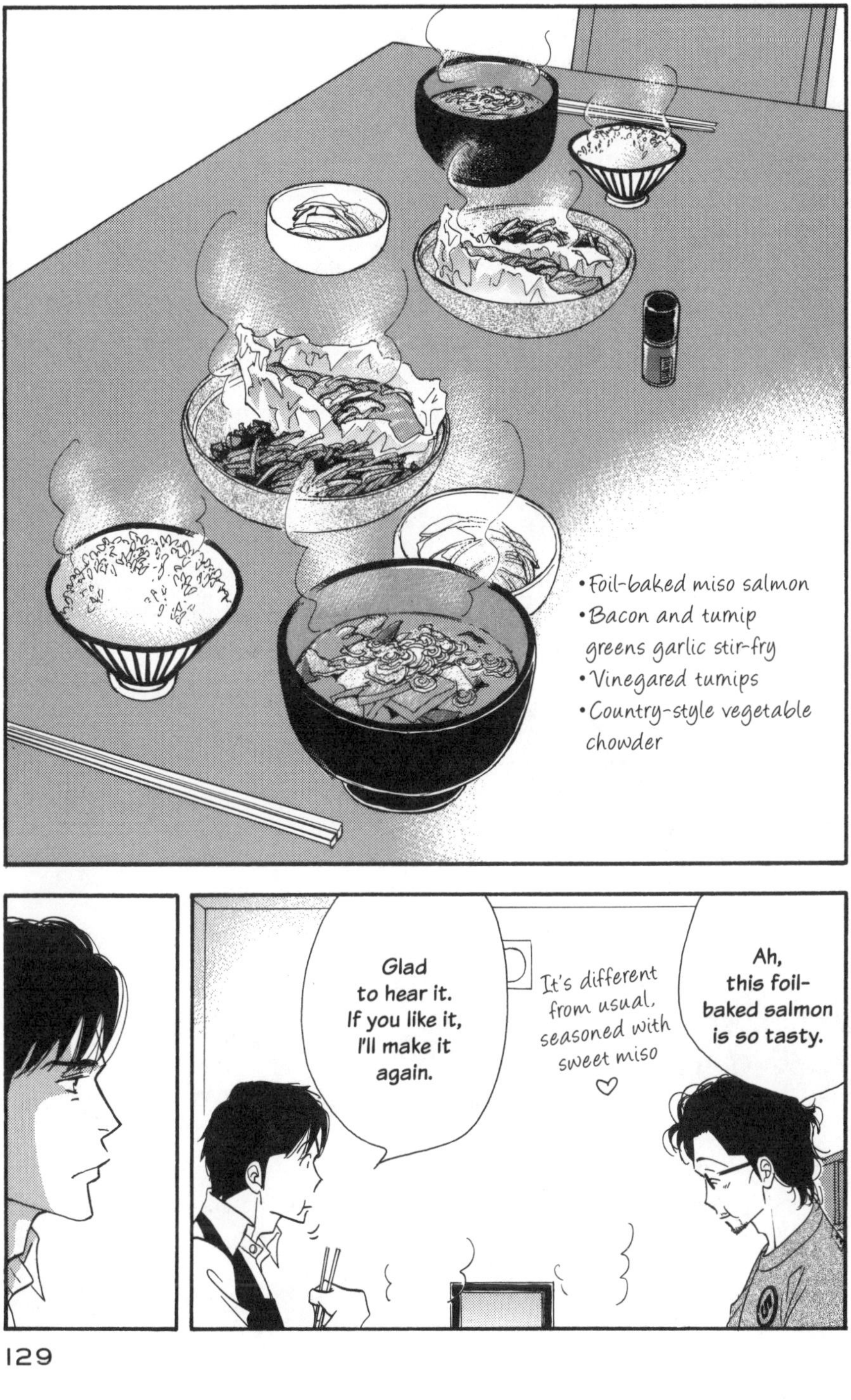
•Foil-baked miso salmon
•Bacon and turnip greens garlic stir-fry
•Vinegared turnips
•Country-style vegetable chowder
Ah, this foil-baked salmon is so tasty.
It's different from usual, seasoned with sweet miso ♡
Glad to hear it. If you like it, I'll make it again.

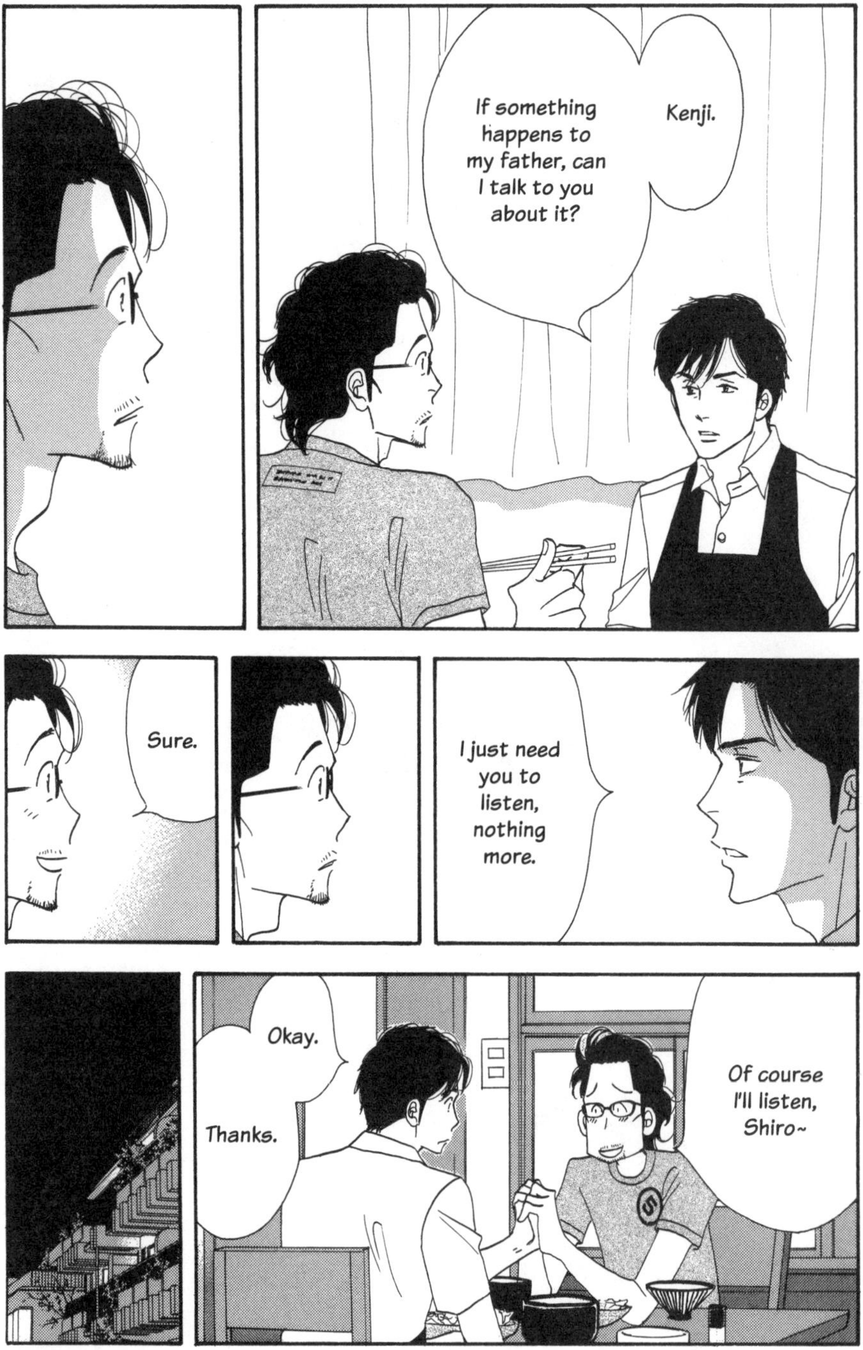
Kenji.
If something happens to my father, can I talk to you about it?
I just need you to listen, nothing more.
Sure.
Of course I'll listen, Shiro~
Okay.
Thanks.

#15 **END**

Country-style vegetable chowder tends to yield a high volume, so try adding a serving of udon noodles to the leftovers for country-style udon.

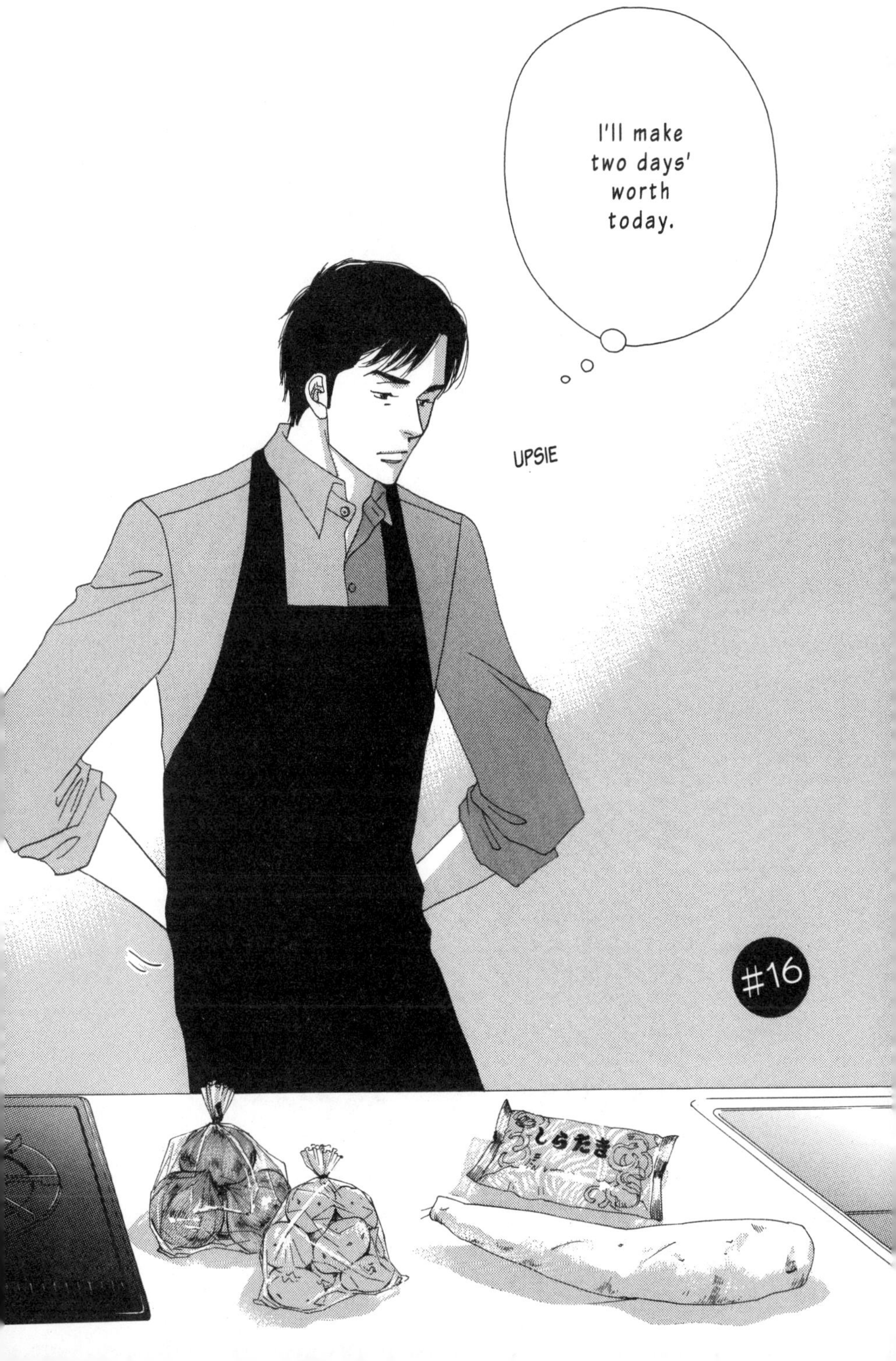
I'll make two days' worth today.
UPSIE
しらたき
#16

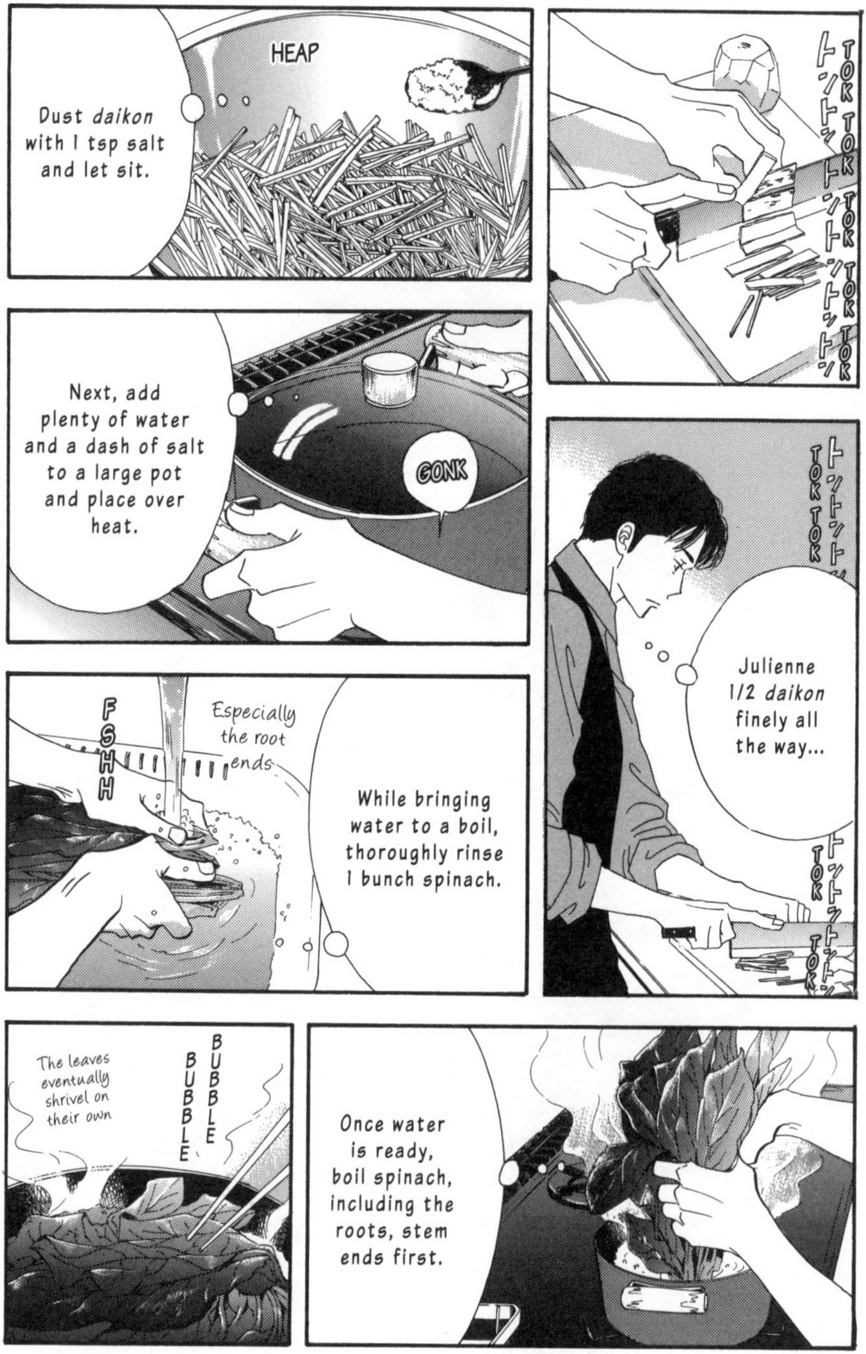
TOK TOK TOK TOK TOK
TOK TOK TOK TOK
Julienne 1/2 *daikon* finely all the way...
HEAP
Dust *daikon* with 1 tsp salt and let sit.
Next, add plenty of water and a dash of salt to a large pot and place over heat.
GONK
While bringing water to a boil, thoroughly rinse 1 bunch spinach.
Especially the root ends
FSHH
Once water is ready, boil spinach, including the roots, stem ends first.
BUBBLE BUBBLE
The leaves eventually shrivel on their own

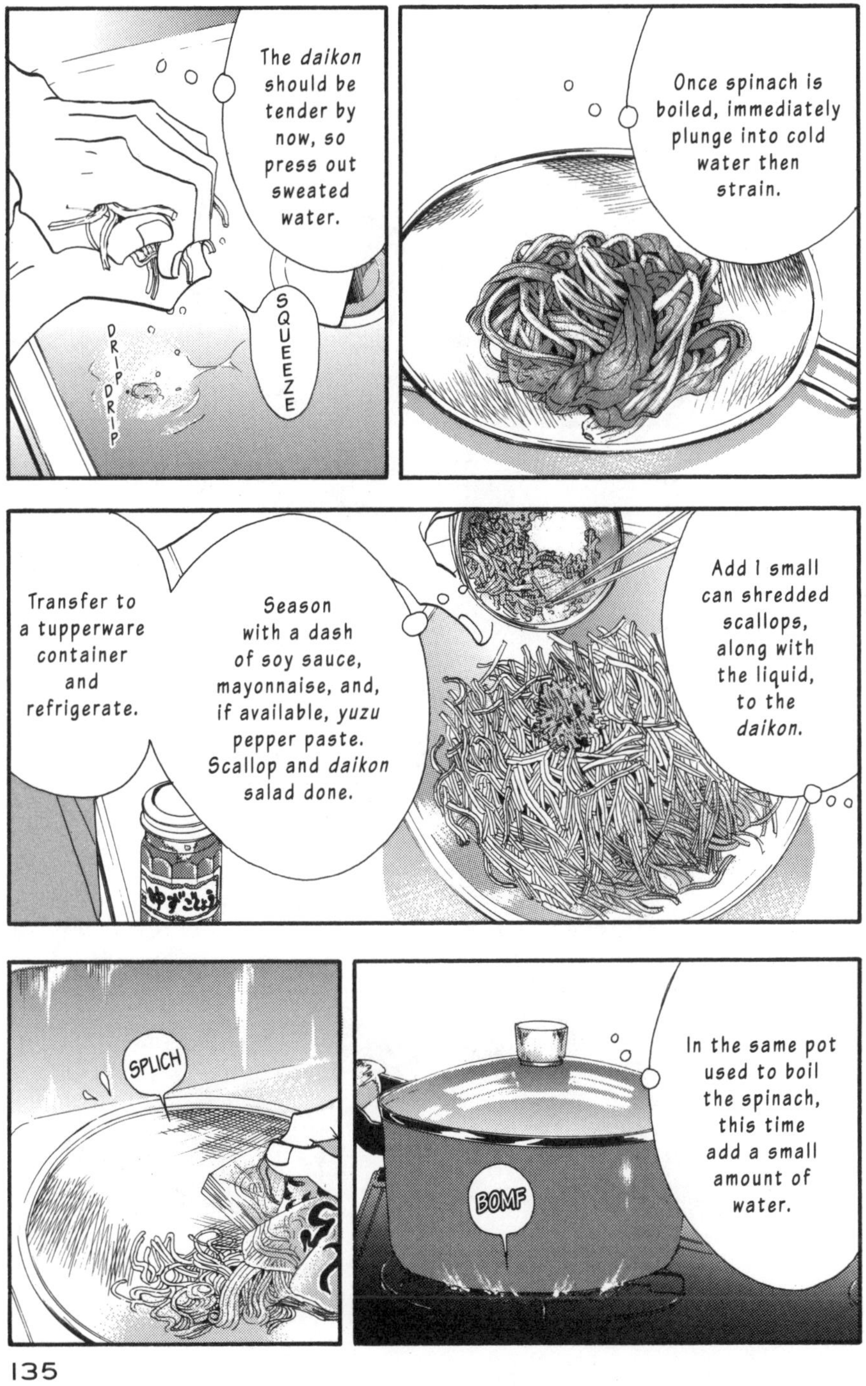
Once spinach is boiled, immediately plunge into cold water then strain.
The daikon should be tender by now, so press out sweated water.
SQUEEZE
DRIP DRIP
Add 1 small can shredded scallops, along with the liquid, to the daikon.
Season with a dash of soy sauce, mayonnaise, and, if available, yuzu pepper paste. Scallop and daikon salad done.
Transfer to a tupperware container and refrigerate.
In the same pot used to boil the spinach, this time add a small amount of water.
BOMF
SPLICH

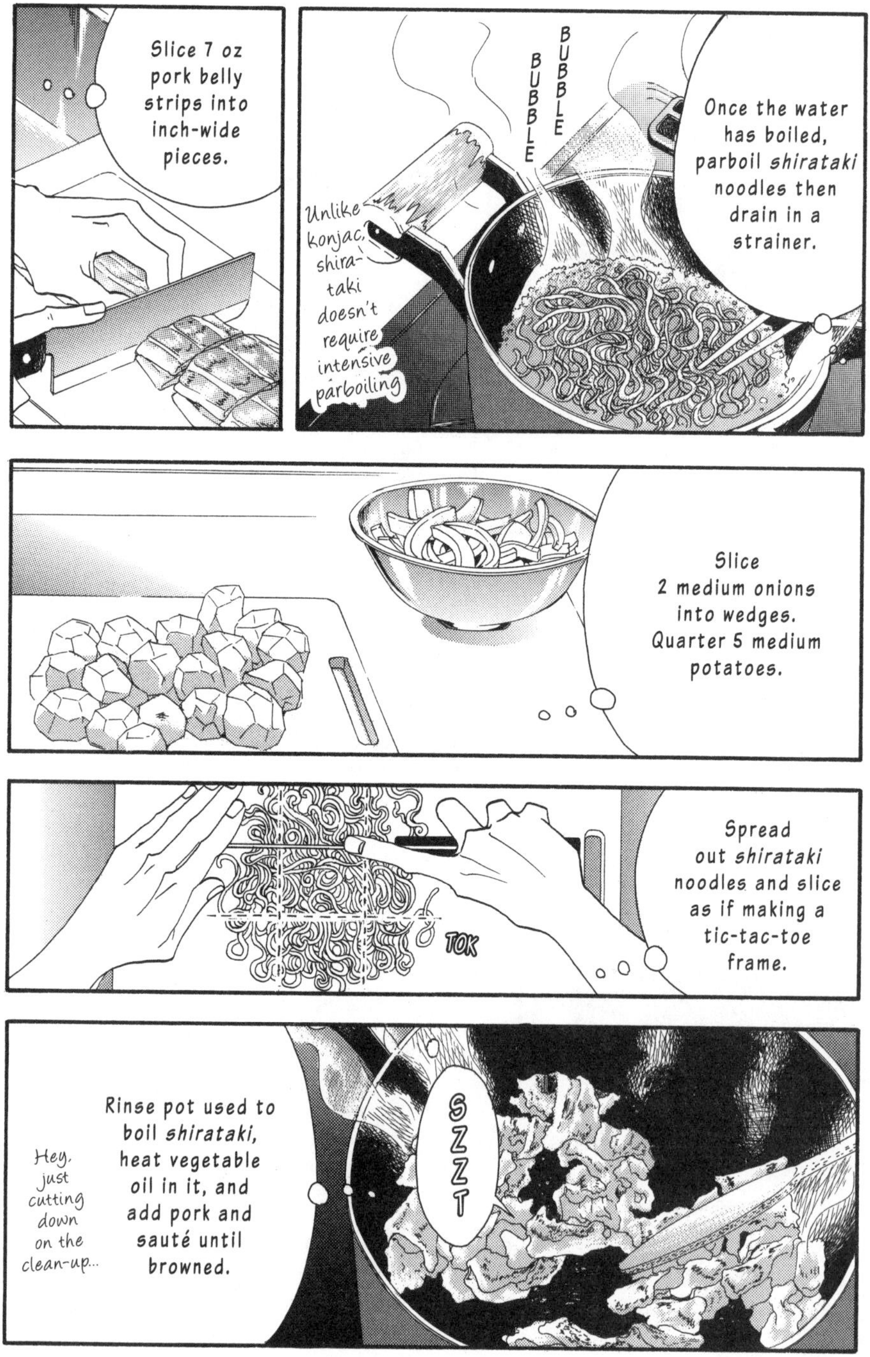
Once the water has boiled, parboil *shirataki* noodles then drain in a strainer.
BUBBLE BUBBLE
Unlike konjac, shirataki doesn't require intensive parboiling
Slice 7 oz pork belly strips into inch-wide pieces.
Slice 2 medium onions into wedges. Quarter 5 medium potatoes.
Spread out *shirataki* noodles and slice as if making a tic-tac-toe frame.
TOK
SZZT
Rinse pot used to boil *shirataki*, heat vegetable oil in it, and add pork and sauté until browned.
Hey, just cutting down on the clean-up...

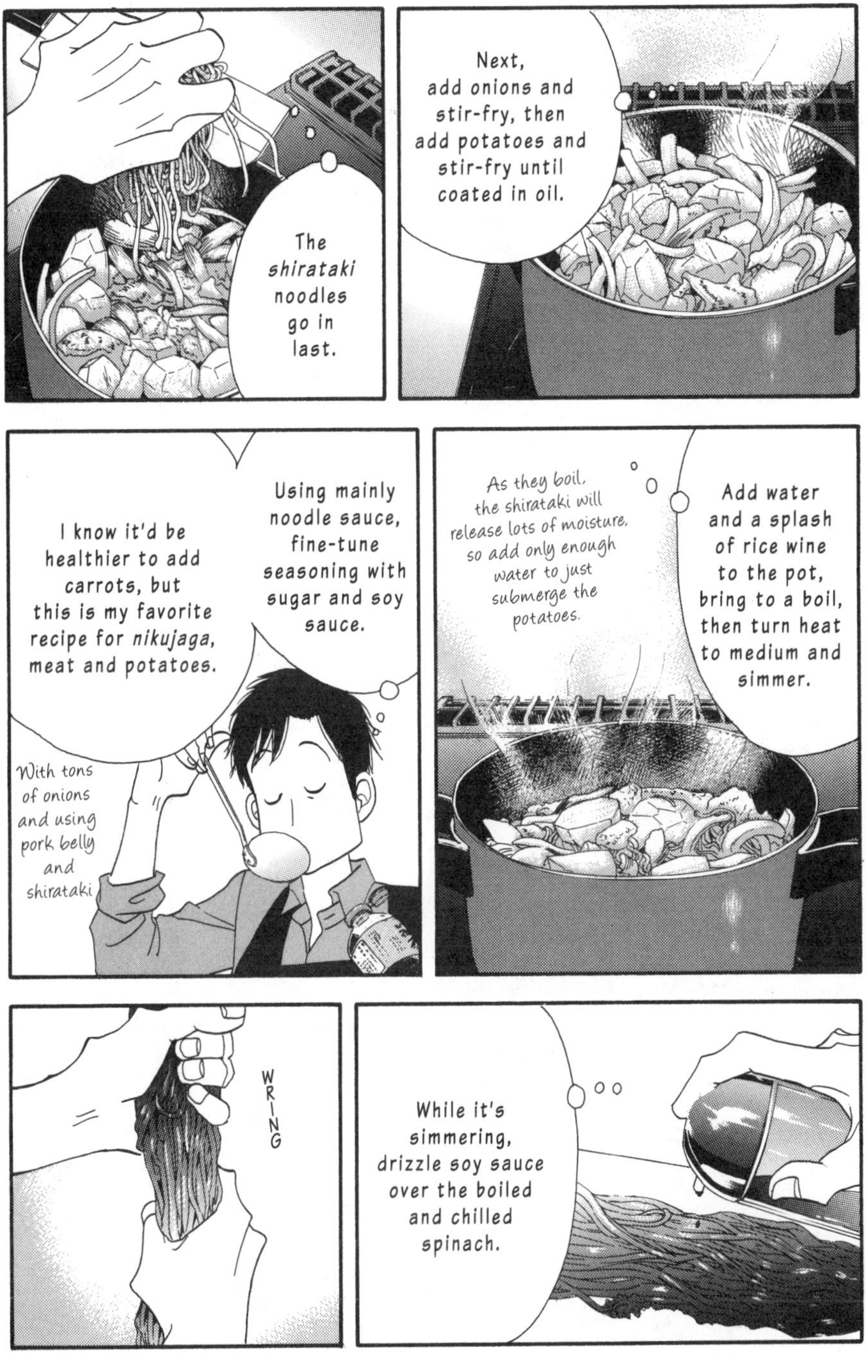
Next, add onions and stir-fry, then add potatoes and stir-fry until coated in oil.
The shirataki noodles go in last.
Add water and a splash of rice wine to the pot, bring to a boil, then turn heat to medium and simmer.
As they boil, the shirataki will release lots of moisture, so add only enough water to just submerge the potatoes.
Using mainly noodle sauce, fine-tune seasoning with sugar and soy sauce.
I know it'd be healthier to add carrots, but this is my favorite recipe for nikujaga, meat and potatoes.
With tons of onions and using pork belly and shirataki
While it's simmering, drizzle soy sauce over the boiled and chilled spinach.
WRING

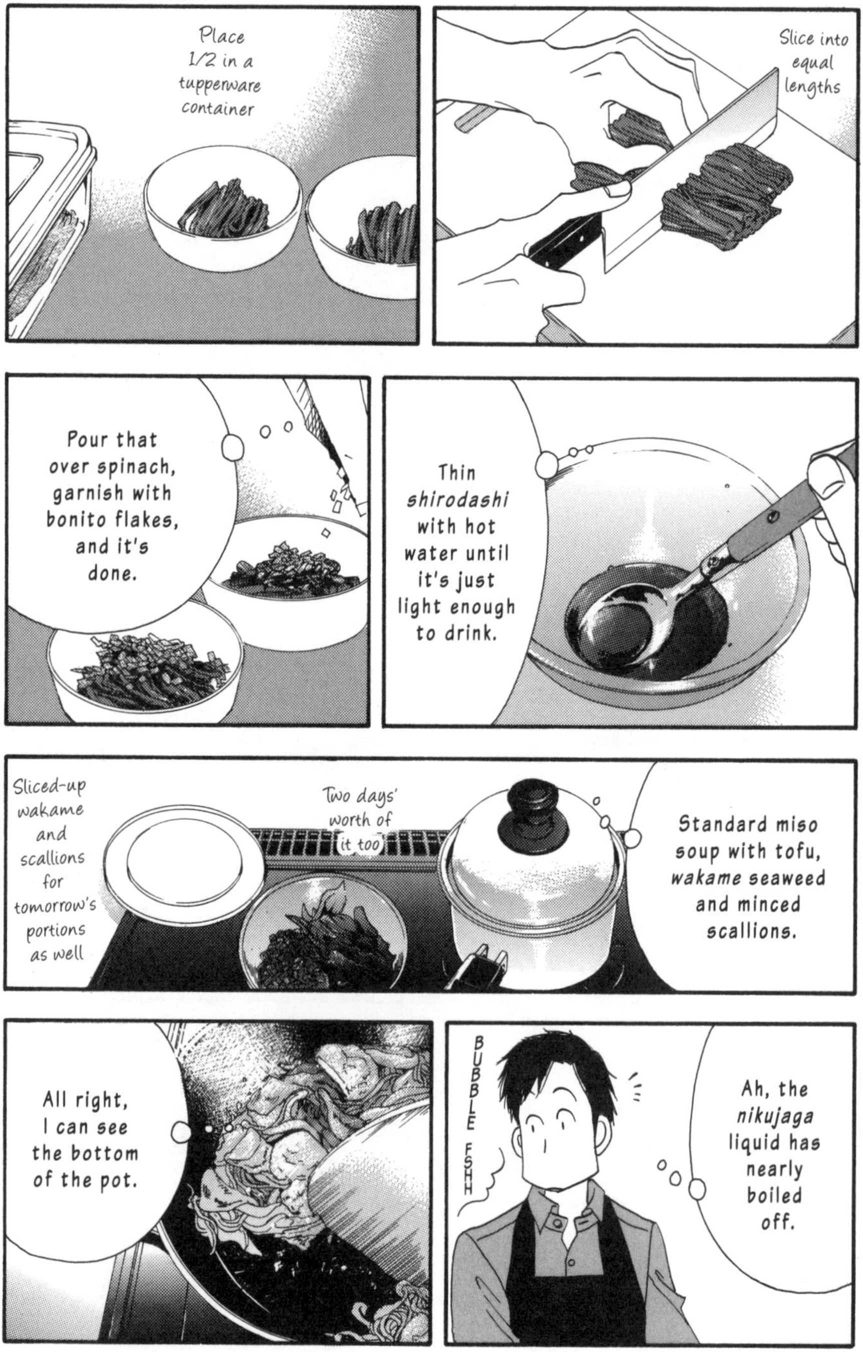
Slice into equal lengths
Place 1/2 in a tupperware container
Thin *shirodashi* with hot water until it's just light enough to drink.
Pour that over spinach, garnish with bonito flakes, and it's done.
Standard miso soup with tofu, *wakame* seaweed and minced scallions.
Two days' worth of it too
Sliced-up wakame and scallions for tomorrow's portions as well
Ah, the *nikujaga* liquid has nearly boiled off.
BUBBLE
FSHH
All right, I can see the bottom of the pot.

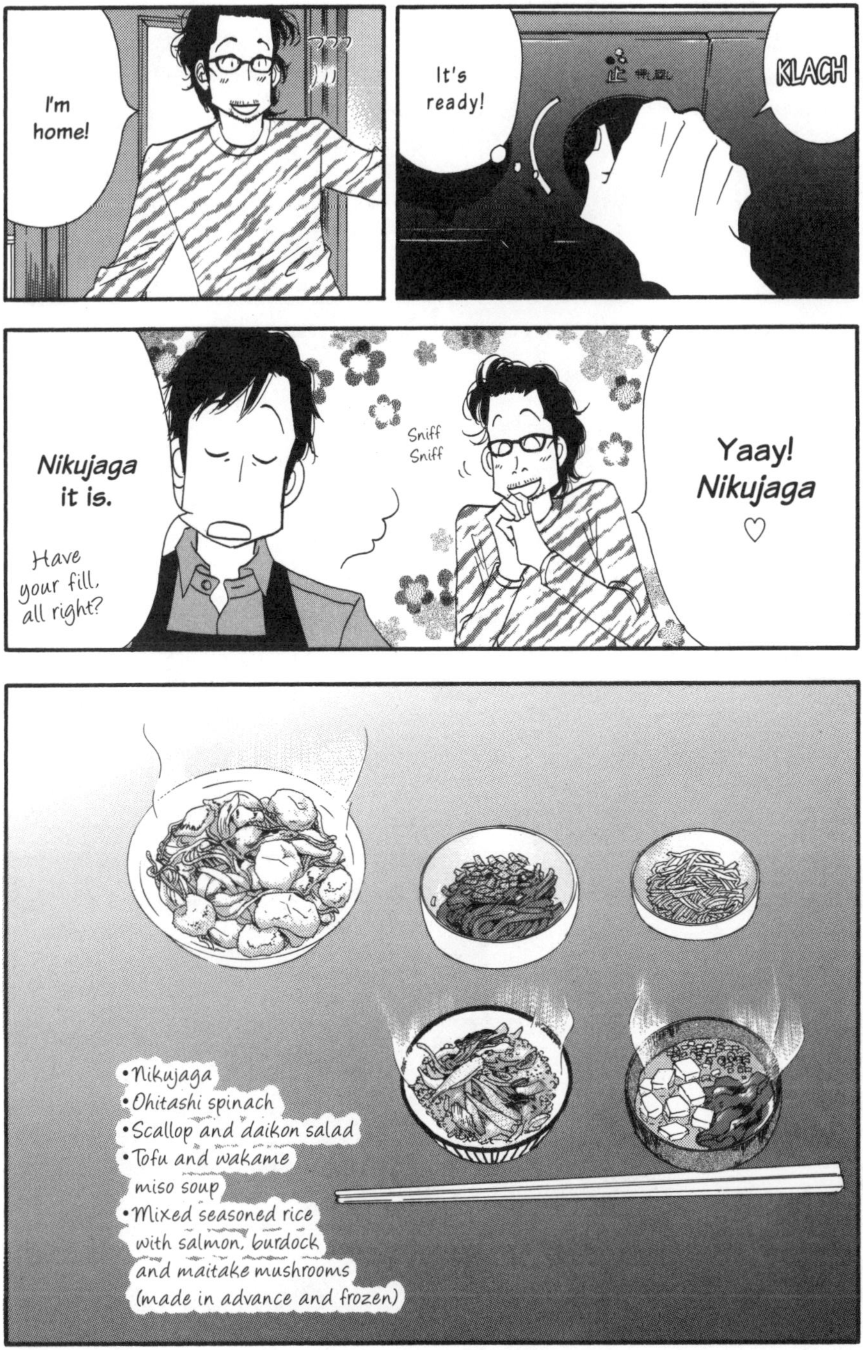
KLACH
It's ready!
I'm home!
Yaay! Nikujaga ♡
Sniff Sniff
Nikujaga it is.
Have your fill, all right?
•Nikujaga
•Ohitashi spinach
•Scallop and daikon salad
•Tofu and wakame miso soup
•Mixed seasoned rice with salmon, burdock and maitake mushrooms (made in advance and frozen)

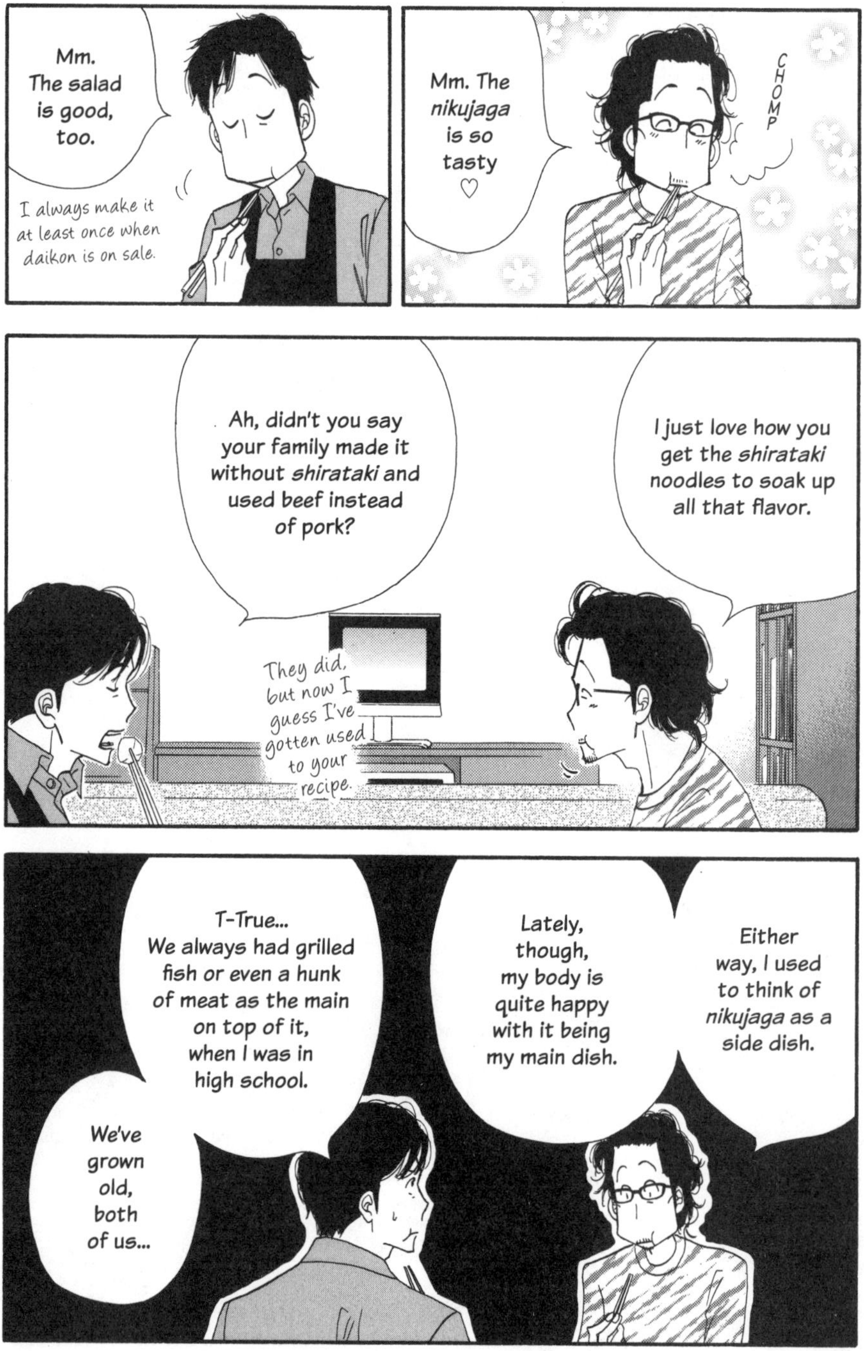
Mm. The *nikujaga* is so tasty ♡
CHOMP
Mm. The salad is good, too.
I always make it at least once when daikon is on sale.
I just love how you get the *shirataki* noodles to soak up all that flavor.
Ah, didn't you say your family made it without *shirataki* and used beef instead of pork?
They did, but now I guess I've gotten used to your recipe.
Either way, I used to think of *nikujaga* as a side dish.
Lately, though, my body is quite happy with it being my main dish.
T-True... We always had grilled fish or even a hunk of meat as the main on top of it, when I was in high school.
We've grown old, both of us...

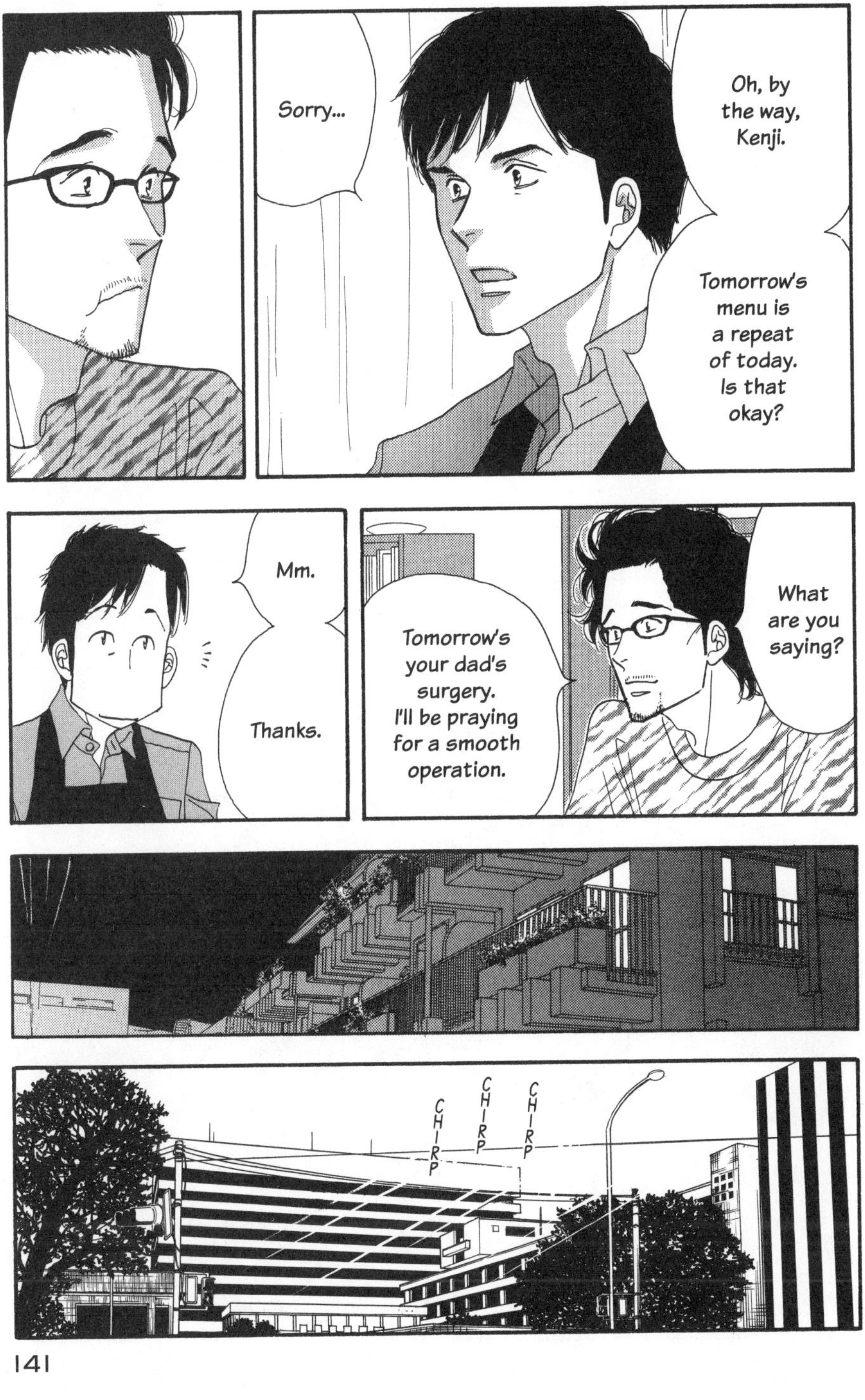
Oh, by the way, Kenji.
Tomorrow's menu is a repeat of today. Is that okay?
Sorry...
What are you saying?
Tomorrow's your dad's surgery. I'll be praying for a smooth operation.
Mm.
Thanks.
CHIRP
CHIRP
CHIRP

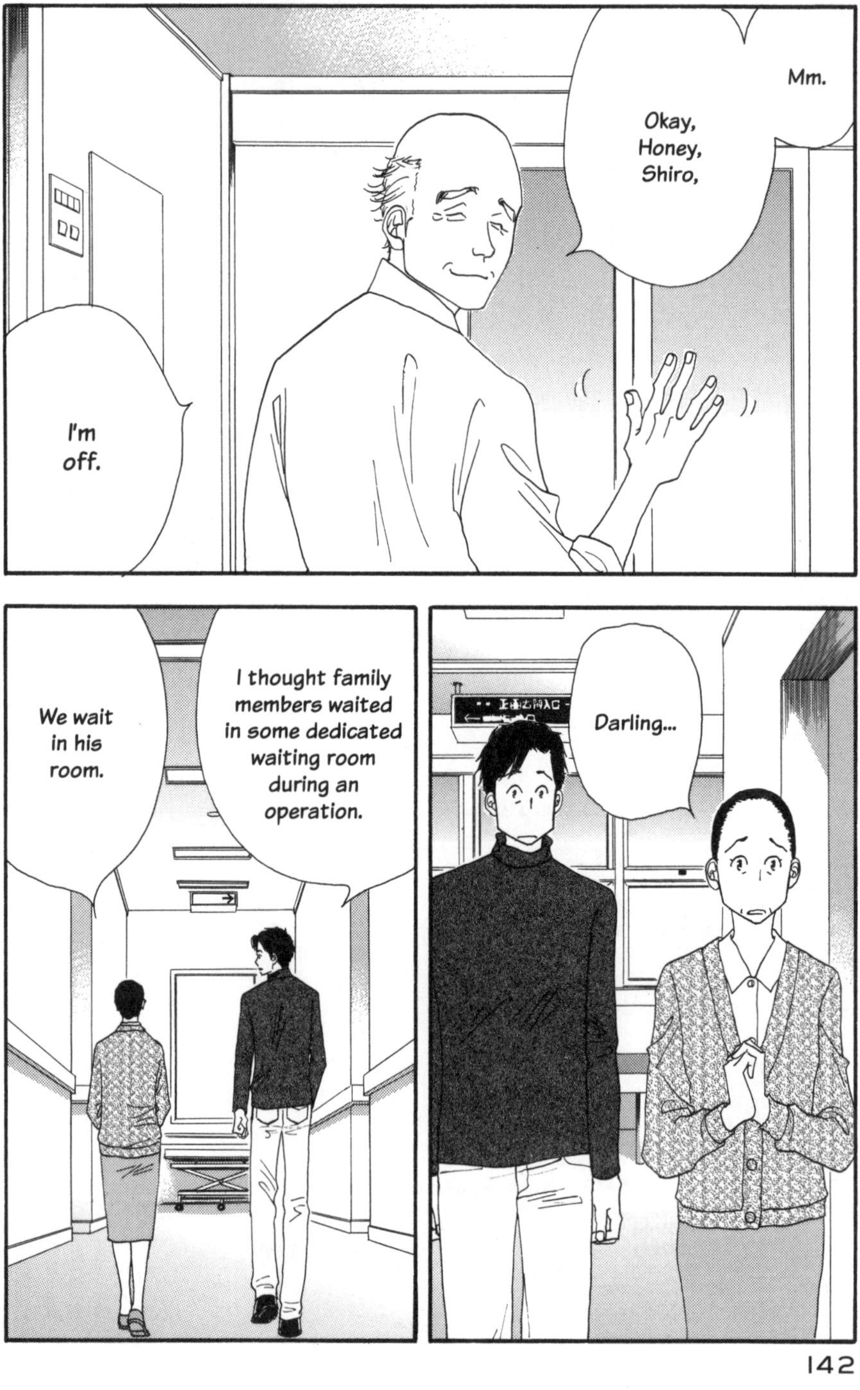
Mm.
Okay, Honey, Shiro,
I'm off.
Darling...
I thought family members waited in some dedicated waiting room during an operation.
We wait in his room.

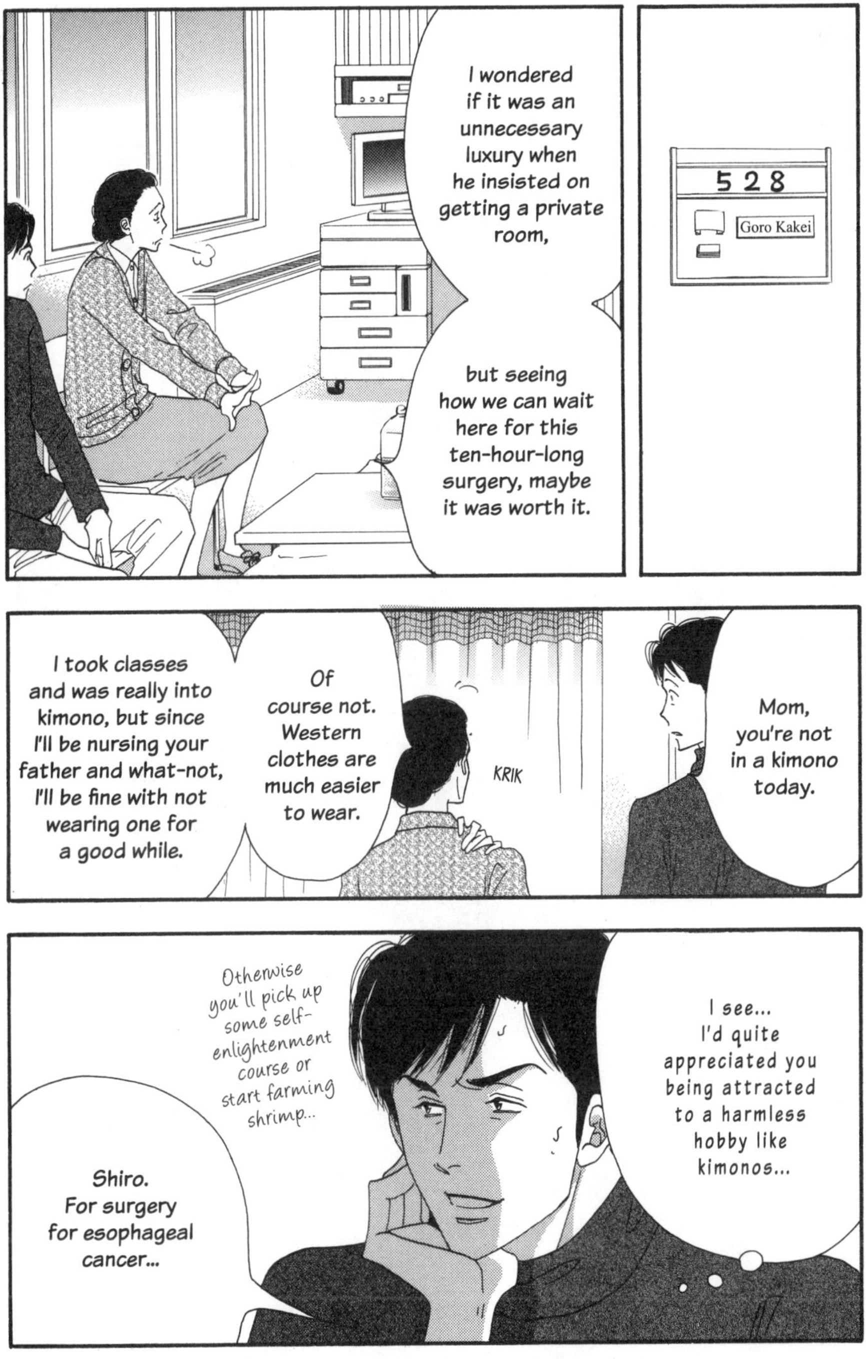
528
Goro Kakei
I wondered if it was an unnecessary luxury when he insisted on getting a private room,
but seeing how we can wait here for this ten-hour-long surgery, maybe it was worth it.
Mom, you're not in a kimono today.
Of course not. Western clothes are much easier to wear.
KRIK
I took classes and was really into kimono, but since I'll be nursing your father and what-not, I'll be fine with not wearing one for a good while.
I see... I'd quite appreciated you being attracted to a harmless hobby like kimonos...
Otherwise you'll pick up some self-enlightenment course or start farming shrimp...
Shiro. For surgery for esophageal cancer...

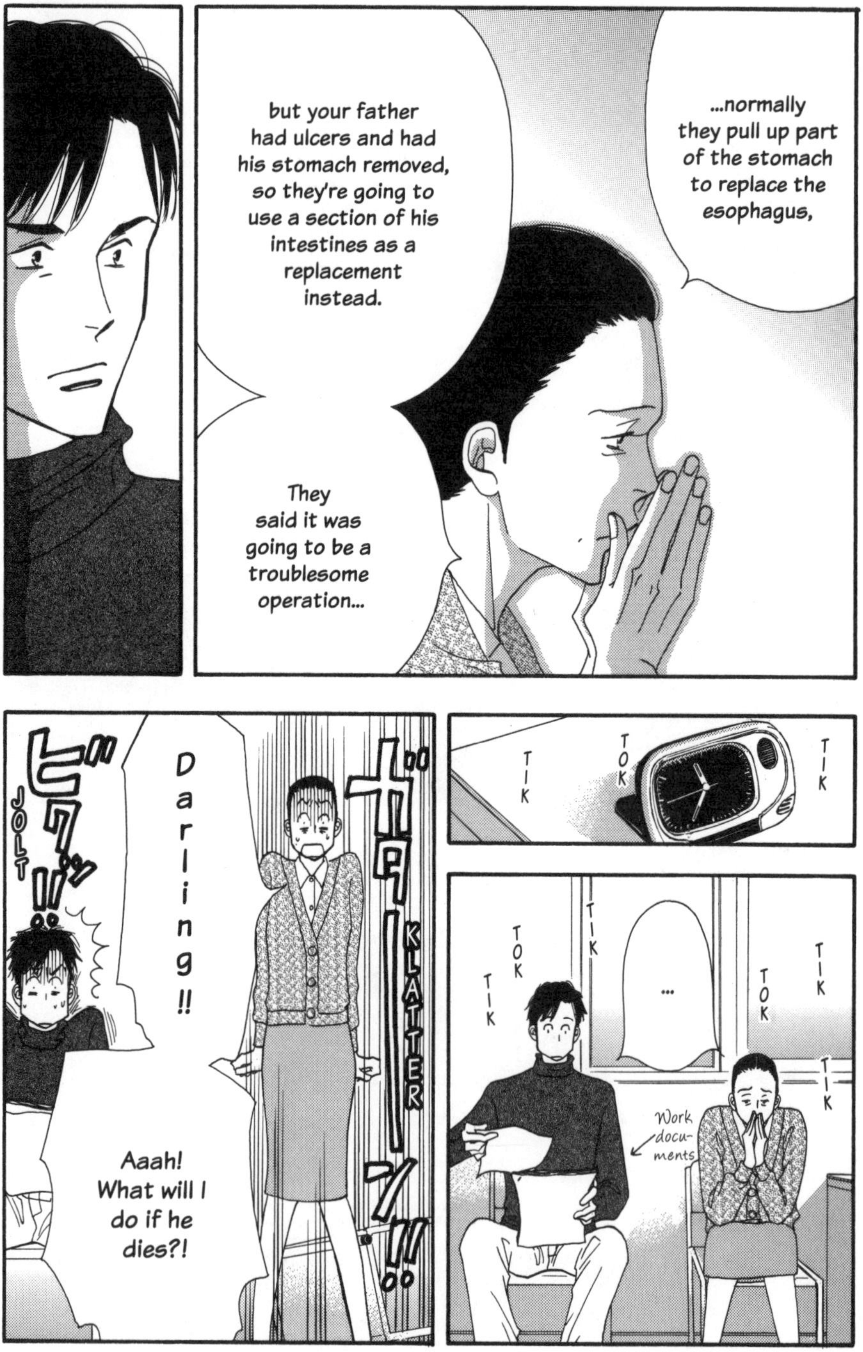
...normally they pull up part of the stomach to replace the esophagus,
but your father had ulcers and had his stomach removed, so they're going to use a section of his intestines as a replacement instead.
They said it was going to be a troublesome operation...
TIK
TOK
TIK
TIK
TOK
TIK
...
TIK
TOK
TIK
TIK
Work documents
Darling!!
KLATTER
JOLT
Aaah! What will I do if he dies?!

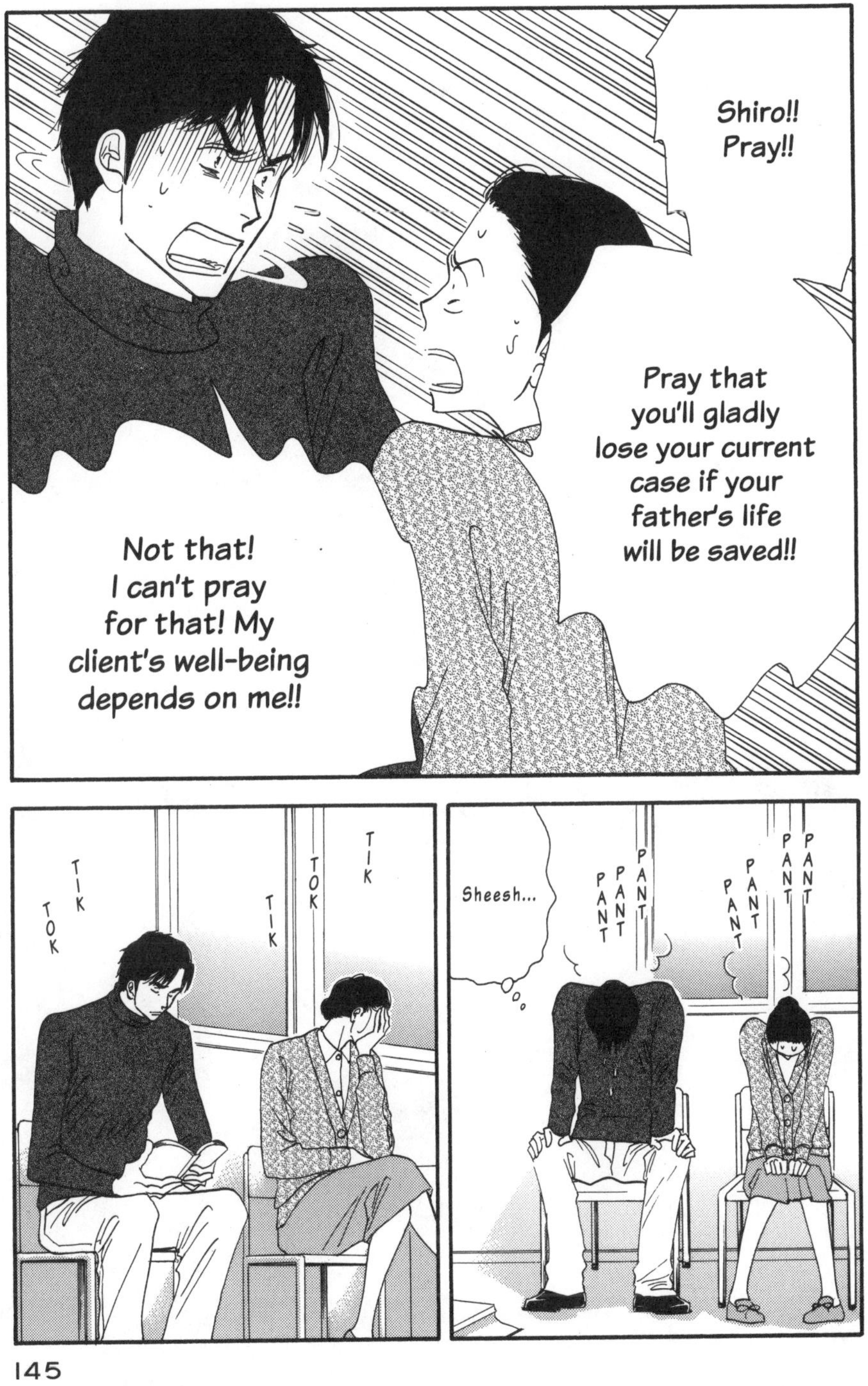
Shiro!! Pray!!
Pray that you'll gladly lose your current case if your father's life will be saved!!
Not that! I can't pray for that! My client's well-being depends on me!!
PANT PANT PANT PANT PANT PANT
PANT PANT PANT
Sheesh...
TIK TIK
TOK
TIK
TOK

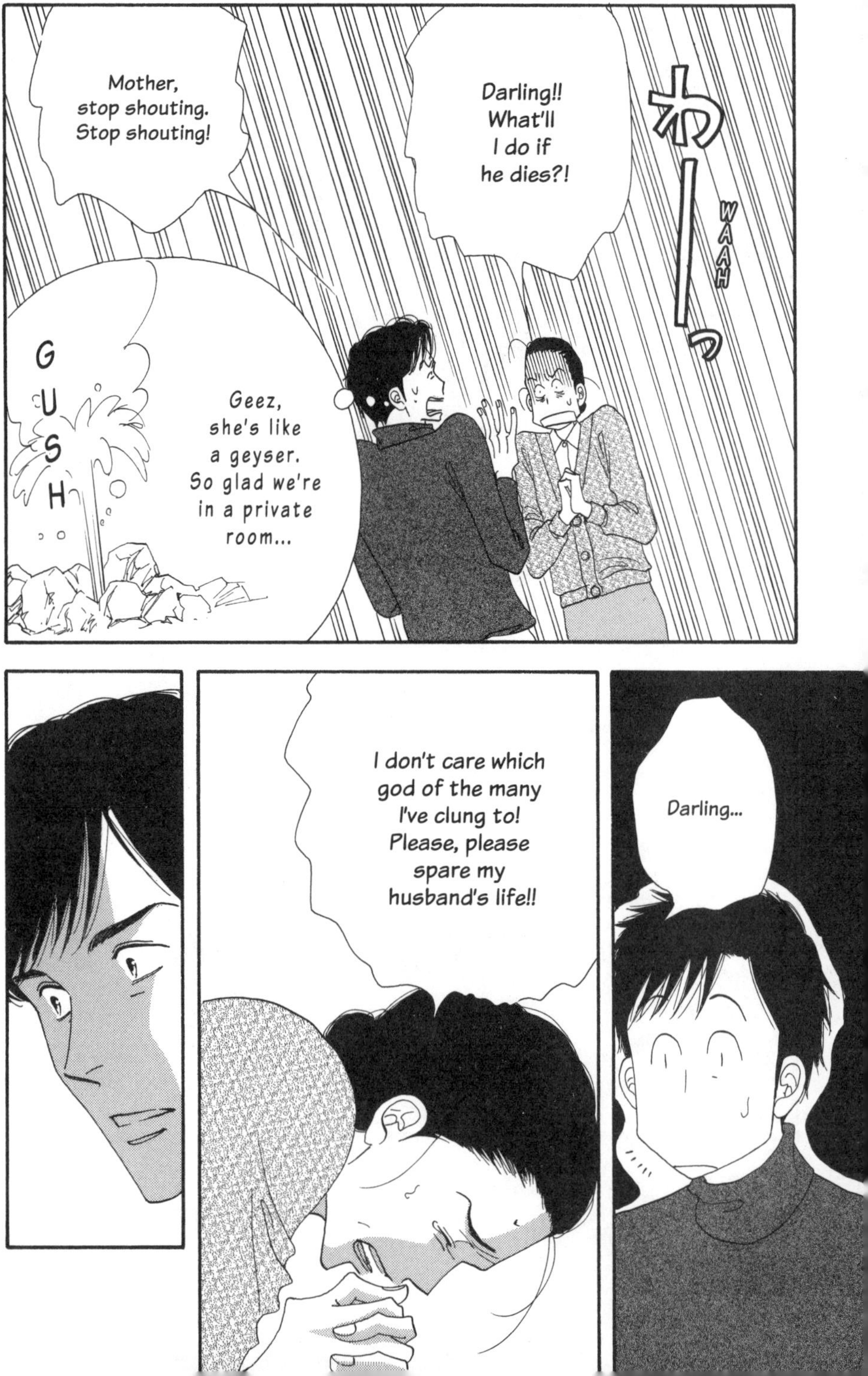
わーっ
WAAAH
Darling!! What'll I do if he dies?!
Mother, stop shouting. Stop shouting!
Geez, she's like a geyser. So glad we're in a private room...
GUSH
Darling...
I don't care which god of the many I've clung to! Please, please spare my husband's life!!

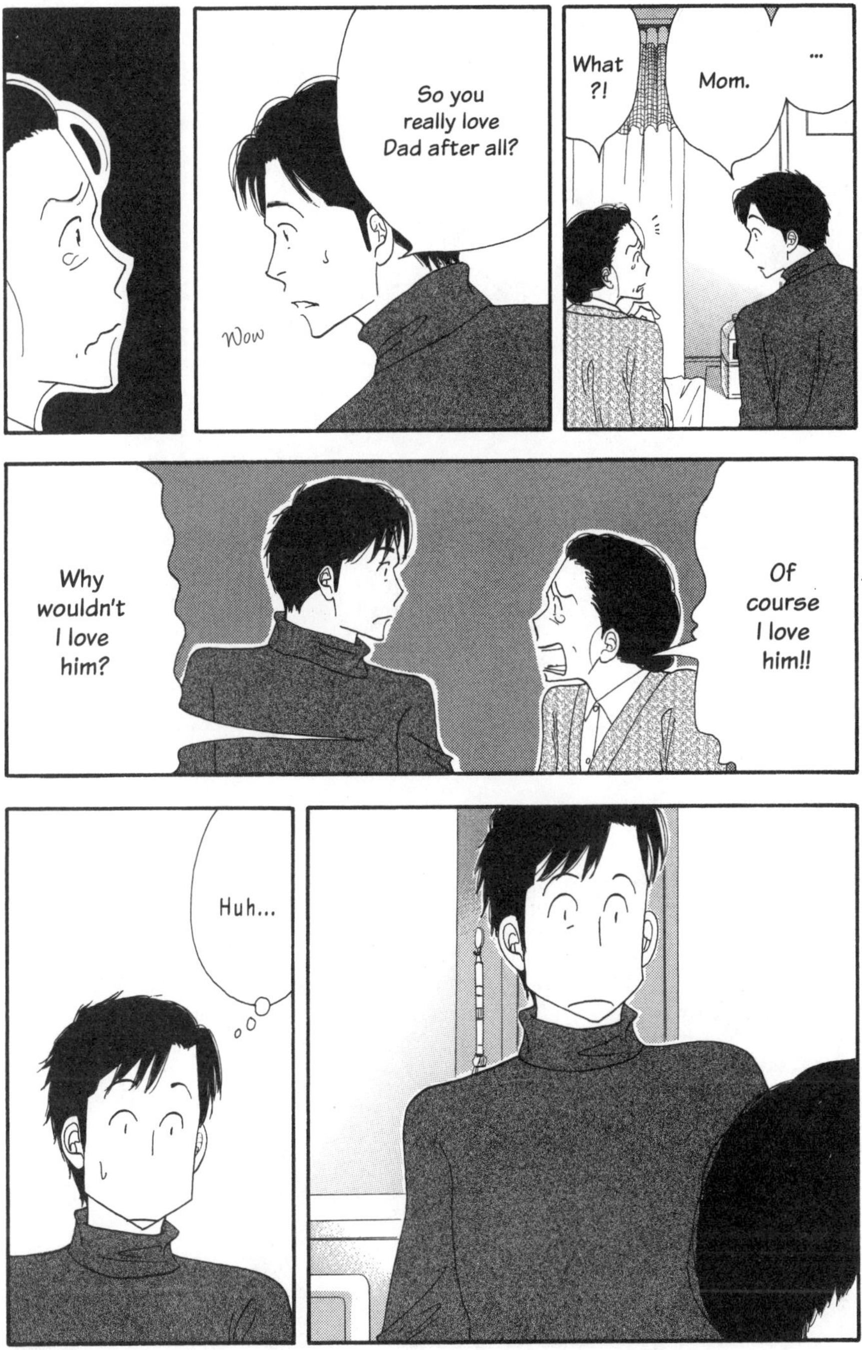
...
Mom.
What ?!
So you really love Dad after all?
Wow
Of course I love him!!
Why wouldn't I love him?
Huh...

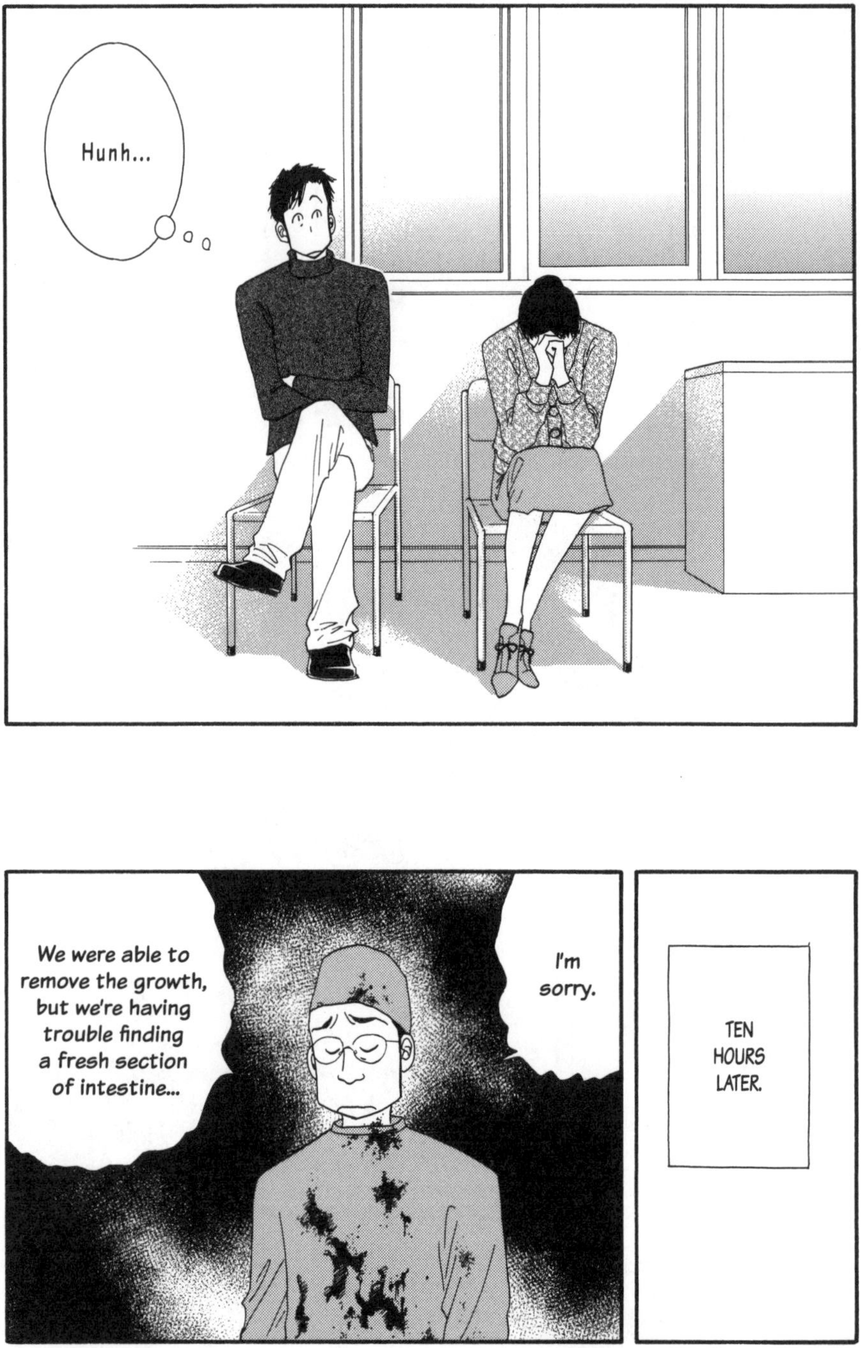
Hunh...
TEN HOURS LATER.
I'm sorry.
We were able to remove the growth, but we're having trouble finding a fresh section of intestine...

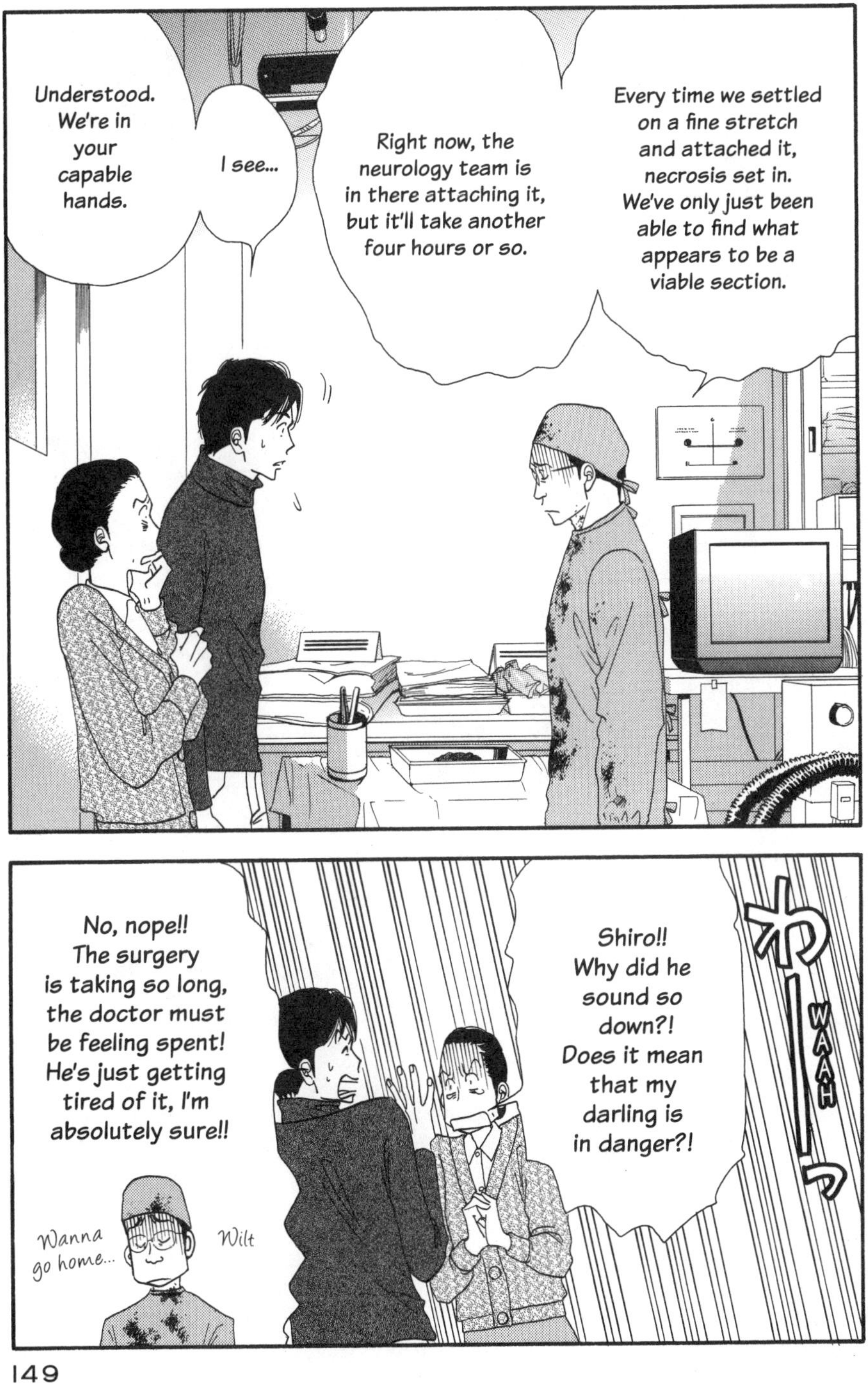
Every time we settled on a fine stretch and attached it, necrosis set in. We've only just been able to find what appears to be a viable section.
Right now, the neurology team is in there attaching it, but it'll take another four hours or so.
I see...
Understood. We're in your capable hands.
わーっ
WAAH
Shiro!! Why did he sound so down?! Does it mean that my darling is in danger?!
No, nope!! The surgery is taking so long, the doctor must be feeling spent! He's just getting tired of it, I'm absolutely sure!!
Wilt
Wanna go home...

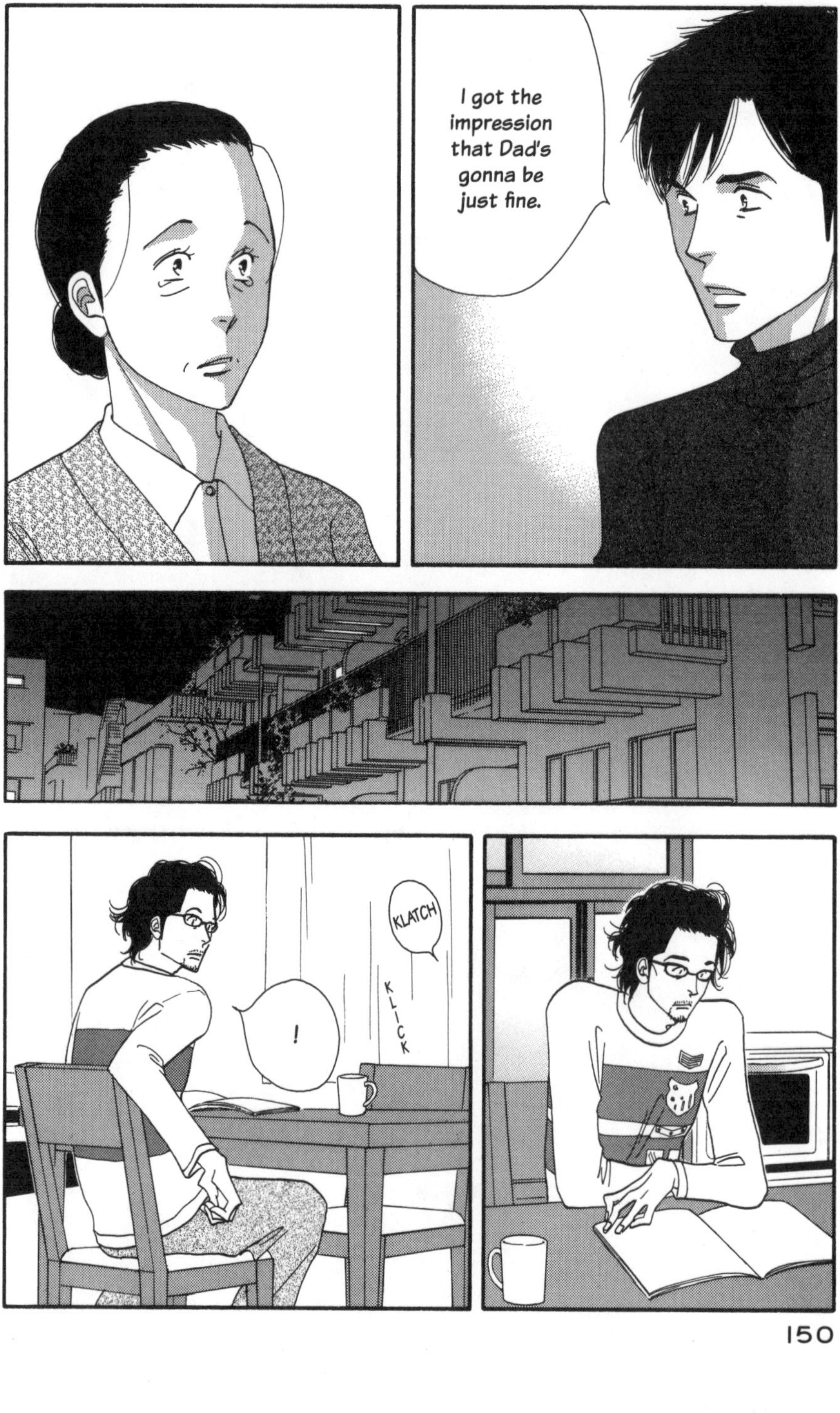
I got the impression that Dad's gonna be just fine.
KLATCH
KLICK
!

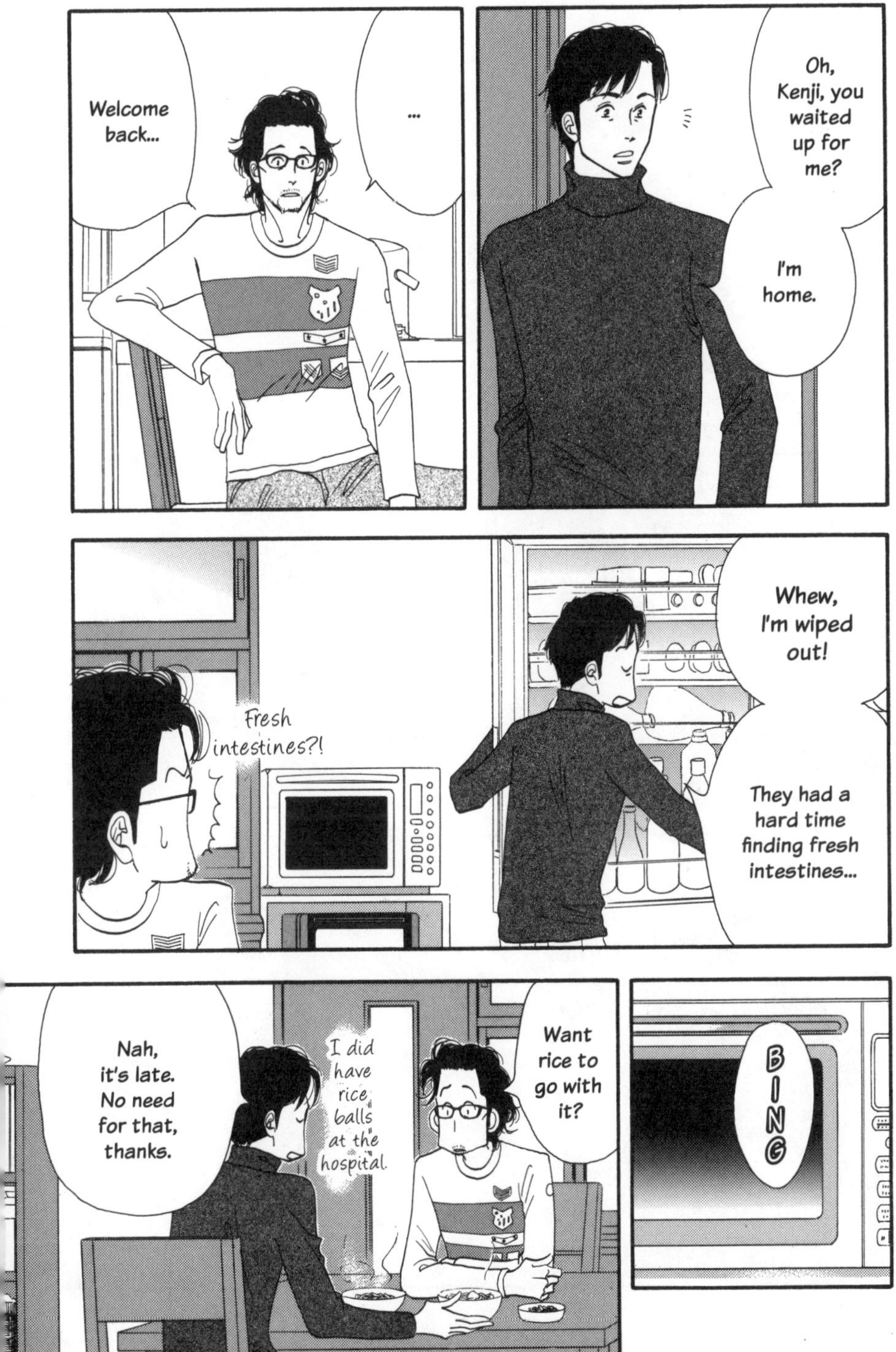

Oh, Kenji, you waited up for me?
I'm home.
...
Welcome back...
Whew, I'm wiped out!
They had a hard time finding fresh intestines...
Fresh intestines?!
BING
Want rice to go with it?
I did have rice balls at the hospital.
Nah, it's late. No need for that, thanks.

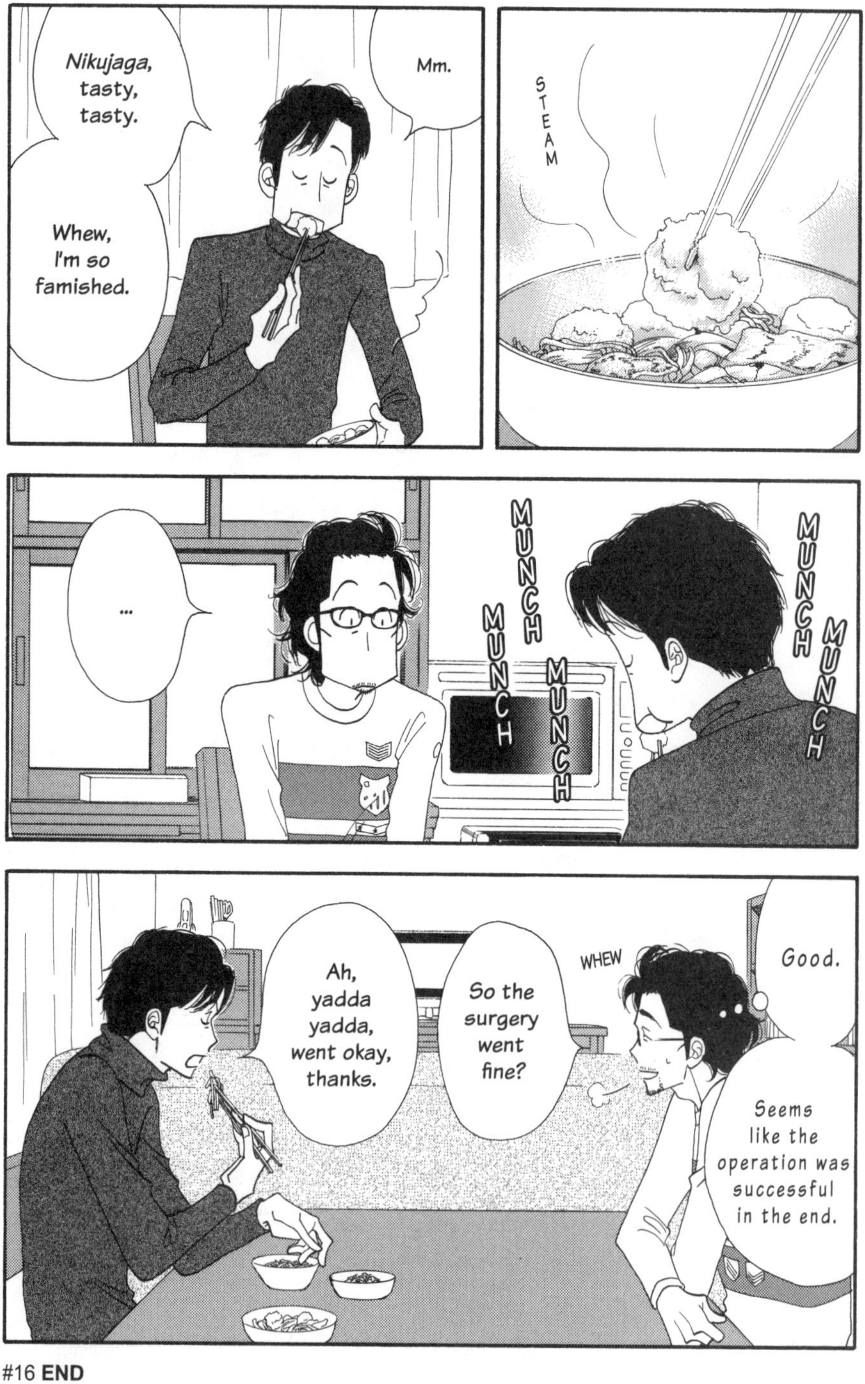
STEAM
Mm.
Nikujaga, tasty, tasty.
Whew, I'm so famished.
MUNCH MUNCH
MUNCH MUNCH
MUNCH MUNCH
...
Good.
Seems like the operation was successful in the end.
WHEW
So the surgery went fine?
Ah, yadda yadda, went okay, thanks.

#16 **END**

For the **scallop and *daikon* salad,**
also try finishing with seven-spice powder
or a dab of wasabi instead of *yuzu* pepper paste.
If spicy isn't your thing, try garnishing with a few slices of
julienned *yuzu* or other citrus peel for an accent flavor.

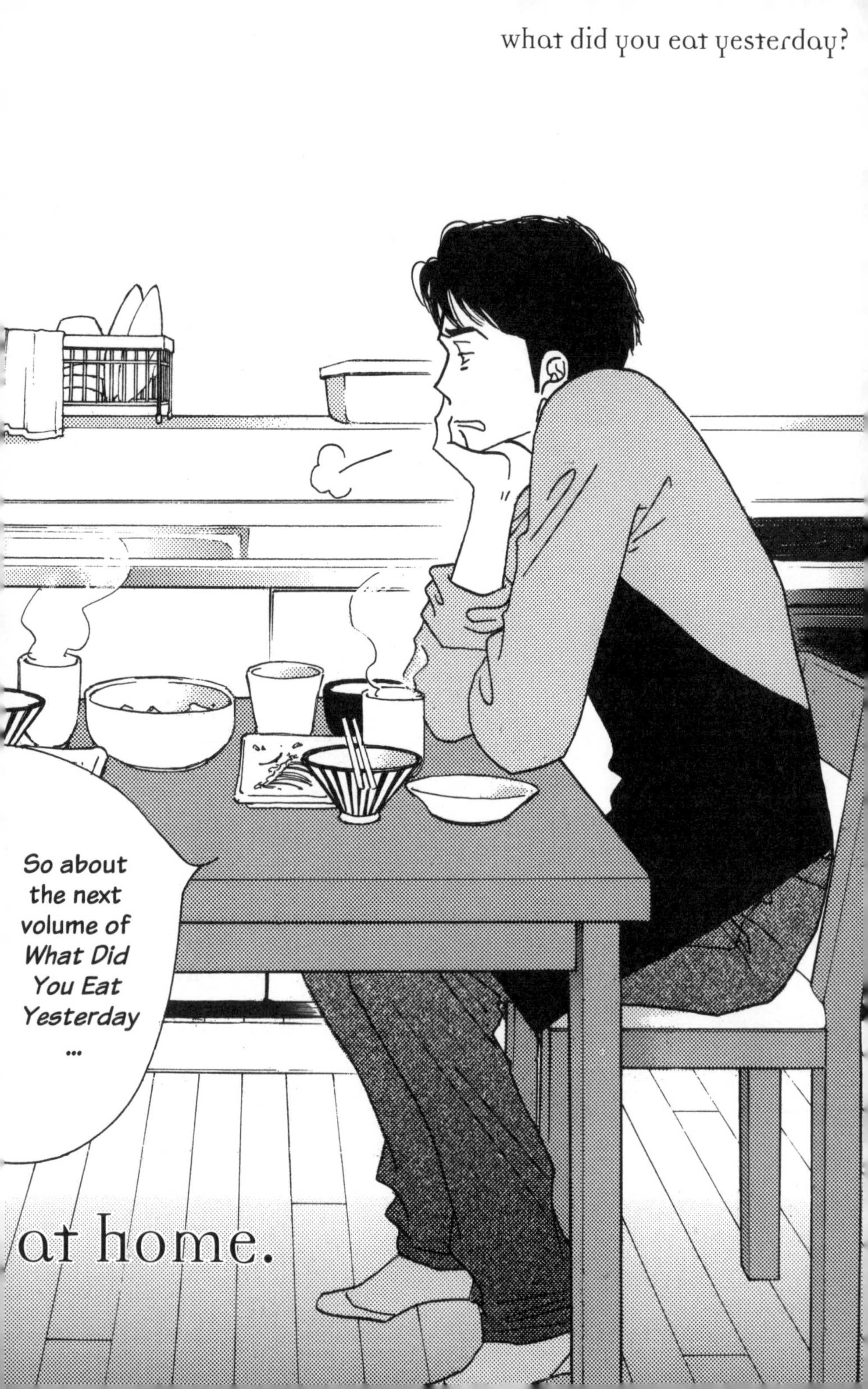
what did you eat yesterday?
So about the next volume of What Did You Eat Yesterday ...
at home.

Miso stir-fried pork over fried rice
sweet and sour soup
citrus dressed napa
chicken and broccoli in oyster sauce
Miso ramen
etc...

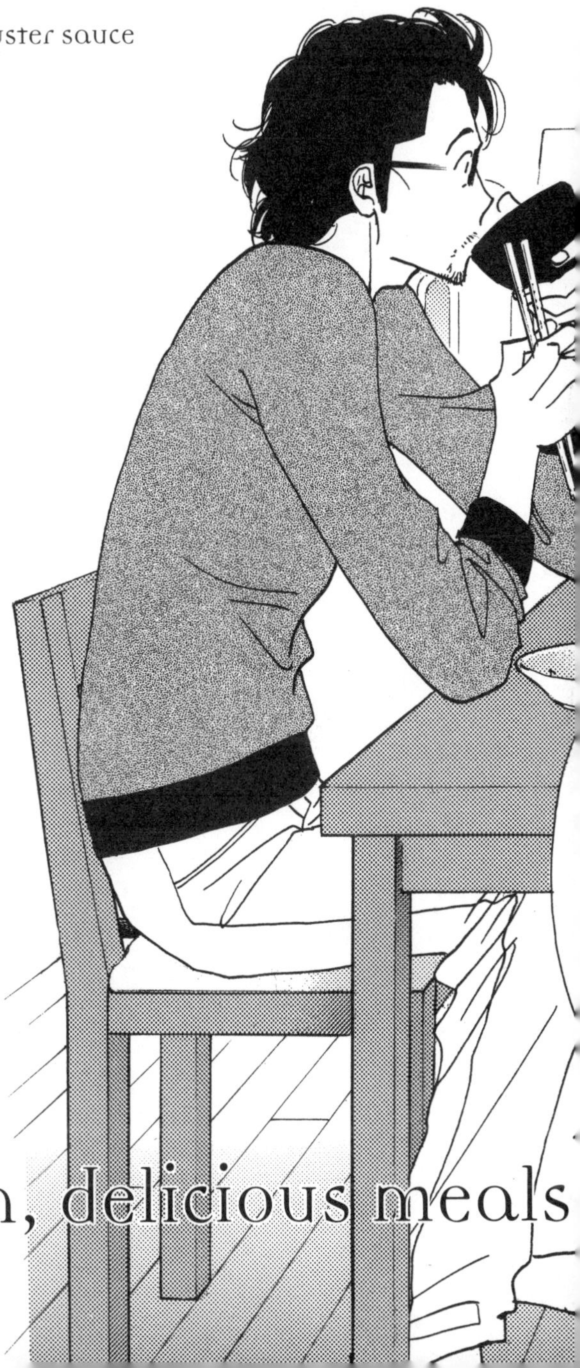

Eating fun, delicious meals

what did you eat yesterday?, volume 2

translation: Maya Rosewood
production: Risa Cho
Tomoe Tsutsumi

© 2014 Fumi Yoshinaga. All rights reserved.
First published in Japan in 2008 by Kodansha Ltd., Tokyo.
Publication rights for this English edition arranged
through Kodansha Ltd., Tokyo.
English language version produced by Vertical, Inc.

Translation provided by Vertical, Inc., 2014
Published by Vertical, Inc., New York

Originally published in Japanese as Kinou nani tabeta? 2 by Kodansha, Ltd.
Kinou nani tabeta? first serialized in Morning, Kodansha, Ltd., 2007-

This is a work of fiction.

ISBN: 978-1-939130-39-6

Manufactured in Canada

First Edition

Vertical, Inc.
451 Park Avenue South
7th Floor
New York, NY 10016
www.vertical-inc.com

Finally available in English: the award-winning comic about wine that has been a hit not just all over Asia but also in France! Learn about legendary bottles as well as affordable secrets while enjoying a page-turner that's not about superheroes but people with jobs to keep. When world-renowned wine critic Kanzaki passes away, his will reveals that his fortune of a wine collection isn't bequeathed as a matter of course to his only son, who in a snub went to work sales at a beer company. To come into the inheritance, Shizuku must identify—in competition with a stellar young critic—twelve heaven-sent wines whose impressions the will describes in flowing terms...

"Arguably the most influential wine publication for the past 20 years."
—*Decanter Magazine*

Volumes 1-4 & New World available now!
approx. 400 pages and $14.95 each

WINNER
GOURMAND COOKBOOK AWARDS
2009

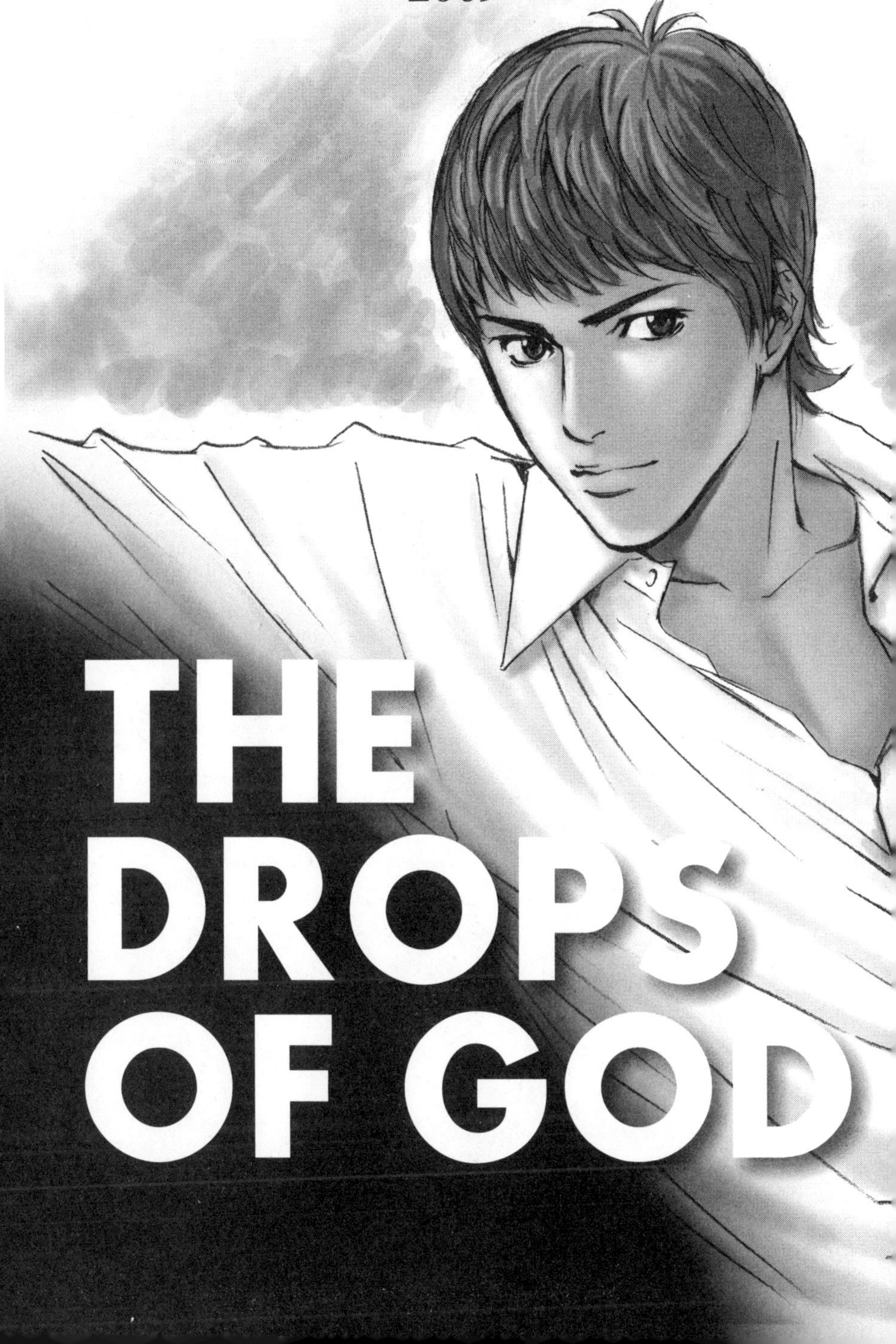
THE DROPS OF GOD

WRONG WAY

Japanese books, including manga like this one,
are meant to be read from right to left.
so the front cover is actually the back cover, and vice versa.
To read this book, please flip it over
and start in the top right-hand corner.
Read the panels, and the bubbles in the panels,
from right to left,
then drop down to the next row and repeat.
It may make you dizzy at first, but forcing your brain
to do things backwards makes you smarter in the long run.
we swear.